Projects for Microsoft® Visual Basic 6

Paul Thurrott

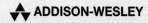

ADDISON-WESLEY

An imprint of Addison Wesley Longman, Inc.

Reading, Massachusetts • Menlo Park, California • New York • Harlow, England
Don Mills, Ontario • Sydney • Mexico City • Madrid • Amsterdam

Executive Editor: Michael Roche
Acquisitions Editor: Anita Devine
Editorial Assistant: Holly Rioux
Senior Marketing Manager: Tom Ziolkowski
Marketing Assistant: Renée Leblanc
Marketing Coordinator: Lauren Morse
Technical Editor: Carl Scharpf
Project Manager: Deanna Storey
Production Supervision: Elm Street Publishing Services, Inc.
Composition and Art: Gillian Hall, The Aardvark Group
Design Supervisor: Regina Hagen
Manufacturing: Sheila Spinney

0-201-45892-6

Ordering from the SELECT System
For more information on ordering and pricing policies for the SELECT Lab Series and supplements, please contact your Addison Wesley Longman sales representative or fax 1-800-284-8292 or email: exam@awl.com. Questions? Email: is@awl.com

Addison-Wesley Publishing Company
One Jacob Way
Reading, MA 01867
http://hepg@awl.com/select

3 4 5 6 7 8 9 10-DOW-01

Preface

Technology is the leading force developing our future at home and at work. Computers are the integral medium; students are scrambling to develop their skills on software applications and the Internet to be competitive in the marketplace. But why stop there? The inner workings of computers are no longer just the business of computer experts. Any individual with some basic Windows knowledge can not only work with software applications and Web browsers, they can create their own with a well developed guide. With this in mind, we are offering this hands-on, project based lab manual for students with little or no previous programming experience. With the *SELECT Lab Series: Projects for Microsoft Visual Basic 6.0*, programming is easy and fun!

As part of the *SELECT Lab Series*, this book follows the same hands-on, project-based approach that you have come to rely on. Each program is developed through several projects, with step-by-step guidance and motivation from Paul Thurrott, an author commended for his casual and clear writing style and authority on computer applications. Students learn the basics of the programming software by developing the well known *Hello, world!* application. They build on these skills to create an energy calculator, a slot machine, and a Web browser.

Student Supplements

- **Visual Basic CD-ROM** – Students receive their own copy of the Visual Basic Working Model and Control Creation Editions, packaged free with the text on one CD-ROM.

- **Web Site** – Students can visit http://hepg.awl.com/select to access files and electronic code needed to complete the projects. They can also link to other Visual Basic sites and further develop their skills through additional projects and exercises.

Instructor Supplements

- **Instructor's Manual** – contains outlines of text material, teaching tips, answers to student study questions, printed test bank, and transparency masters.

On the Web:

The following supplements are available on the Instructor's Web Site at http://hepg.awl.com/select. Please contact your local sales representative for your ID and password.

- **Instructor's Manual** – Download outlines of text material, teaching tips, and answers to student study questions.

- **Start and solution files** – Start files are available for all projects so that they may be completed out of order if desired. Solution files are provided for assessment purposes.

- **Art files** – Create your own transparency masters and presentation slides using screen shots from the text.

- **Electronic Test Bank** – With our test generating software, you can create tests to print, administer on a network, or convert to HTML for students to access via the Internet.

1 PROJECT

Building Your
First Program

In the programming world, there is perhaps no more famous sample program than *"Hello, world!"* For that reason, the projects in Part One of this module will acquaint you with Visual Basic 6.0 using this classic example. Unlike the dry programming projects of the past, however, you will be tackling the *"Hello, world!"* example the *visual* way, using the world's easiest software development tool. Using only controls and properties, you will create your first real Windows application. Sure, it will be a modest program, but it is your first step toward a greater understanding of Visual Basic and the way its tools work together. You will also be improving this program somewhat over the course of the next three projects.

Objectives

After completing this project, you will be able to:

➤ Create and save a Visual Basic project
➤ Change form properties using the IDE
➤ Run Visual Basic programs from the IDE
➤ Use system colors

The Challenge

Your goal first is to get acquainted with the Visual Basic environment and the way its tools allow you to construct the user interface for your programs visually. Each of the subsequent projects in Part One builds on the program you design here so that when you're done you will have created a fully functional Visual Basic application.

VB-28

The Introduction sets the stage for the project and explains its purpose.

Clearly defined and measurable **Objectives** outline the skills covered.

The **Challenge** expains how the objectives are met and the approach that students will use to complete the project.

While you're probably ready to sit down and start playing with Visual Basic, programming requires a little more forethought than that. You first need to spend some time away from the computer to plan your solution. Don't make the classic mistake of sitting down immediately at the computer and attacking the problem without understanding the overall goals of the project. In this case, the program you will create is small and fairly easy to understand, so it won't require much advance planning.

The Solution

The specifications for this first program are as follows:

* The program will display a single window with a title containing your name followed by a colon, a space, and the phrase *Project 1*.
* The window will have a fixed border so that the user cannot resize it.
* The background color of the window will match the system background color for windows.

When this project is complete, your program should resemble Figure 1.1.

Figure 1.1 The specifications call for Project 1 to resemble this when complete.

The Setup

OK, it's time to get your hands dirty! Place this module near a computer, turn it on if required, and boot into Windows 98 (Windows 95 or NT 4.0+ will work as well). Since this is the first time you will actually use Visual Basic, you should first become familiar with some VB terminology. As mentioned in the Overview, Visual Basic uses a *solution file* to store any projects you create with the program. Visual Basic **solutions** consist of the windows—which Visual Basic calls forms—and code files that you create, along with other types of files that you or the system may create. This collection of files (the solution) as a whole represents the project—or

---

The **Solution** states the specifications required for the project to be complete.

An illustration shows the outcome of the project.

The **Setup** outlines the steps that students should take to begin the project.

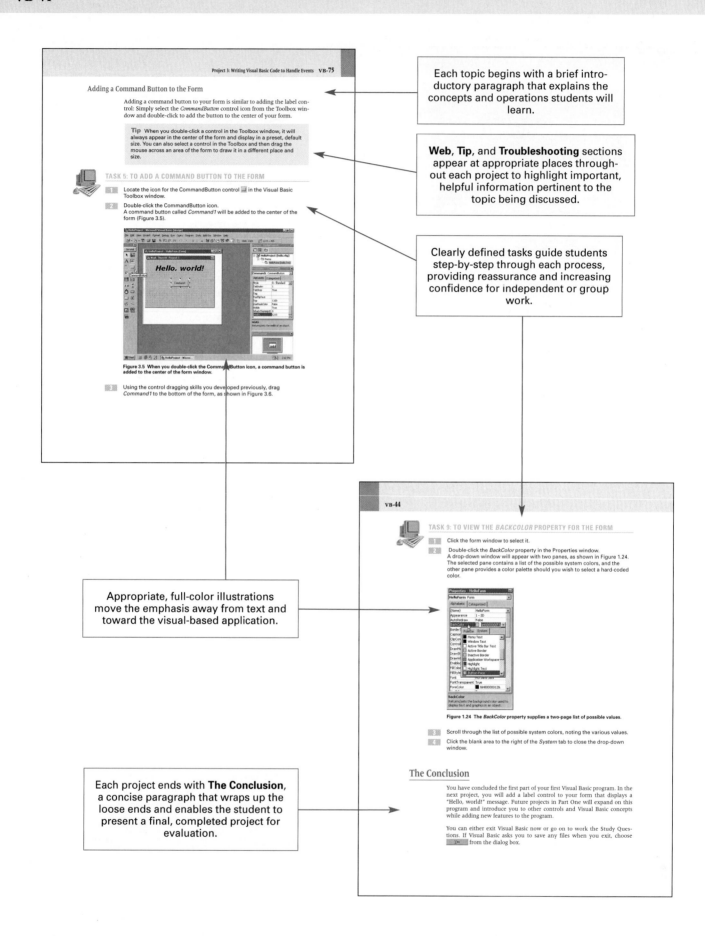

Each topic begins with a brief intro-ductory paragraph that explains the concepts and operations students will learn.

Web, **Tip**, and **Troubleshooting** sections appear at appropriate places through-out each project to highlight important, helpful information pertinent to the topic being discussed.

Clearly defined tasks guide students step-by-step through each process, providing reassurance and increasing confidence for independent or group work.

Appropriate, full-color illustrations move the emphasis away from text and toward the visual-based application.

Each project ends with **The Conclusion**, a concise paragraph that wraps up the loose ends and enables the student to present a final, completed project for evaluation.

Summary and Exercises

Summary

- Projects and forms are saved separately as part of a Visual Basic solution.
- The *Caption* property of a form changes the form's title bar text.
- The *BorderStyle* property of a form determines the type of border on the form window.
- The *Name* property determines the internal name of a form or control.
- The *BackColor* property determines the background color of the form.

Key Terms and Operations

Key Terms	Operations
BackColor property	create and save a VB project
BorderStyle property	run a program from the IDE
Caption property	save the project and form files
FRM file	separately as part of a solution
hard-code	use the Properties window to set form
internal names	properties
Name property	
project type	
solutions	
system colors	
VBP file	

Study Questions

Multiple Choice

1. The form is saved separately from the project, but you should save them
   a. in the same folder.
   b. on the same hard drive.
   c. on the same network.
   d. in the same code segment.

2. The form's *Caption* property changes the
   a. text on the form window.
   b. text on the form's status bar.
   c. text on the form's title bar.
   d. text on the form's input.

3. What are the two primary file types that Visual Basic will save in a Standard EXE project type?
   a. EXE and COM
   b. FRM and MAK
   c. MAK and VBP
   d. FRM and VBP

VB-45

A **Summary** in bulleted-list format further reinforces the Objectives and the material presented in the project.

Key terms are boldface and italicized throughout each project, and then listed for handy review in the summary section at the end of the project.

Study questions, **Hands-On**, and **On Your Own Exercises** bring the content of the project into focus again and allow for independent or group review of the material learned.

---

7. It is impossible to hard-code color values into the *BackColor* property.

8. Properties can be set in the Visual Basic IDE with the Properties window.

9. Visual Basic uses internal names for objects in your programs.

10. Visual Basic 6.0 projects use a .mak extension.

Short Answer

1. If you want the user to be able to resize the form's border, what is the correct value for *BorderStyle*?

2. What types of files make up a Visual Basic solution?

3. What type of project would you start if you want to create a typical Windows application?

4. What does the .frm file extension stand for?

5. Would the Visual Basic IDE allow you to enter the nonsensical phrase **jfdklfjdklk123** as the caption for a form window?

6. What happens when you double-click a property in the Properties window that displays a drop-down list of values?

7. Why is it important to give objects internal names?

8. How do you tell Visual Basic where you want your program to appear when it runs?

9. How do you change the text in the title bar of the form?

10. What is the color setting for Button Face on your system?

Group Discussion

1. The program you created in this project did not require you to write any code, yet you can run the program and it does work. What do you think Visual Basic is doing for you in the background?

2. Visual Basic lets you save form files separately from the rest of the project so that you can easily reuse those windows in other solutions. Why is this beneficial?

3. Because Visual Basic is so easy to use, a lot of non-programmers have started using it. What might be the downside to this?

4. Using MSDN Library, search for the term *hello, visual basic* and look over the document titled "Hello, Visual Basic" to get you prepared for the next project.

Hands-On

1. Practice with properties
Create a form with a hard-coded light blue background, a caption of **My little blue form**, and a sizable border.

2. Working with border styles
Start a new Visual Basic project and experiment with the different form border styles. Explain how each is different and, if possible, find an example of each style somewhere else in the Windows user interface.

Hands-On exercises present tasks for building on the skills acquired in the project.

VB-48

On Your Own

1. Writing specifications
Sometimes program specifications resemble clear English instructions that might be given to a person for a certain task. On a piece of paper or in a word processing program, write specifications for the computation of gross pay based on the following information.

a. The pay rate is $10.00 per hour.

b. Hours worked above 40 are paid at a rate of time and a half (that is, one and a half times the pay rate).

> **Tip** These kinds of instructions are sometimes referred to as *pseudocode*. Programmers use pseudocode to map out the solution to a programming problem in English. The pseudocode is then used as the basis for the actual programming language code they need to write to solve the problem.

2. Working with colors
Create a new Visual Basic project and set the *BackColor* property of the form window to Teal, which is the default color of the desktop (if your desktop is a different color, try to set it to the closest color you can find to the desktop color). Create a second project, this time setting the form *BackColor* to the system color "Desktop." Now, change the color of the system's desktop background using Display Properties. Run both programs again and describe what happens in each.

On Your Own assignments invoke critical thinking and integration of project skills.

More about the SELECT Lab Series:

The *SELECT Lab Series* is a complete learning resource for information systems users. We invite you to explore the latest releases of computer software using our up-to-date learning packages. Hands-on project based lab manuals make it quick and easy for anyone to develop computer skills for the home or workplace. To meet the individual needs of your course we offer the following:

- **Lab Manuals**: Dozens of proven and class tested *SELECT Lab Series* manuals are available, from the latest operating systems and browsers to the most popular applications software for word processing, spreadsheets, databases, and presentation graphics. The *SELECT Lab Series* also offers coverage on Web page creation and software programming and several of our manuals prepare students for the Microsoft Office User Specialist exams. A complete listing of titles can be found on the back cover of this book or visit our Web Site at http://hepg.awl.com.

- **Bundling:** Our TechSuite program allows you to choose the combination of lab manuals that best suits your classroom needs. These lab manuals can also be bundled with computer concepts texts, allowing students to purchase their books in one convenient package with a significant discount.

- **Software Donation:** Your school may qualify for upgrades or full software licenses for your labs. Contact your local sales representative for more information.

Your local representative will be happy to work with you and your bookstore manager to provide the most current menu of software applications lab manuals. Your representative will also outline the ordering process, and provide pricing, ISBNs, and delivery information. Please call 1-800-447-2226 or visit our Web site at http://hepg.awl.com.

Acknowledgments

I would like to thank Anita Devine and Holly Rioux for their patience and understanding during the development of this book. You were both incredible. Also thanks to Stephanie and Mark for giving up the time needed to complete this project.

But perhaps most importantly, thanks to Gary Brent for getting me started with computer book writing. Gary and I worked on the first edition of this book together (VB 3.0) years ago and I will fondly remember those days forever. Thanks Gary.

Paul Thurrott

Contents

PART FOUR Web Browser

Programming
Using Visual Basic

Overview

When the first Personal Computers burst on the scene some 25 years ago, they were lumbering, unfriendly beasts designed for the die-hard technical users looking for something more than ham radios and electronic breadboard kits. Today, the nearly ubiquitous *Personal Computer (PC)* is found in more homes than are VCRs. Moreover, a stand-alone computer that is not connected to the global *Internet* is becoming more and more rare; we live in a truly connected society. This day was predicted in numerous science fiction stories of the past, but no one really believed it would happen this quickly.

And even though this power has been available for only a short time, many computer users have a hard time remembering the days before the Internet opened the doors to vast realms of information sharing, gaming, and correspondence. Today, it is a trivial matter to converse at any time with a friend on the far side of the planet, without even picking up a telephone. With Web browsers, we can connect to distant sites on the Internet as easily as we can open a file on our own computer.

Have you ever wondered how this all works? Although it may seem like magic, in reality someone using *Visual Basic (VB)* or a similar tool created all of the computer software that makes your computer and even the Internet hum. In this module, you will learn how to create your own software, some of which will actually connect to distant sites over the Internet. As a user of Visual Basic, you are in an enviable position; just a few short years ago Internet programming required extensive knowledge of arcane codes and languages. Today, with the latest version of Visual Basic, such programming is fun and easy. Creating your own Windows programs—those that don't require any Internet connectivity—is even easier.

You've got the tools, and this module will get you started. It's time to create some magic of your own.

Objectives

After completing this project, you will be able to:

➤ **Understand Visual Basic's role in programming history**

➤ **Understand Visual Basic 6.0 basics**

➤ **Start Visual Basic**

➤ **Identify key parts of the Visual Basic IDE**

➤ **Access the MSDN Library to get help**

➤ **Exit Visual Basic**

Programming the Computer

At its most basic level, a computer *program* is a series of codes that instructs the computer to perform certain tasks. When the computer follows these instructions, it is said to *execute* or *run* the program. A computer is capable only of executing programs that were written in its native *machine language*, a generally nasty collection of 1s and 0s unintelligible to most humans. *Programmers*, who use a *programming language* that is much easier to understand than machine language, write the programs you typically run, such as Microsoft Windows and Microsoft Office. There are numerous programming languages available, but they all have one thing in common: In the end, they translate the code of the programming language into the machine language the computer understands. This allows programmers to use a more friendly language when they write computer programs.

When it comes to programming languages, programmers are a dogmatic bunch, generally sticking with—and vigorously defending—their language of choice. The creators of *Fortran*, one of the first programming languages, attempted to create a programming language that could be easily read by humans. Those who came up with later languages, such as *Pascal*, *C*, *C++*, and *Java*, gave up readability to enable more powerful features. Of the numerous programming languages available today, only Visual Basic combines an easily used, easily read, and easily understood language with the most advanced programming features currently available.

> **Tip** Microsoft makes many programming language products for its Windows family of operating systems. You may have seen its *Visual C++* (for C and C++ programming) and *Visual J++* (for Java programming) products. These products are often used in tandem with Visual Basic in large programming projects, so they are also sold together in a package called *Visual Studio*. The current version of Visual Studio is 6.0.

A Short History of BASIC

After the creation of Fortran, an attempt was made in the 1960s to create an even more readable computer language for ordinary people. Dubbed *BASIC* (Basic All-Purpose Symbolic Instruction Code) by its creators, this new language was an instant success with programmers because of its simple, English-like syntax. Versions of BASIC were created for virtually every kind of computer ever made and most up-and-coming programmers of the 1970s began their careers by learning this language.

In the late 1970s, the personal computer revolution began when **MITS**, a tiny company in Albuquerque, New Mexico, introduced the **Altair** computer. Microsoft's first product was for this computer—a version of BASIC co-written by CEO Bill Gates, then only a teenager. Over the years, Microsoft ported BASIC to numerous personal computer systems and released a series of upgrades for the **IBM PC** such as GW-BASIC, QBasic, and QuickBasic. All of these BASIC derivatives ran on **MS-DOS**, the command line operating system that Microsoft had developed for IBM and the vast array of IBM-compatible PCs.

Then came **Windows**, the graphical successor to MS-DOS. At first, Windows programs were incredibly hard to create, and programmers struggled with the arcane C programming language and a bewildering collection of new concepts. Then Microsoft created the first version of Visual Basic, designed to take the complexity out of Windows programming and make the process genuinely *fun*. It was an instant success. Indeed, the product was so successful that many of its users weren't even programmers.

The initial release of Visual Basic was quickly followed by several major updates, including version 3.0 (1993), 4.0 (1995), 5.0 (1997), and now, version 6.0. Each version has added to the power of the product while retaining its famous ease of use. Visual Basic 4.0 was the first version to support 32-bit Windows programming, introducing its users to the capabilities of Windows 95 and Windows NT. Early versions of Visual Basic used a confusing Single Document Interface (SDI) with multiple floating windows (Figure O.1), but Microsoft did away with this in version 5.0 (although it's still an option for the old-school diehards).

Introduction to Visual Basic

Now that you've got a grasp on where Visual Basic came from, let's take a look at the actual product and explore some of the thinking behind the Visual Basic way. Visual Basic is, quite simply, the easiest, fastest, and yes, most fun way to create programs for Windows 95, 98, and NT. In fact, Visual Basic is so popular that many other programming languages have tried to copy its look and feel. Tools like Visual Basic are now referred to as **RAD (Rapid Application Development)** because they make it so easy to create application programs. Still, Visual Basic is by far the easiest and the fastest of these languages.

The word *visual* in Visual Basic is telling: The biggest change that Visual Basic brought to programming was the idea that the elements of a Windows application—windows, buttons, menus, and other controls—could

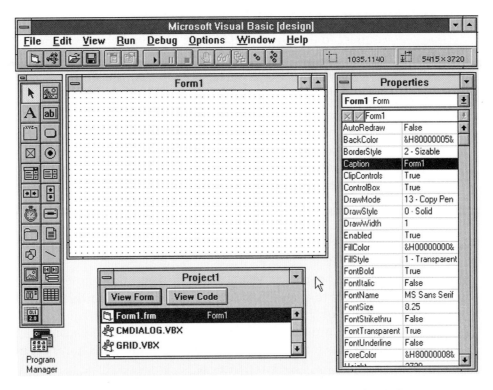

Figure O.1 Early versions of Visual Basic featured a confusing Single Document Interface with multiple floating windows.

be manipulated *visually* and then simply tied together with code. In fact, for most applications, you essentially *draw* the application with a collection of window elements in a virtual toolbox, and then connect it all together with VB code. Compare this to the old method where the weary programmer would sit at a text terminal typing endless lines of essentially unreadable C code and you'll see why Visual Basic is so popular.

The essential Visual Basic concept, which eventually found its way to all kinds of other programming methodologies (including Web development) is called **event-driven programming**. With the event-driven programming model used by Visual Basic, everything in your application is an **object**. These objects have **properties**, or attributes, that determine how objects look and act. A command button object, for example, has height and width properties.

These objects can handle **events**, which are, as you might suspect, things that *happen* to objects. For example, the command button object can handle an *OnClick* event, which occurs when the user clicks that button. Different objects can handle different events, just as different objects have different properties. When you create a Visual Basic program, then, you visually arrange objects on a window (which VB refers to as a **form**) and decide which events you want to handle. It's that simple.

Objects also support **methods**, which describe the *capabilities* of the object. A method is basically something the object does. For example, you might have an object that accesses a database. One thing this object could do is connect to the physical database file somewhere on the computer or over a network, so the database object might have a *Connect* method that would make that happen. We will be looking into objects and their properties, events, and methods as we progress through the module.

> **Tip** Objects can be compared to nouns, properties to adjectives, and methods to verbs. For example, a dog is an object that has properties such as size and color. And the dog can perform actions such as bark and run, which can be compared to an object's methods.

Visual Basic Editions

Microsoft packages Visual Basic in three separate editions, each designed to appeal to a specific audience. The projects in this module, with the exception of Project 8, will work with any of these editions. (Project 8 requires a database library not found in the Learning Edition. Your instructor will have instructions for obtaining this library if needed.)

- *Control Creation Edition*   Though this hasn't been updated since Visual Basic 5.0, the VB Control Creation Edition (CCE) is still a viable way to use Visual Basic to create ActiveX controls that run in Web browsers on the Internet. The VB 5.0 CCE is included on the CD-ROM that accompanies this text.

- *Learning Edition*   Geared toward beginners, this edition includes some nice printed documentation (programmer-speak for "a book"), lots of online documentation (a CD-ROM) and a special "Learn VB Now" CD-ROM. This is a great package for anyone learning Visual Basic for the first time.

- *Working Model Edition*   Also included on the enclosed CD-ROM, it offers the same development environment as the Learning Edition, though it doesn't allow you to create executable files, Web pages, or ActiveX controls. These are minor limitations in learning Visual Basic, given the amount of tools you're getting at such a low cost. To access the help files, you will need to register on line with the MSDN Library at http://msdn.microsoft.com/developer/.

- *Professional Edition*   This midlevel edition includes all of the features in the Learning Edition plus additional controls, an integrated database, and Web development tools.

- *Enterprise Edition*   Designed with distributed application development in mind, this edition is for the most adept Visual Basic programmers. It supports a list of technologies too long and complicated to mention here and is as complete as is possible.

Visual Basic is also available as part of an expensive—and huge—package called **Visual Studio**. Visual Studio includes all of Microsoft's software and Web development tools in one box. It is designed for professional programmers who require multiple programming languages.

Visual Basic Derivatives

Microsoft also has created a family of products based on Visual Basic, each of which fills a specific niche. Together with VB itself, they form the culmination of Bill Gates' promise of "Visual Basic everywhere." So learning Visual Basic isn't the end, but rather the start of a journey. And once you've learned one of these derivatives, it's easy to use any of the others.

- *Visual Basic Scripting Edition (VBScript)*   This lightweight *scripting language*, which is used to provide interactivity in Web pages, brings the power of the Visual Basic language (but not the visual design tools) to HTML, the language of the Web. VBScript code (Figure O.2) can be embedded in the HTML code to create Web pages and provide features that normal HTML cannot.

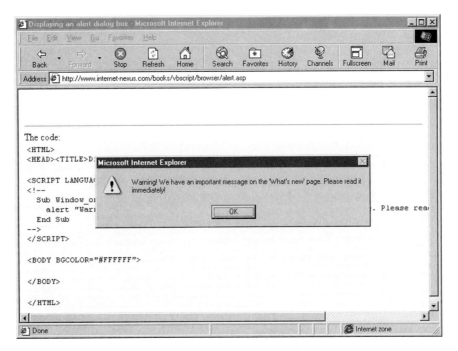

Figure O.2 VBScript makes Web pages more powerful.

- *Visual Basic Applications Edition (VBA)*   Typically used as a macro language for application programs such as Microsoft Word and Microsoft Excel, VBA allows the use of Visual Basic language (and a visual environment very similar to VB itself) to modify and enhance other programs. Applications that use VBA are extensively and easily programmable, giving users the power to handcraft their own modifications. The VBA editor from Microsoft Office is shown in Figure O.3.

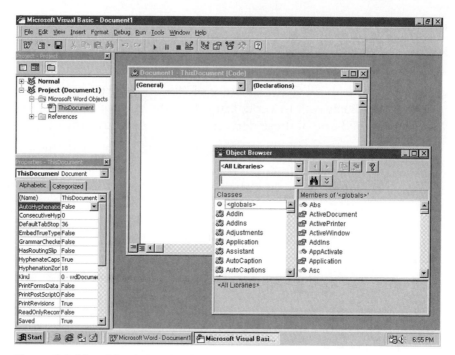

Figure O.3 Visual Basic for Applications offers a full VB environment for macro users.

- *Windows CE Toolkit for Visual Basic* This package allows the creation of applications for Windows CE, a new version of Windows designed for handheld and palm-sized PCs, using Visual Basic.

Web Tip For more information on Visual Basic or its many derivatives, please visit the Microsoft Web site at http://www.microsoft.com.

What's New in Visual Basic 6.0

With each new release of Visual Basic, Microsoft has targeted the product to specific enhancements and features, and version 6.0 is no exception. Released in September 1998, Visual Basic 6.0 is designed to make Web and database programming easier than ever. On that note, the product is quite successful, but VB 6.0 includes much, much more than that. In keeping with VB's ease of use, Microsoft has added numerous new Wizards—like the ones you might have seen in Microsoft Office—to guide you step by step through specific tasks. New Windows 98 controls, such as the Internet Explorer Coolbars shown in Figure O.4, have been added, and existing controls have been enhanced to take advantage of new features. These additions, the aforementioned Web and database enhancements, and a long list of language improvements make Visual Basic 6.0 an important release.

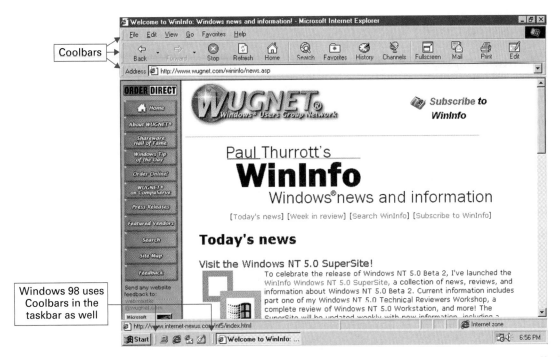

Figure O.4 Internet Explorer versions 4.0 and higher use new Coolbars, offering users a customizable user interface.

Starting Visual Basic

Depending on how Visual Basic was installed in your computer—as a stand-alone product or as part of a Visual Studio installation—the standard program group containing the shortcut to Visual Basic will be found in *Microsoft Visual Basic 6.0, Microsoft Visual Studio 6.0,* or similar. Ask your instructor or lab assistant if you can't find the shortcut to Visual Basic. In this module, we will assume that the Visual Basic shortcut is found in Start→Programs→Microsoft Visual Studio 6.0.

In the following steps, you will launch Visual Basic and make sure that some of its options are correctly set up.

TASK 1: TO FIND THE PROGRAM GROUP

1 Click the ⚑Start button to open the *Start* menu.

2 Open the *Programs* submenu and navigate to the group called *Microsoft Visual Studio 6.0.*

> **Troubleshooting Tip** The name of the Visual Basic program group could be different. If you are using the stand-alone Visual Basic product (not as part of Visual Studio), the group will be called *Visual Basic 6.0,* for example. If you can't find the correct program group, ask your instructor or lab assistant.

3 Select the shortcut 🗓 Microsoft Visual Basic 6.0 .

Visual Basic will start. When Visual Basic starts, you should see a New Project window as shown in Figure O.5.

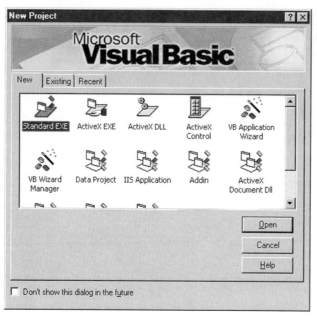

Figure O.5 Visual Basic displays the New Project dialog box when it first starts.

TASK 2: TO SET OPTIONS

1 If the New Project dialog box appeared, click the [Open] button to start a new Standard Exe project. (The different **project** types will be explained in Project 1.) If the New Project dialog does not appear, select *New Project* from the *File* menu.

2 Choose *Options* from the *Tools* menu to open the Visual Basic Options dialog box.

3 On the *Editor* page, check the *Require Variable Declaration* choice as shown in Figure O.6.

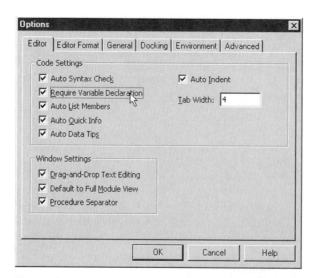

Figure O.6 The default for *Require Variable Declaration* is off.

4 On the *Environment* page, make sure the choice *Prompt for project* is selected under the *When Visual Basic starts* option.

5 On the *Advanced* tab, make sure the *SDI Development Environment* is not checked. This module assumes that you are *not* using the SDI Development Environment.

6 Click [OK] to close the dialog box.

Introducing the Visual Basic IDE

The ***Visual Basic Integrated Development Environment (IDE)*** consists of a main window and numerous subwindows (or child windows), as shown in Figure O.7. Many subwindows in Visual Basic are typically ***docked***, or attached to a side of the main window.

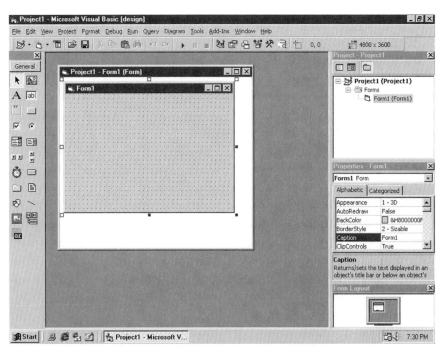

Figure O.7 The Visual Basic IDE in all its glory. This is the default view, which you can customize.

If your Visual Basic IDE hasn't been modified, you will typically see the following five subwindows in Visual Basic, four of which are docked.

- ***Toolbox*** A collection of controls you can add to your Visual Basic program (Figure O.8).

Figure O.8 The Toolbox window offers a palette of controls.

- *Form1* The basis of your Visual Basic program (Figure O.9). You add controls to this form to present a user interface for your program, if it requires one. Some Visual Basic programs do not use a form window.

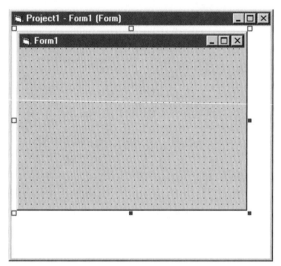

Figure O.9 The default form window is an empty canvas for you to work with.

- *Project Explorer* A hierarchical list of the files that constitutes your Visual Basic program (Figure O.10).

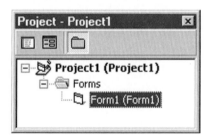

Figure O.10 You can use the Project Explorer window to view the files in your solution.

- **Properties**   A list of the properties of the currently selected object (Figure O.11). When you begin a new project, the form window will be selected, so the list of properties you first see will pertain to the form. You can modify default values for object properties with this window.

Figure O.11 Properties for the currently selected object are listed in the Properties window.

- **Form Layout**   Determines where your program will appear on the Windows desktop when it is run (Figure O.12).

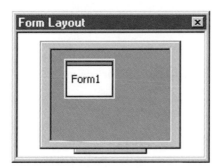

Figure O.12 You can specify where your program will appear visually with the Form Layout window.

Troubleshooting Tip   If you don't see some or all of these windows, do not fear. You can open them by selecting the correct option from the Visual Basic *View* menu. If, for example, the Properties window is not available when you use Visual Basic, simply choose *Properties Window* from the *View* menu.

The Visual Basic IDE is easily modified. As you work with Visual Basic, you may find yourself using some windows but not others, and you may wish to dock or undock windows. In the following steps, you will examine how the various windows in the Visual Basic IDE work.

TASK 3: TO DOCK AND UNDOCK WINDOWS

1 Locate the Project Explorer window (it should be labeled *Project1 - Project1*). If you don't see it, select *Project Explorer* from the *View* menu.

2 Click the titlebar of the Project Explorer window but do not release the mouse button.

3 Drag the window into the center of the Visual Basic IDE, as shown in Figure O.13, and release the mouse button. This is known as undocking the window.

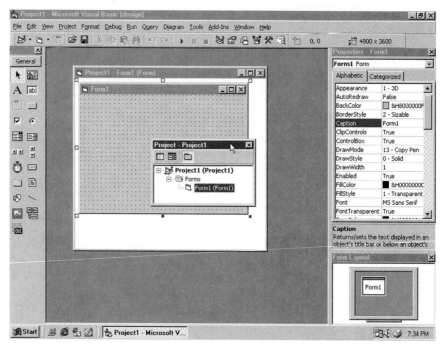

Figure O.13 An undocked window floats inside the Visual Basic IDE, unattached to the sides of the main window.

4 Drag the window over to the left side of the Visual Basic IDE and release the mouse button.
Notice that the window docks there as well, as shown in Figure O.14 (*Note*: It can also dock above the toolbox, depending on where you drag the window.)

5 Drag the Project Explorer window back to its original location at the top right of the Visual Basic IDE and release the mouse button. Watch the outline as you drag it to ensure that it docks in the correct location.

As you can see, any of the dockable windows in the Visual Basic IDE can be moved around or undocked. They can also be resized or removed if you desire. You will be using most of these windows quite extensively over the course of this module, so don't worry if you don't quite understand how it all comes together quite yet. In the first project, you will spend more time actually using the windows and seeing how they work together. As you gain experience with Visual Basic, you will probably develop your own personal way to arrange these windows; feel free to do so, remembering that you can regain any missing windows by visiting the *View* menu.

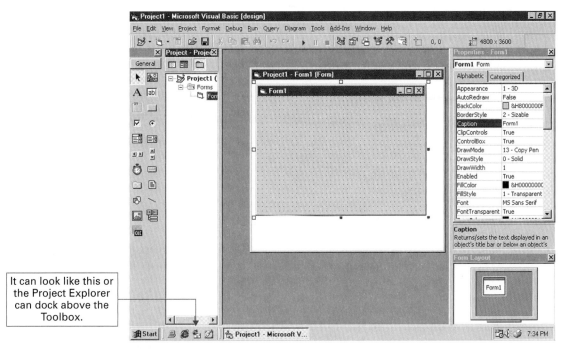

It can look like this or the Project Explorer can dock above the Toolbox.

Figure O.14 Subwindows in the Visual Basic IDE can be docked on any side of the main window.

Tip Dockable windows in the Visual Basic IDE have a smaller title bar than normal windows, which feature only a close window icon ☒ and a title. "Normal" child windows, such as the form window, cannot be docked, but they can be maximized, minimized, and restored within the space in the IDE not occupied by the docked windows.

Getting Assistance

The key to programming is knowing where to get help, and Visual Basic offers an extensive collection of online assistance that can be found in a separate Web browser-based help system known as the ***MSDN Library***. The MSDN Library uses the same familiar *hypertext* system found on the Web, making it intuitive and easy to use.

Web Tip   The letters in MSDN stand for Microsoft Developer Network, Microsoft's support network for software and Web developers. MSDN maintains an incredible Web site for developers at http://msdn.microsoft.com.

MSDN Library uses an Explorer-like window with *Contents*, *Index*, *Search*, and *Favorites* options in the left pane. These options allow you to find information in a variety of ways.

TASK 4: TO OPEN MSDN LIBRARY

1 Choose *Contents* from the *Help* menu in Visual Basic.
The MSDN Library window will open, as shown in Figure O.15.

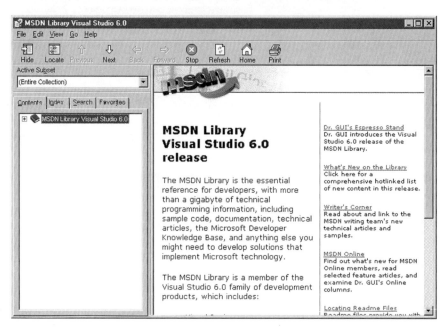

Figure O.15 The MSDN Library is an extensive collection of online help for all of Microsoft's developer tools.

2 Maximize the window if it isn't already maximized.

Because the MSDN Library is used to provide assistance for all of Visual Studio, you may find lots of information in the library that is not related to Visual Basic. It is possible, however, to narrow down the available choices to only display Visual Basic topics.

TASK 5: TO MAKE SURE THAT VISUAL BASIC HELP IS DISPLAYED

1 Take a look at the *Active Subset* drop-down list box near the top-left corner of the MSDN Library window. It probably will be set to *Entire Collection*.

2 Drop-down the list box to display the list of help subsets you can work with, as shown in Figure O.16.

3 Scroll down the list until you find "Visual Basic Documentation" and choose that option. Each time you open MSDN Library, you will want to make sure that this subset is selected.

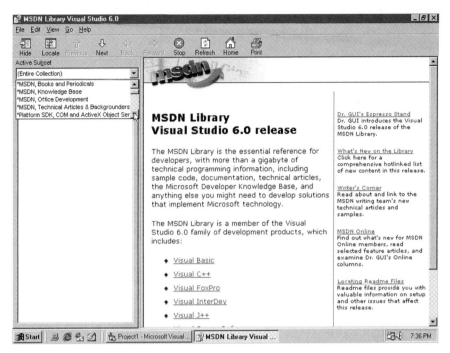

Figure O.16 MSDN Library allows you to trim back the amount of information it will display.

TASK 6: TO SCAN INFORMATION BY TOPIC

1 Expand the view in the Contents pane (if it isn't already) by clicking the plus sign (+) next to the title, "MSDN Library Visual Studio 6.0."
A number of topics will appear, as shown in Figure O.17.

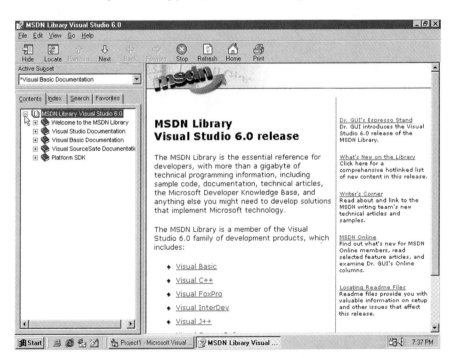

Figure O.17 The tree view used in MSDN Library lets you display the information you need.

2 Expand the entry titled "Visual Basic Documentation" (Figure O.18).

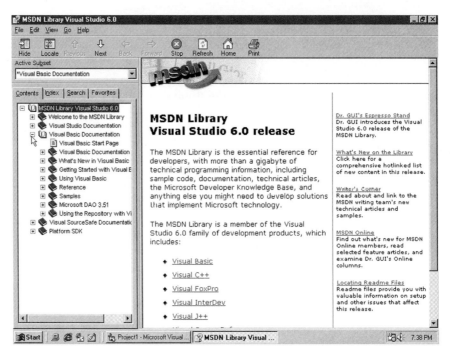

Figure O.18 The documentation choices for Visual Basic can be seen when that topic is expanded.

3 Single-click the entry titled "Visual Basic Start Page" to display the entry point for Visual Basic help topics (Figure O.19).
There are a number of topics available, including tutorials, reference material, and what's new items.

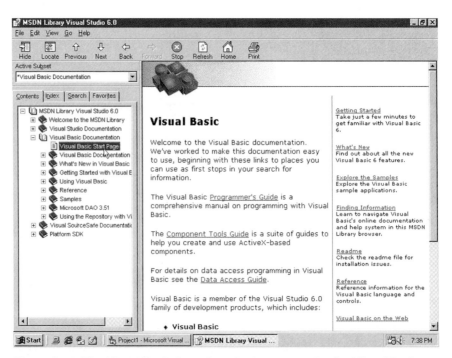

Figure O.19 The Visual Basic Start Page is the entry point for Visual Basic documentation in MSDN Library.

TASK 7: TO USE THE INDEX

1 Select the Index pane in the left column of MSDN Library.
The index will appear in the left pane, as shown in Figure O.20. Items in the index are listed alphabetically, and you can type the beginning of a help topic into the edit box. MSDN Library will "auto-complete" your index topic as you type. (It's a little weird at first, but you'll grow to enjoy this feature.)

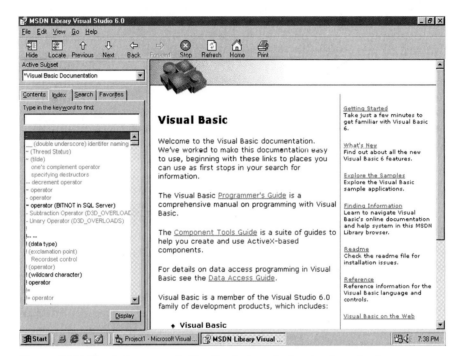

Figure O.20 The Index page is like the Index of a book where topics are arranged alphabetically.

2 Type **V** in the edit box.
The index list will jump to items that begin with the letter V, as shown in Figure O.21.

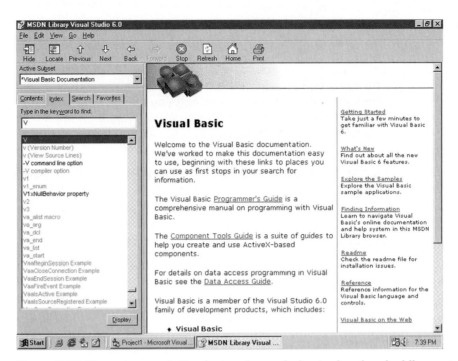

Figure O.21 The auto-completion feature jumps index topics ahead while you type.

3 Type **isual Basic** to complete the index navigation.

4 Double-click the item titled "Visual Basic 6.0 New Features" to view information about the new features in Visual Basic (Figure O.22).

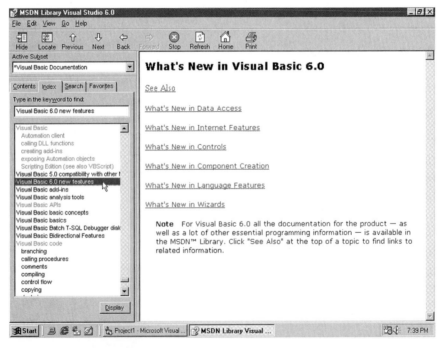

Figure O.22 "What's New in Visual Basic 6.0" provides a quick look at new features.

TASK 8: TO SEARCH FOR INFORMATION

1 Select the Search pane in the left column of MSDN Library.
The search feature will appear in the left pane.

2 Type **ADO** in the text box labeled "Type in the word(s) to search for" and press (ENTER).
After a moment, a list of search results will appear in the left pane, as shown in Figure O.23. These results can be sorted for relevance using a number of criteria. In this case, you want to see the information that pertains to Visual Basic, not the rest of Visual Studio (this won't be a problem if Visual Basic is installed without the rest of Visual Studio).

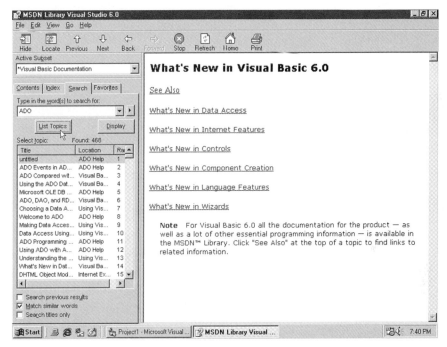

Figure O.23 The default view in Search is somewhat a mess.

3 Click the header labeled "Location" at the top of the search results.
The search results will be sorted by their position in MSDN Library (that is, by topic subsets), as shown in Figure O.24.

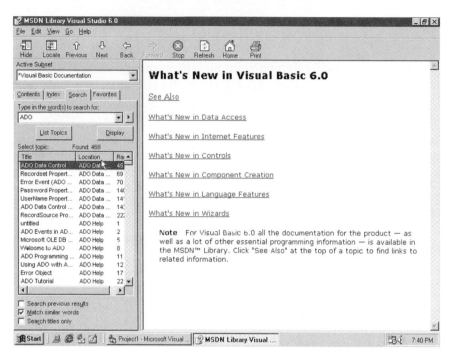

Figure O.24 You can sort search results by topic location.

4   Scroll down the list of search results.
    You will see results in "ADO Data Control," "ADO Help," and other
    locations. You will be learning more about ADO in a later project.

TASK 9: TO USE FAVORITES

1   Select the Favorites pane in the left column of MSDN Library.
    The Favorites feature will appear. Like Internet Explorer, the MSDN Library
    Favorites feature lets you save your favorite locations (in this case, within
    MSDN Library) for later retrieval. This way, you can always get back easily
    to an important document in *Help* if you need to.

2   Return to the Contents pane and double-click "Visual Basic Start Page" from
    within the Visual Basic Documentation section.
    The Visual Basic Start Page will appear in the right pane of MSDN Library.

3   Return to the Favorites pane and click the Add button.
    This adds the Visual Basic Start Page to your Favorites list (Figure O.25). The
    next time you visit MSDN Library, you will be able to get to this page with-
    out navigating through the Contents or Index and without searching for it.

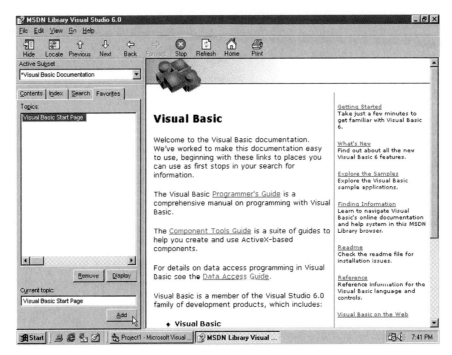

Figure O.25 Adding a Favorites item is very similar to adding one in Internet Explorer and enables you to return easily to this topic later.

TASK 10: TO EXIT MSDN LIBRARY

1 Click the ⊠ button in the top right of the MSDN Library or choose *Exit* from the *File* menu.

> **Tip** Throughout the course of this module, you will frequently run into new and potentially confusing topics. Programming isn't like other computer-related tasks where it is sometimes obvious where to turn for help. If you don't understand something, remember that you can always turn to MSDN Library for help.

Exiting Visual Basic

Now that you've had a short tour of the Visual Basic interface and MSDN Library, you can exit Visual Basic.

TASK 11: TO EXIT VISUAL BASIC

1 Open the *File* menu and choose *Exit*. Visual Basic will often ask you if you'd like to save changes.

2 Click the No button if the Save dialog box appears.

Naturally, you can also choose to exit Visual Basic by clicking the ⊠ button in the top right of the main Visual Basic window.

> **Tip** Visual Basic projects are sometimes referred to as **solutions** because it is easy to think of anything you create in VB as a solution. As such, Visual Basic will save your solution if you so desire, including all the changes you have made, the positions and sizes of windows in the IDE, and the like. Visual Basic will always remember the way you set up the IDE and return it to that state the next time you use it.

The Conclusion

You are about to enter the exciting world of Windows programming with Visual Basic 6.0. In the coming projects, you will explore the core features of Visual Basic while you develop useful—and we hope fun—applications all on your own! Your first program will emulate the classic introductory programming assignment, the famous *Hello, world!* For now, you have concluded your overview of Visual Basic 6.0; you can either exit Visual Basic now or go on and work the Study Questions.

Summary and Exercises

Summary

- A program is a series of instructions for a computer, written in a programming language.
- Visual Basic allows you to create easy yet powerful event-driven programs for Microsoft Windows.
- A typical Visual Basic Integrated Development Environment (IDE) will have five main subwindows: Toolbox, Form, Project Explorer, Properties, and Form Layout.
- The main window contains the menu bar and toolbars; subwindows are typically docked to the main window.
- The Toolbox window is a palette of controls.
- The Form window provides the basis for your Standard EXE program.
- The Project Explorer window lists the files that make up the current solution.
- The Properties window is used to set attributes for the currently selected object.
- The Form Layout window is used to determine where your program will appear on the Windows desktop.
- MSDN Library provides extensive online help for Visual Basic and other Visual Studio 6.0 applications.

Key Terms and Operations

Key Terms

Altair	object
BASIC	Pascal
C	Personal Computer (PC)
C++	program
docked	programmers
event-driven programming	programming language
events	project
execute	properties
form	Rapid Application Development
Fortran	(RAD)
hypertext	run
IBM PC	scripting language
Internet	solution
Java	Visual Basic IDE
machine language	Visual C++
methods	Visual J++
MITS	Visual Studio
MSDN Library	Windows
MS-DOS	

Operations

access MSDN Library to get help
dock child windows
exit Visual Basic
start Visual Basic
undock child windows

Study Questions

Multiple Choice

1. In Visual Basic terminology, a window is called a
   a. file.
   b. form.
   c. Microsoft Windows.
   d. project.

2. Programmers write programs in a human-readable format with
   a. machine code.
   b. assembly language.
   c. a programming language.
   d. a Web scripting language.

3. The key programming concept in Visual Basic is
   a. procedural.
   b. object-oriented.
   c. event-driven.
   d. modal.

4. Which window in the Visual Basic IDE is a palette of controls?
   a. Properties window
   b. Toolbox window
   c. Project Explorer window
   d. Form window

5. Which kind of help would you not find in MSDN Library?
   a. Visual Basic
   b. Visual Studio
   c. Visual C++
   d. Windows 98

True/False

1. More people have computers than have VCRs.

2. Visual Basic is harder to use than other programming languages.

3. RAD stands for Really Advanced Development.

4. Visual Basic is an object-based programming language.

5. You should always enable forced variable declaration.

Short Answer

1. What is the native language of a computer?

2. When the user clicks a command button, what is that an example of?

3. What does RAD stand for?

4. What is the suite of programming tools that Visual Basic is a part of?

5. When was BASIC originally developed?

Group Discussion

1. How is Visual Basic different from other versions of BASIC?

2. Why is event-driven programming so natural in Windows?

3. Why is Visual Basic an important tool to master?

4. Where do you see programming tools heading next?

PART ONE

Hello World!

PROJECT

Building Your First Program

In the programming world, there is perhaps no more famous sample program than *"Hello, world!"* For that reason, the projects in Part One of this module will acquaint you with Visual Basic 6.0 using this classic example. Unlike the dry programming projects of the past, however, you will be tackling the *"Hello, world!"* example the *visual* way, using the world's easiest software development tool. Using only controls and properties, you will create your first real Windows application. Sure, it will be a modest program, but it is your first step toward a greater understanding of Visual Basic and the way its tools work together. You will also be improving this program somewhat over the course of the next three projects.

Objectives

After completing this project, you will be able to:

➤ **Create and save a Visual Basic project**

➤ **Change form properties using the IDE**

➤ **Run Visual Basic programs from the IDE**

➤ **Use system colors**

The Challenge

Your first goal is to get acquainted with the Visual Basic environment and the way its tools allow you to construct the user interface for your programs visually. Each of the subsequent projects in Part One builds on the program you design here so that when you're done you will have created a fully functional Visual Basic application.

While you're probably ready to sit down and start playing with Visual Basic, programming requires a little more forethought than that You first need to spend some time away from the computer to plan your solution. Don't make the classic mistake of sitting down immediately at the computer and attacking the problem without understanding the overall goals of the project. In this case, the program you will create is small and fairly easy to understand, so it won't require much advance planning.

The Solution

The specifications for this first program are as follows:

- The program will display a single window with a title containing your name followed by a colon, a space, and the phrase *Project 1*.

- The window will have a fixed border so that the user cannot resize it.

- The background color of the window will match the system background color for windows.

When this project is complete, your program should resemble Figure 1.1.

Figure 1.1 The specifications call for Project 1 to resemble this when complete.

The Setup

OK, it's time to get your hands dirty! Place this module near a computer, turn it on if required, and boot into Windows 98 (Windows 95 or NT 4.0+ will work as well). Since this is the first time you will actually use Visual Basic, you should first become familiar with some VB terminology. As mentioned in the Overview, Visual Basic uses a *solution file* to store any projects you create with the program. Visual Basic **solutions** consist of the windows—which Visual Basic calls forms—and code files that you create, along with other types of files that you or the system may create. This collection of files (the solution) as a whole represents the project—or projects—you are working with. Generally speaking, the Visual Basic projects you'll be working through in this module aren't very large, but you should consult your instructor about the location(s) to which you should save your projects. It's not a good idea to randomly place files on the computer or network.

Beginning a New Project

There are two crucial elements to starting a new project in Visual Basic: (1) Choosing the correct *project type* and (2) naming your files in a logical manner when you save the project. Visual Basic supports a number of project types, including *Standard EXE* (the type you will normally work with), *ActiveX EXE*, *ActiveX DLL*, and many others. When you first run Visual Basic, you will be presented with a dialog box that will ask you about the type of project you'd like to create. Naming your files will occur the first time you save your project. In the following steps, you will create a new Visual Basic project and then save the project to disk so you can access it later.

TASK 1: TO START VISUAL BASIC

1 Open the *Start* menu, navigate to the appropriate Program group, and click the *Microsoft Visual Basic 6.0* item.
The Visual Basic IDE will open and the New Project dialog box will appear.

2 Select *Standard EXE* and click ⬚Open⬚.
This will create a new Visual Basic project, as shown in Figure 1.2.

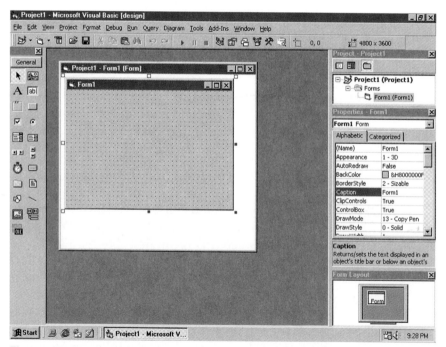

Figure 1.2 A new project is loaded into the Visual Basic IDE.

TASK 2: TO SAVE YOUR VISUAL BASIC PROJECT

1 From the *File* menu, choose *Save Project*.
The Save File As dialog box will appear, as shown in Figure 1.3. The first item Visual Basic wants you to save is the form window.

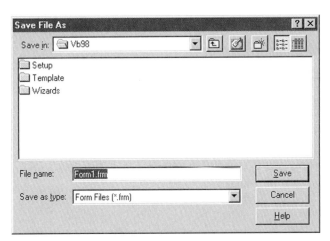

Figure 1.3 When you save your project, the form file is saved first.

2 Navigate to the location where you will save your Visual Basic projects (consult your instructor or lab assistant) and create a new folder called *Hello, world!* as shown in Figure 1.4.

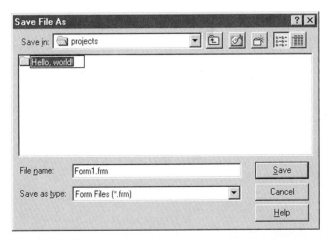

Figure 1.4 Create a new folder to hold the files in your solution.

3 Select all of the text in the File name text box, type **hello** and then press (ENTER) to save the form as *hello.frm*.
Now the Save Project As dialog box will appear (Figure 1.5).

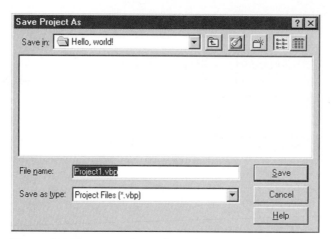

Figure 1.5 The second step in saving the project involves saving the project file.

4 Select all of the text in the File name text box, type **hello**, and then press
(ENTER) to save the project as *hello.vbp* (Figure 1.6).
The dialog box will close, and you will be returned to the Visual Basic IDE.

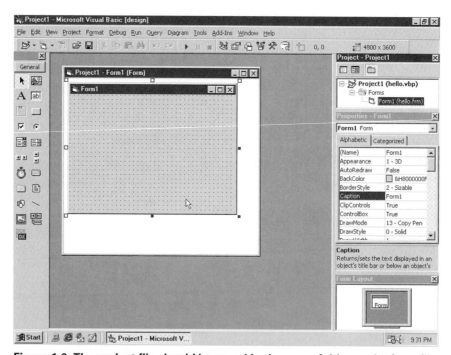

Figure 1.6 The project file should be saved in the same folder as the form file.

If you look at the Project window in the Visual Basic IDE, you will see that
the file name of the project has changed (to *hello.vbp*) and the file name of
the form has also changed (to *hello.frm*) (see Figure 1.7). These names are
used by the Windows file system to locate and use the files. Internally, Visual Basic has other names for the project and form, however, and you
can change those to be friendlier as well.

Figure 1.7 Once you've saved the project files, the Project Explorer updates to reflect the new file names.

Tip The *.frm* extension obviously stands for "form" but can you guess what the *.vbp* extension stands for? If you guessed "Visual Basic project," you are correct. Older versions of Visual Basic used the extension *.mak* for project files. Go figure.

Exploring the Properties Window

The Properties window in the Visual Basic IDE contains a list of attributes for the object that is currently selected in the Project window. In a Standard EXE project like the one you are creating, the form window is selected by default. You can see that it has a long list of *properties*—attributes you can change or retrieve—with which to work. When you think about the things you can do with a form window, some of the properties (*Caption*, *Height*, and *Width*, for example) probably make sense immediately. Others such as *DrawStyle*, *OLEDropMode*, and the like are probably more confusing right now (thank goodness for the excellent online help!). Every item you work with in Visual Basic will have a property list like this.

Using the Properties window is straightforward: You select the property you'd like to change by clicking the property name in the left column and then pull down a list of options in the right column or type in a new value. Many properties, such as *Enabled*, have a limited range of potential values. For example, *Enabled* can only be set to True or False; if you type a value such as **Bob** into the Enabled property, Visual Basic will not accept it. For this reason, it's a good idea to use the Properties window when you can to take advantage of Visual Basic's built-in error-checking: It will never let you enter an incorrect value. On the other hand, some properties, such as *Caption*, do let you type in a value and you are free to create whatever text you'd like, as shown in Figure 1.8.

BorderStyle	2 - Sizable
Caption	Ramalamadingd
ClipControls	True
ControlBox	True
DrawMode	13 - Copy Pen

Figure 1.8 Properties that accept text will accept just about any text you can think of.

Properties that offer drop-down lists of choices (Figure 1.9) can be navigated in other ways as well. For instance, you can double-click on these properties to cycle through the list of possible values. Each double-click will move the value forward to the next choice. When the end of the list of values is encountered, the list cycles back to the beginning. If you encounter a property with numerous possible values, however, double-clicking will quickly become tiresome. In this case, simply click the down-arrow in the right side to find the value you need.

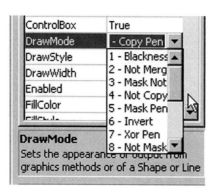

Figure 1.9 Some properties provide a drop-down list of possible values.

Moving Around the Properties Window

The default view in the Properties window is alphabetical, but you can also choose to sort properties by category. To do so, simply select the *Categorized* tab in the window. This view, shown in Figure 1.10, can actually be more confusing than the alphabetical view, especially when the selected item has a large number of properties, like form windows do. In this module, we won't be using the categorized view, but you are free to do so if you find it more logical.

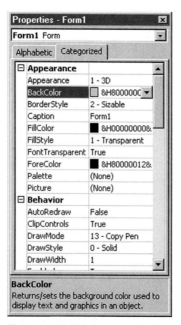

Figure 1.10 The categorized view in the Properties window segregates properties into logical groups.

One other note about the Properties window: You will notice a drop-down list box at the top of the window, which should now read *Form 1 Form* (Figure 1.11). This list offers one method of choosing the item for which you like to see properties: Simply select the item you want from the list. Right now, you should only see one item in the list box; you don't yet have a list of choices.

Figure 1.11 The drop-down list at the top of the Properties window allows you to choose from the available objects.

Changing the Properties

Now that you've had a chance to explore the Properties window, it's time to get to work. In the following subsections you will make changes to four properties: *Name, Caption, BorderStyle,* and *BackColor.*

Changing the *Name* Property

First, you will change the **internal names** for the form and project by changing the **Name** property. The internal names for items in your projects will become more important when you begin writing Visual Basic code (starting in the next project), but it's a good idea to get in the habit of naming things logically from the start.

TASK 3: TO RENAME THE INTERNAL PROJECT NAME

 Click the text *Project 1 (hello.vbp)* in the Project window to select it. Notice that the view in the Properties window changes to display the properties for the project, not for the form, now that the project is the selected item. This is shown in Figure 1.12.

Figure 1.12 **The project properties are not as extensive as the form properties.**

2   Select the text to the right of the (*Name*) property.

3   Type **HelloProject** as the project name and press (ENTER).
The caption in the Visual Basic IDE will change to reflect the new name, as will the name of the project in the Project window (Figure 1.13).

Figure 1.13 **Once you change the name of the project, the Project Explorer will automatically reflect that change.**

TASK 4: TO RENAME THE INTERNAL FORM NAME

1   Select the form in the Project window.
The Properties window view will change to show the properties for *Form1*.

2   Select the text to the right of the (*Name*) property.

3   Type **HelloForm** as the form name and press (ENTER).
The caption in the floating form window will change, as will the name of the form in the Project window (Figure 1.14).

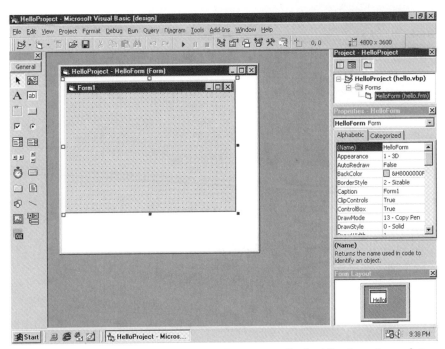

Figure 1.14 Changing the form name also causes Project Explorer to update.

4   Save the Project by clicking the 🖫 button on the toolbar or by choosing *Save Project* from the *File* menu.
Because you have already named your form and project, you will not see a dialog box; your work is automatically saved.

Running the Program

Admittedly, you haven't actually done anything to affect the appearance of your program yet, but it's always fun to see it come to life for the first time. In the following steps, you will run the program from the IDE. During the development of a Visual Basic project, you might do this hundreds of times.

TASK 5: TO RUN THE PROGRAM FROM THE IDE

1   Run the program by clicking the ▶ button on the toolbar or by choosing *Start* from the *Run* menu.
The program window will appear, as shown in Figure 1.15.

Figure 1.15 Here it is—your first program!

2 You can play with the window a bit by resizing it or minimizing, maximizing, and restoring it.

3 Close the window when you are done by clicking its ⊠ button.

Tip You can also run programs from the IDE by clicking the (F5) key.

One thing you might have noticed when you ran your program is that it appeared near the upper-left corner of the screen. Typically, you want your programs to start in a specific location; the Visual Basic IDE offers a way to do this without having to write any code. In the lower-right corner of the IDE, you should see the Form Layout window (if not, choose *Form Layout Window* from the View window). This window, which shows a graphical representation of your form window on the desktop, lets you determine where your form will appear when the program runs (Figure 1.16). In the following steps, you will ensure that your program begins in the center of the screen.

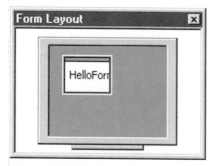

Figure 1.16 The Form Layout window shows a graphical representation of where your program will appear on the desktop.

TASK 6: TO MAKE SURE THE PROGRAM RUNS IN THE CENTER OF THE SCREEN

1 Right-click the representation of your form in the Form Layout window of the Visual Basic IDE.
A pop-up menu will appear, as shown in Figure 1.17.

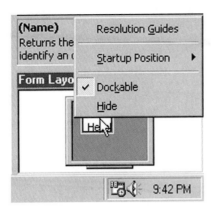

Figure 1.17 The pop-up menu for the Form Layout window appears.

2 Choose *Startup Position* and then *Center Screen.*
The little form window representation will change position to reflect its new startup position (Figure 1.18).

Figure 1.18 When you change the startup position of your form, the Form Layout window will update to reflect that change.

3 Run the program again and see that it starts in the center of the screen (Figure 1.19).

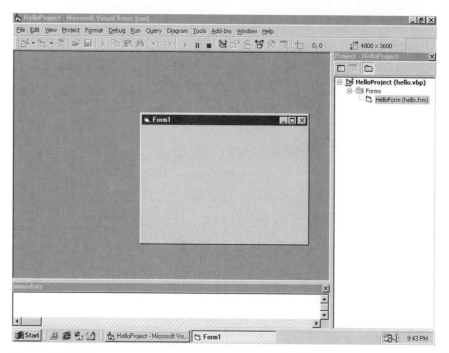

Figure 1.19 Now your program starts in the center of your screen.

4   Close your program and return to the Visual Basic IDE.

Changing the *Caption* Property

You will now change the **Caption property** of the form. The form's *Caption* property is used to set the text you see in the form's title bar. The form in your project is currently set to its default value of *Form1*.

TASK 7: TO CHANGE THE *CAPTION* PROPERTY

1   Select the form. You can do this by clicking the form itself in the floating window labeled *HelloProject – (Form1)*, or by selecting *HelloForm* from the Project window.

2   In the Properties window, double-click the *Caption* property.
This will highlight the text in the value side of the *Caption* property (Figure 1.20).

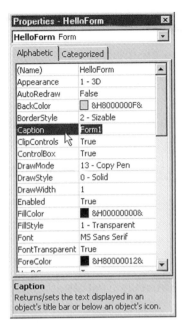

Figure 1.20 When you double-click the *Caption* property, its value is highlighted.

3 Type your name, a colon, a space, and then **Project 1**.
The screen should resemble Figure 1.21, with your name instead of *Mark Thurrott*.

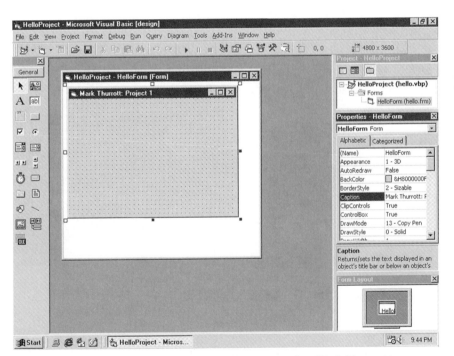

Figure 1.21 You should substitute your own name for *Mark Thurrott*.

4 Press (ENTER) and run the program to see your changes.

5 Quit the program when you are done.

Changing the *BorderStyle* Property

You will recall from the list of specifications for this project that the window should not be resizable but should rather feature a fixed border. The border style of a form window, logically enough, is set with the **Border-Style property**. Using this property, you can enable or disable the window's resize capability, make the window look like a dialog box or tool window, or remove the border altogether. In the following steps, you will change the style of the form window's border.

TASK 8: TO CHANGE THE *BORDERSTYLE* PROPERTY

1 Click the form window to select it.

2 Click the *BorderStyle* property in the Properties window. The current border style is set to *2 – Sizable*.

3 Pull down the drop-down list for *BorderStyle* values and choose *1 – Fixed Single*, as shown in Figure 1.22.

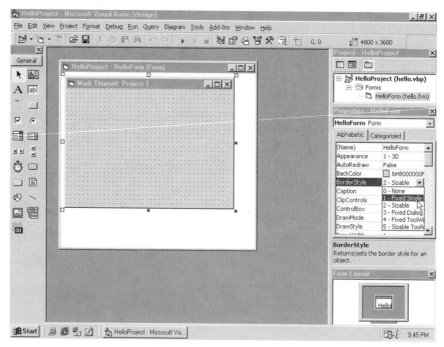

Figure 1.22 The *BorderStyle* property offers a list of preset values.

4 Press (ENTER).

5 Run the program and note the change in its border style.
You are now unable to resize the window while the program is running. The program is shown in Figure 1.23.

Figure 1.23 Now your program window cannot be resized by the user.

6   Close the program and return to the Visual Basic IDE.

Setting the *BackColor* Property

In the bad old days before Windows 95, software developers used to force, or **hard-code**, color values into their programs, pushing their aesthetic ideals on unwary users. The problem with this approach is that Windows supports **system colors** that can be modified in Display Properties. Whereas many users are happy with blue title bars, gray windows, and a teal desktop, others spend considerable time changing the colors of almost every item in their systems. A good program will respect these system colors and not change a title bar to green, for example. Rather, it will set the color of the title bar to the system color for title bars. This means that any user—whether they've changed the color of their title bars or not—can see the color they want to see when they run your program.

Of course, Visual Basic supports both ways of setting values: You can specify a specific color for various properties when needed, or you can tell your program to use a user-configurable system color such as *Menu Text* or *Button Face*. Sometimes it really is appropriate to hard-code color values, but some poorly-written programs throw up an obnoxious white window on your otherwise grayscale-colored screen. In this module, the programs will generally keep to the system colors and not unwisely force color ideals on the user.

On that note, it's time to take a look at a property that sets a color: the **BackColor property**. In the case of a form window, the *BackColor* property does, indeed, set the background color of the form window. If you haven't changed the system colors on your system, this means that your window will appear in a medium gray color. This color is actually set by the system color "Button Face," which, as you might suspect, is also the default color for command buttons in your system. You won't need to change the value of *BackColor* property—it's already set to Button Face—but this is a good time check out this property and see how these colors are set. The specification for the project calls for the background color of the window to match the background color of other windows in your system.

TASK 9: TO VIEW THE *BACKCOLOR* PROPERTY FOR THE FORM

1 Click the form window to select it.

2 Double-click the *BackColor* property in the Properties window.
A drop-down window will appear with two panes, as shown in Figure 1.24. The selected pane contains a list of the possible system colors, and the other pane provides a color palette should you wish to select a hard-coded color.

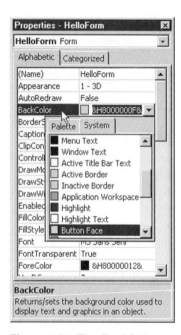

Figure 1.24 The *BackColor* property supplies a two-page list of possible values.

3 Scroll through the list of possible system colors, noting the various values.

4 Click the blank area to the right of the *System* tab to close the drop-down window.

The Conclusion

You have concluded the first part of your first Visual Basic program. In the next project, you will add a label control to your form that displays a "Hello, world!" message. Future projects in Part One will expand on this program and introduce you to other controls and Visual Basic concepts while adding new features to the program.

You can either exit Visual Basic now or go on to work the Study Questions. If Visual Basic asks you to save any files when you exit, choose Yes from the dialog box.

Summary and Exercises

Summary

- Projects and forms are saved separately as part of a Visual Basic solution.
- The *Caption* property of a form changes the form's title bar text.
- The *BorderStyle* property of a form determines the type of border on the form window.
- The *Name* property determines the internal name of a form or control.
- The *BackColor* property determines the background color of the form.

Key Terms and Operations

Key Terms

BackColor property
BorderStyle property
Caption property
FRM file
hard-code
internal names
Name property
project type
solutions
system colors
VBP file

Operations

create and save a VB project
run a program from the IDE
save the project and form files
   separately as part of a solution
use the Properties window to set form
   properties

Study Questions

Multiple Choice

1. The form is saved separately from the project, but you should save them
   a. in the same folder.
   b. on the same hard drive.
   c. on the same network.
   d. in the same code segment.

2. The form's *Caption* property changes the
   a. text on the form window.
   b. text on the form's status bar.
   c. text on the form's title bar.
   d. text on the form's input.

3. What are the two primary file types that Visual Basic will save in a Standard EXE project type?
   a. EXE and COM
   b. FRM and MAK
   c. MAK and VBP
   d. FRM and VBP

4. Which window contains a list of attributes for the currently selected object?
    a. Form window
    b. Project Explorer window
    c. Visual Basic window
    d. Properties window

5. Double-clicking the *Caption* property in the Properties window will
    a. cause the computer to beep.
    b. move to the next property in the list.
    c. select the current value of the property.
    d. do nothing.

6. To run your program from within the IDE, you can choose
    a. *Run* from the *File* menu.
    b. *Make Exe* from the *File* menu.
    c. *New Form* from the *Edit* menu.
    d. *Start* from the *Run* menu.

7. If you don't want the user to resize the form window while the program is running, which property would you change?
    a. *BorderStyle*
    b. *BorderWidth*
    c. *Resize*
    d. *BorderType*

8. The property used to identify an object internally is called the
    a. *Title* property.
    b. *Name* property.
    c. *ID* property.
    d. *InternalName* property.

9. You want the background color of the form to match the color of the desktop. Which property must you change?
    a. *Background* property
    b. *Back* property
    c. *BackColor* property
    d. *BackStyle* property

10. Which one of these choices is *not* a way to run your program from the Visual Basic IDE?
    a. Choose Start from the Run menu.
    b. Press (F5).
    c. Click the *Run* button ▶ on the toolbar.
    d. Double-click the EXE file for your program in My Computer.

True/False

1. Visual Basic uses a solution file to store the projects you create.

2. Typically, you work with an ActiveX DLL project when you want to create a Windows application in Visual Basic.

3. A form is a window.

4. You can set the value of a *Name* property to a string of characters that includes a space.

5. The *Text* property is used to set the text you see in the form's title bar.

6. You can use the *BorderStyle* property to determine whether the user can resize a form.

7. It is impossible to hard-code color values into the *BackColor* property.

8. Properties can be set in the Visual Basic IDE with the Properties window.

9. Visual Basic uses internal names for objects in your programs.

10. Visual Basic 6.0 projects use a .mak extension.

Short Answer

1. If you want the user to be able to resize the form's border, what is the correct value for *BorderStyle*?

2. What types of files make up a Visual Basic solution?

3. What type of project would you start if you want to create a typical Windows application?

4. What does the .frm file extension stand for?

5. Would the Visual Basic IDE allow you to enter the nonsensical phrase **jfdklfjdklk123** as the caption for a form window?

6. What happens when you double-click a property in the Properties window that displays a drop-down list of values?

7. Why is it important to give objects internal names?

8. How do you tell Visual Basic where you want your program to appear when it runs?

9. How do you change the text in the title bar of the form?

10. What is the color setting for Button Face on your system?

Group Discussion

1. The program you created in this project did not require you to write any code, yet you can run the program and it does work. What do you think Visual Basic is doing for you in the background?

2. Visual Basic lets you save form files separately from the rest of the project so that you can easily reuse those windows in other solutions. Why is this beneficial?

3. Because Visual Basic is so easy to use, a lot of non-programmers have started using it. What might be the downside to this?

4. Using MSDN Library, search for the term *hello, visual basic* and look over the document titled "Hello, Visual Basic" to get you prepared for the next project.

Hands-On

1. Practice with properties
Create a form with a hard-coded light blue background, a caption of **My little blue form**, and a sizable border.

2. Working with border styles
Start a new Visual Basic project and experiment with the different form border styles. Explain how each is different and, if possible, find an example of each style somewhere else in the Windows user interface.

On Your Own

1. Writing specifications

Sometimes program specifications resemble clear English instructions that might be given to a person for a certain task. On a piece of paper or in a word processing program, write specifications for the computation of gross pay based on the following information.

a. The pay rate is $10.00 per hour.

b. Hours worked above 40 are paid at a rate of time and a half (that is, one and a half times the pay rate).

> **Tip** These kinds of instructions are sometimes referred to as *pseudocode*. Programmers use pseudocode to map out the solution to a programming problem in English. The pseudocode is then used as the basis for the actual programming language code they need to write to solve the problem.

2. Working with colors

Create a new Visual Basic project and set the *BackColor* property of the form window to Teal, which is the default color of the desktop (if your desktop is a different color, try to set it to the closest color you can find to the desktop color). Create a second project, this time setting the form *BackColor* to the system color "Desktop." Now, change the color of the system's desktop background using Display Properties. Run both programs again and describe what happens with each.

Using Controls

As your experience with Visual Basic grows, you will need to learn how to use, manipulate, and program Visual Basic controls. In this project, you will take the first step toward this goal by adding your first control to your *Hello, world!* program. You will also learn how to create an executable program that can be run without the Visual Basic IDE.

Objectives

After completing this project, you will be able to:

➤ **Reload a Visual Basic project**

➤ **Place text on a form with a label control**

➤ **Change label control properties**

➤ **Create an executable program**

➤ **Print a Visual Basic program**

The Challenge

You will recall from Project 1 that you are creating a program that will display the text *Hello, world!* In Project 1, you created the basis for this program: a new Visual Basic project that contains a single form window. You modified the name of the project, the name of the form, and the title bar caption. You also ensured that users of the program would not be able to resize the window.

For the second installment of this program, you will need to add a text label to the form so that you can display the caption phrase indicated in the specifications. The Visual Basic label control will work nicely, and you will work with this control's properties so that the text of the label matches the requirements of the specifications. Then, using options in the Visual Basic IDE, you will create an executable version of your program and print out the pertinent information.

The Solution

The specifications for this program are as follows:

- The phrase *Hello, world!* will appear in the center of the form, aligned to the center.

- The text will be rendered using the 24-point bold italic Verdana font.

- The default system color will be used for the text.

- An executable version of the program will be created so that users without Visual Basic will be able to run it.

- The form image and properties will be outputted to a printer.

The Setup

You will need to reload your Visual Basic solution so that you may continue working with it. In Project 1, two files were saved, hello.frm (the form file) and hello.vbp (the project file). You reload the program by selecting the correct project file when Visual Basic starts.

TASK 1: TO RELOAD THE *HELLO, WORLD!* PROJECT

 Start Visual Basic with its shortcut in the *Start* menu.

 In the New Project window that appears, select the *Existing* tab as shown in Figure 2.1.

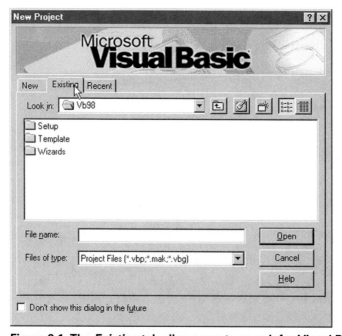

Figure 2.1 The *Existing* tab allows you to search for Visual Basic solutions that have been saved to disk.

3 In the *Existing* page of the dialog box, navigate to the location where you stored your project and double-click hello.vbp to reload the project. Your *Hello, world!* project will appear.

4 In the Project window, expand the *Forms* folder and double-click *HelloForm (hello.frm)* to display the form (Figure 2.2).

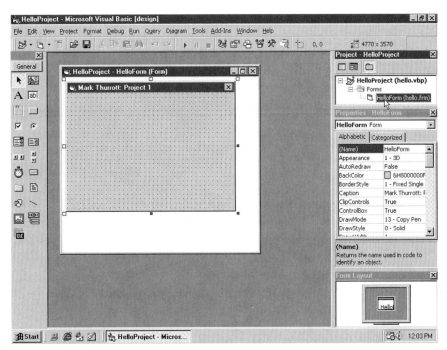

Figure 2.2 The form window is not automatically displayed when your project reloads.

Naming Conventions Overview

You may recall from Project 1 that we named the form and the project with easily understood names—*HelloForm* and *HelloProject*. Although these names are certainly readable and understandable, it would be hard to maintain this program if it had many named items. What if, for example, the program had 20 menu items? Names such as *HelloMenu1, HelloMenu2,* and so on would quickly confuse any programmer. For this reason, different **naming conventions** have developed over the years to provide standardized ways of naming items used in any programming language, be it Visual Basic, C++, or whatever.

The most successful of these naming conventions is the **Hungarian Notation** developed by Charles Simonyi, a famous programmer from Microsoft who is Hungarian by birth. Simonyi decided that the best way to name an item would be to add a descriptive prefix to its name. For example, Form windows get the prefix **frm**; a form you might otherwise call *MainWindow* would be named *frmMainWindow* using Hungarian Notation. Before you understand the notation, the name might look like gibberish. But once you get used to it, it makes good sense. This early in your Visual Basic experience you might question the need for such a naming convention, but when you start writing actual Visual Basic code, you will be happy to have such a naming convention to to keep things coherent.

In fact, you'll soon be adding a *label control* to your form that will allow you to display a string of text to the user. The label control, like other controls used by Visual Basic, can use any name you see fit, but it's a good idea to get used to the naming conventions you'll see in other projects in this module. So you will begin using Hungarian Notation names almost immediately. The prefix for a label control, by the way, is **lbl**.

Using a Label Control

Looking back to the specifications for this project, you'll notice that we need to display some text in the center of the form. This sounds like the sort of thing a control might be used for, and you will find that the Toolbox window in the Visual Basic IDE contains a palette of controls you can add to your form. One such control, the **label control**, is indeed specifically designed to display text.

Adding a Label Control to Your Form

In the following steps, you will add a label control to your form.

TASK 2: TO ADD A LABEL CONTROL TO THE FORM

1 Locate the label control A in the Toolbox window (if the Toolbox is not available, choose *Toolbox* from the *View* menu).

2 Double-click the label control icon A to add a label to your form. A label with the caption *Label1* will appear in the center of the form (Figure 2.3).

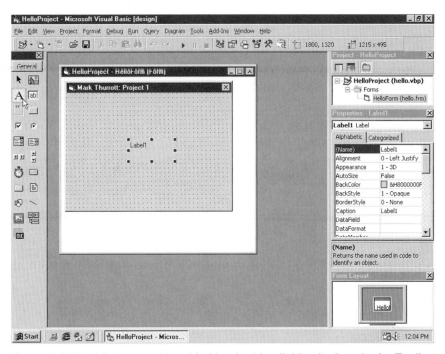

Figure 2.3 The label control is added by double-clicking its icon in the Toolbox.

Resizing the Label Control

Since the label control appears in the center of the form window by default, you won't need to move it but you will want to resize it so that it occupies the width of the window. Controls can be moved by clicking and dragging, similar to the way you move icons around on the Windows desktop. You can resize most controls using the resizing boxes found around the edges of the control when it is selected. In the following steps, you will resize the label control to occupy the full width of the form window.

TASK 3: TO RESIZE THE LABEL CONTROL

1   Select the label control on the form window.

2   Move the mouse pointer to the left edge of the control.
Note that the pointer changes into a double-sided arrow, indicating that you can drag the edge to resize the control. This is shown in Figure 2.4.

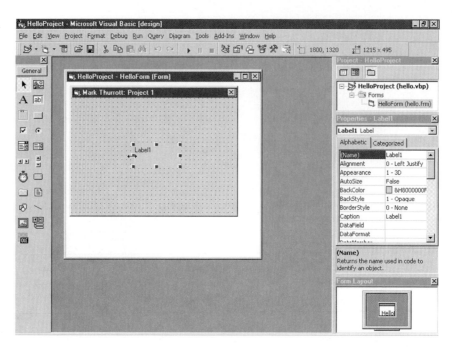

Figure 2.4 When you hover over the edge of most controls, the mouse cursor changes to allow you to resize the control.

3   As shown in Figure 2.5, drag the left edge of the control to the left edge of the form window and release the mouse button.

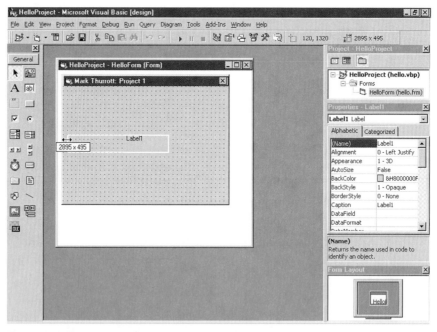

Figure 2.5 To resize a control, grab one of its sides with the mouse cursor and drag it away from the control.

4   Repeat step 3 for the right side of the control.
When you are done, the label control should resemble Figure 2.6.

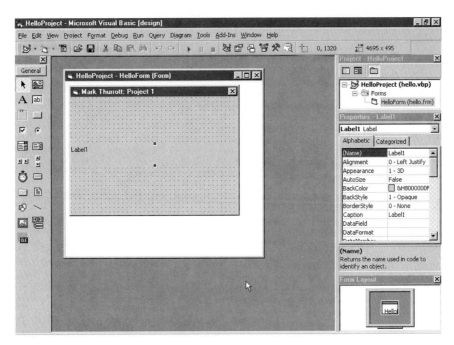

Figure 2.6 The resized label control now occupies the width of the form.

Modifying the *Name* Property

Per the earlier discussion of naming conventions, it's now time to honor Charles Simonyi by renaming your new label control with something more befitting a true Visual Basic program. The **Name property** (which is conveniently located at the top of the properties list as (*Name*) in the Properties window) provides this ability.

TASK 4: TO CHANGE THE *NAME* PROPERTY

1   Select the label control.

2   Locate the (*Name*) property at the top of the Properties window.

3   Double-click the property name and type **lblHello** as the name for the label control (Figure 2.7).

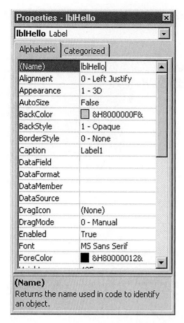

Figure 2.7 You can rename the label control by changing the *Name* property.

4 Press (ENTER) for the change to take effect.

Modifying the *Alignment* Property

Now that the label control is properly situated on the form and has been renamed, you will need to center the text that it displays. You can modify the label's ***Alignment property*** to achieve this effect. Text in a label control can be aligned three ways: *left-aligned* (the default), *right-aligned*, or *centered*. In the following steps, you will center the text in the label control.

TASK 5: TO CHANGE THE *ALIGNMENT* PROPERTY

1 Select the label control if it isn't already selected.

2 In the Properties window, locate and select the *Alignment* property.

3 In the value column, select *2 - Center* from the drop-down list box and press (ENTER).
The text in the label control will be centered, as shown in Figure 2.8.

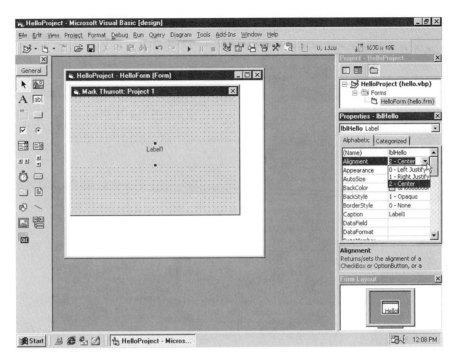

Figure 2.8 The *Alignment* property offers a drop-down list of possible choices.

Modifying the *Caption* Property

According to the specifications for this project, the label control should display the text *Hello, world!* in the center of the window. You've already centered the text, but it still displays *Label1*. In the following steps, you will change the text displayed by the label. This is done by changing its ***Caption* property**.

TASK 6: TO CHANGE THE *CAPTION* PROPERTY

1 Select the label control if it isn't already selected.

2 Locate the *Caption* property and double-click it to highlight the existing caption.

3 Type **Hello, world!** as the new caption.

4 Run the program by choosing *Start* from the *Run* menu or by pressing the ▶ button on the toolbar.
You're getting close! The program should now display the correct message (Figure 2.9).

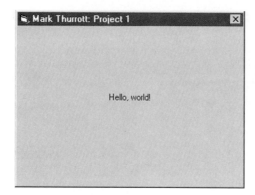

Figure 2.9 Hello, world!

Changing the Text Properties

Now you need to modify the font of the text in the label control so that it is the right typeface, style, and size. The specification for this project calls for the Verdana font rendered in 24-point bold italic text. The text should match the system color for text.

For controls that use text, Visual Basic supplies a **Font property** to set the font and font styles displayed. Attempting to modify this control launches a separate Font selection window that may be familiar to you: It's the same one used by programs like Microsoft Notepad. In the following steps, you will modify the *Font* property and the **ForeColor property**, which is used to set the foreground color of the control (which in this case is the text of the control).

TASK 7: TO CHANGE THE *FONT* PROPERTY

1 Select the label control.

2 Double-click the *Font* property in the Properties window. The Font dialog box will appear, as shown in Figure 2.10.

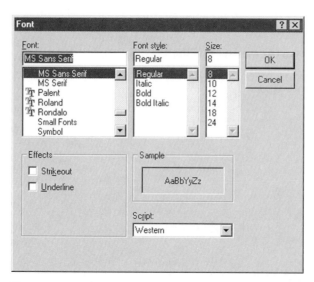

Figure 2.10 The font dialog box appears when you change the Font property.

3 Select *Verdana* from the Font list box.

4 Select *Bold Italic* from the Font style list box.

5 Select *24* from the Size list box and click ⬚ OK to close the dialog box (Figure 2.11).

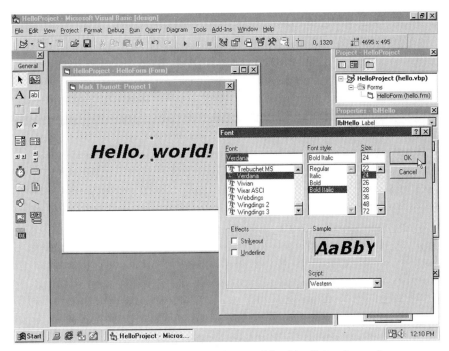

Figure 2.11 Your font selection should resemble this dialog box when you are done.

TASK 8: TO CHANGE THE *FORECOLOR* PROPERTY

1 Select the label control.

2 Double-click the *ForeColor* property in the Properties window. A drop-down window will appear with two tabs. Note that the default choice for the text is *Button Text,* as shown in Figure 2.12.

Figure 2.12 The *ForeColor* property displays a drop-down list identical to the one used by *BackColor*.

3 Change the value to *Window Text*.

4 Run the program as shown in Figure 2.13.

Figure 2.13 Now it looks correct: *Hello, world!* in all its glory.

5 Quit the program when you are done.

Creating an Executable Program

The program you've created is now complete, but if you'd like to run it outside of the Visual Basic IDE, you will need to make an *executable file*. This is a file that will run when you double-click it with the mouse, and it will have a .exe extension. For this reason, executable files are sometimes referred to as **EXEs** (pronounced "ee-ex-ease"). Visual Basic can create a single stand-alone executable file for you if you'd like. In the following steps, you will do so.

Tip   Versions of Visual Basic before version 5.0 could not create true
stand-alone executable files. For your EXE to run, the system would
have to have certain support files installed as well. This is no longer
the case: Your Visual Basic EXEs should run on any Windows 95/98/NT
system.

TASK 9: TO CREATE AN EXE

1   In the Visual Basic IDE, choose *Make hello.exe* from the *File* menu.
The Make Project dialog box will appear, with the project directory loaded
by default. This is shown in Figure 2.14.

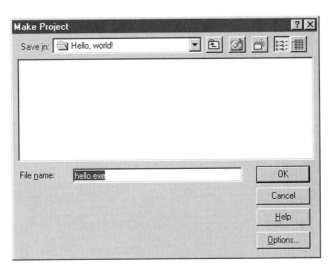

**Figure 2.14 The Make Project dialog box allows you to create an executable (EXE)
file.**

2   Since the default name, *hello.exe*, is acceptable, click   OK   to create the
executable file.
You will see two status bars flash on the Visual Basic toolbar. After a short
time, your executable file will be complete.

3   Navigate to the folder where your project is saved by using My Computer or
Windows Explorer.
You will see a file named *hello.exe,* as shown in Figure 2.15.

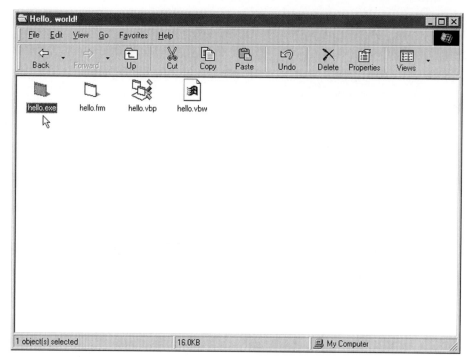

Figure 2.15 Your executable file is saved in the folder you chose earlier.

4 Double-click this file and your program will run.

Congratulations! You've created your first Windows program with Visual Basic.

Printing Your Visual Basic Program

Visual Basic offers a variety of printing options, allowing you to print an image of any form windows, text code listings, and even a text version of a form (which looks like a list of properties and corresponding values). Since the existing project doesn't have any code, your printing tasks will include printing an image of your completed form and a text printout of the form.

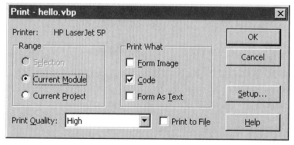

Figure 2.16 The Print dialog box allows you to print information from a Visual Basic solution.

To print in Visual Basic, you must access the *Print* option from the *File* menu. The resulting Print dialog box, shown in Figure 2.16, may seem complex, but a quick overview should get you started. In the left half of the dialog box, under the *Range* section, you can choose whether to print all of the items in the project or just from within the current **module** (also called a code module). A module is simply a file that contains Visual Basic source code; a form is a special kind of module because it also includes visual information (the form and its controls). (We'll be discussing modules in more detail later on.)

In the *Print What* section, you will see three choices. The *Form Image* option will print a graphical image of the form. The Code option, which is selected by default, will print any source code you may have created (so far, you haven't created any source code). Finally, the *Form As Text* option will spit out a list of properties and corresponding values. This can be valuable in some situations, and it's likely that some instructors will ask for this list with your completed projects. For complex projects, however, this list can easily span several pages of paper.

Now that you have an understanding of the Print dialog box, it's time to print your project.

TASK 10: TO PRINT YOUR VISUAL BASIC PROGRAM

1 Choose *Print* from the *File* menu.
The Print dialog box will appear.

2 Uncheck the *Code* option.

3 Select the *Form Image* and *Form As Text* options.

4 Click OK to print as shown in Figure 2.17 and examine the printouts.

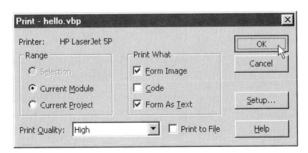

Figure 2.17 Use these options to print information about your Visual Basic program.

5 Close the Visual Basic IDE. Click Yes when the dialog box asks you if you'd like to save changes.

The Conclusion

You have concluded Project 2, which is a continuation of your first Visual Basic program. In the next two projects, you will enhance this program further by adding user interaction and some new Visual Basic controls, including a text box, some command buttons, and other features. You will also learn to write Visual Basic code, which is very similar to English and to HTML, the language of the Web.

You can either exit Visual Basic now or go on to work the Study Questions.

Summary and Exercises

Summary

- The label control is used when you want to display text.
- Controls are added to a form by using the Toolbox window.
- The label's *Caption* property determines what text is displayed.
- The label's *Font* property determines the font and font styles used to display text.
- The label's *Alignment* property determines how text is aligned within the control.
- The label's *ForeColor* property determines the foreground color of the label control.
- Visual Basic can easily create true executable programs (EXEs).
- You can print information about your Visual Basic solution using the Print feature.

Key Terms and Operations

Key Terms
Alignment property
Caption property
executable files (EXEs)
Font property
ForeColor property
Hungarian Notation
label control
module
naming conventions
Name property

Operations
add controls with the Toolbox window
change properties for a label control
create an executable (EXE) file
print a program listing
reload an existing project
run an EXE file from Windows

Study Questions

Multiple Choice

1. The label control is used to
   a. call a procedure.
   b. allow input from the user.
   c. name a variable.
   d. display text.

2. Which window contains a palette of the controls you can add to a form?
   a. Palette window.
   b. Project Explorer window.
   c. Toolbox window.
   d. Form window.

3. To create an executable program in Visual Basic, you must choose
   a. *Make* from the *File* menu.
   b. *Create* from the *File* menu.
   c. *Make EXE* from the *Tools* menu.
   d. *Make* from the *Project* menu.

4. In Hungarian Notation, what is the prefix for a label control?
   a. lab
   b. label
   c. lbl
   d. l

5. The property that determines the color of a label control's text is
   a. *Color.*
   b. *BackColor.*
   c. *TextColor.*
   d. *ForeColor.*

6. You would like to display green text on a black background using a label control. Which two properties would you need to change?
   a. *TextColor* and *BackColor*
   b. *ForeColor* and *BackColor*
   c. *TextColor* and *bgColor*
   d. *ForeColor* and *bgColor*

7. What property would you change if you wanted to right-justify text in a label?
   a. *Align*
   b. *RightJustify*
   c. *Justify*
   d. *Alignment*

8. How would you change the display of a label to Times New Roman 24-point text?
   a. Change the *Font* property
   b. Change the *ForeColor* property
   c. Change the *Text* property
   d. Change the *FontStyle* property

9. When you create an executable file, you can run this file
   a. on Windows 3.1, Windows 95/98, and Windows NT.
   b. on Windows 95/98 and Windows NT.
   c. only from within the Visual Basic IDE.
   d. from any version of Windows as long as Visual Basic is installed.

10. What three things can you print from Visual Basic?
    a. *Form As Text, Form As Image, Module As Image*
    b. *Module Image, Module Code, Module As Code*
    c. *Form Image, Code, Form As Text*
    d. *Form Image, Form As Module, Module Image*

True/False

1. You can reload a project you've worked on in the past by using the *Existing* tab of the New Project window.

2. Hungarian Notation is so named because its creator, Charles Simonyi, is Polish.

3. The label control displays text messages.

4. The *Text* property of the label control is used to specify the text it displays.

5. If you wanted the text in a label control to be aligned with the right edge of the control, you would set its *Alignment* property to right-aligned.

6. If you'd like the text in a label control to be bold, you could set the *Bold*

property to *True*.

7. The color of the text in the label control is determined by the *TextColor* property.

8. Visual Basic 6.0 allows you to create executable files.

9. The programs you create in Visual Basic 6.0 will run on Windows NT.

10. A code module contains Visual Basic source code.

Short Answer

1. How do you create an executable file?

2. Which property specifies the text that will appear in a label control?

3. In Hungarian Notation, what is the prefix attached to the file name supposed to remind the programmer of?

4. Will the *Alignment* property of a label change the alignment of text within the label or the alignment of the label within the form?

5. What three-letter extension describes an executable file?

6. What is the Hungarian Notation prefix for a form window?

7. How do you reload a project you've worked on previously?

8. Why is Hungarian Notation called "Hungarian"?

9. Is it consistent for the label control and the form to both have a property named *Caption*?

10. What is a code module?

Group Discussion

1. Visual Basic doesn't enforce the use of Hugarian Notation or any other naming convention. Why is it still a good idea for programmers to use such a convention?

2. The stunning ease with which you can create a true Windows executable in Visual Basic belies the true power of this environment. How has Visual Basic made Windows programming easier?

Hands-On _____

Creating an address form
Design a form window that displays your name and address in Arial 18-point bold type with a red background and yellow text. Use separate labels for the name and address. Allow the form to be resizable. Experiment with resizing the form to see what effect it has on the displayed text.

On Your Own _____

1. Practicing with properties
Try to duplicate the font and alignment of the form and controls shown in Figure 2.18. The background of the form should be medium blue and the labels should be white text on green backgrounds. The font used in the top label is Arial. The middle label uses the Courier New font and the bottom label uses MS Sans Serif.

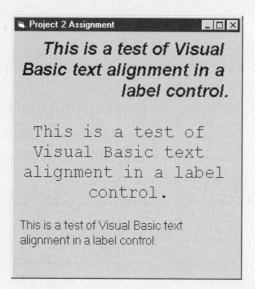

Figure 2.18 Use these options to print information about this Visual Basic program.

2. Working with other label Properties

Create a new Visual Basic project that has a single label control on the form. The caption of the label should be your name rendered in a 24-point bold italic Times New Roman font. The form's border style should resemble a dialog box and should not be resizable. The form window should be just wide enough to accommodate the width of the label control (make sure your name fits on one line).

Change the background color of the form to dark blue (hard-code it using the color palette) and then make it so that the color of the form passes through and is visible through the text of the label. To do this, you must set one of the other label properties (in other words, do not set the *BackColor* property of the label to the same color as the form). Describe how you did this and which property needed to be changed.

> **Tip** Use MSDN Library, if desired, to examine the other properties of the label control.

3. Creating a label window

Create a new Visual Basic program with a dialog-style form (that is, a form that cannot be resized). Add a label control to the form and size it so that it occupies the entire form surface. Center the text in the label and change the caption to ENTER. The font should be Times New Roman bold, colored red with a white background. Size the font to the largest possible size that will fit within the space provided.

Writing Visual Basic Code to Handle Events

In the first two projects, you created a simple Visual Basic program without using any code at all. This speaks volumes about the power of Visual Basic! But to create truly useful Windows applications you will need to write some code. In this project, you will write your first Visual Basic code as you expand the *Hello, world!* program by adding new controls.

Objectives

After completing this project, you will be able to:

➤ **Hone your ability to position controls on a form**

➤ **Create command buttons**

➤ **Attach VB code to event-handler procedures**

The Challenge

In the first two parts of this project, you developed your first Windows application—a window that displays the phrase *Hello, world!* to the user. This was a simple way to introduce you to the Visual Basic IDE and how it is used to create a stand-alone executable program.

As in the real world, specifications change. For the final two projects in Part One, you will develop a better version of the *Hello, world!* program that builds on your original program and adds new features. The existing program was created solely by modifying properties in the Properties window of the Visual Basic IDE: To produce a more useful program, you will also need to use some Visual Basic code. As you will see, Visual Basic code is easy to read and write.

Your original program offers no interaction with the user. It also only offers one way to exit—through the *Close Window* button in the title bar. Most Windows programs are more powerful than that. In this and the following project, you will produce a version of the *Hello, world!* program that allows users to input their name and get a personalized greeting. You will learn to use some of the other common Visual Basic controls, such as the text box and the command button. And, you will also learn to handle control events, such as the events that occur when the user clicks a command button.

The Solution

You will eventually modify the program you created in the first projects so that it allows users to input their name and, upon clicking a command button labeled *Greeting*, see the name combined with the greeting *Hello* and an exclamation point. For example, if the user types **Gary** for the name and clicks the *Greeting* button, the words *Hello, Gary!* will be displayed.

In this project, your goal is to to add new controls to the form and cause the *Hello, world!* message to display in response to a button click, rather than just appear when the program loads. The specifications for this program are as follows:

- The *Hello, world!* message will appear when the user clicks a *Greeting* command button.

When this project is complete, your program should resemble Figure 3.1.

Figure 3.1 Your program should resemble this when you have completed this project.

The Setup

Since this program is based on the first two projects, you will continue using your existing *Hello* solution to complete this project as well. As with

Project 2, you will need to reload your Visual Basic solution so that you may continue working with it. You reload the solution by selecting the correct project file when Visual Basic starts.

TASK 1: TO RELOAD THE *HELLO, WORLD!* PROJECT

1. Start Visual Basic.

2. In the New Project window that appears, select the *Existing* tab and navigate to the location where you stored your project.

3. Double-click *hello.vbp* to reload the project.

4. In the Project window, expand the *Forms* folder and double-click *HelloForm (hello.frm)* to display the form.

Resizing the Form Window

The first thing you want to do is resize the form window. Until now the window has only held a single label control, so the default size of the window was appropriate. Now, however, you will be adding other controls so a slightly larger window will be needed to accommodate them. The border style of the window—fixed single—will not change, so the user will still be unable to change the size of the window when your program runs.

A Note on Screen Measurements

Visual Basic uses a curious coordinate system for measuring the width and height of objects as they appear on screen. You may be familiar with the term *pixel*, which is the smallest dot or image that you can display on your screen. Most computer screens are 800 pixels wide by 600 pixels tall, which is commonly referred to as 800 x 600 (read as "800 by 600"). Measurements such as 800 x 600 are referred to as *resolution*: Other common computer resolutions are 640 x 480, 1024 x 768, and 1280 x 1024.

You might expect Visual Basic to use pixels to determine the width and height of objects such as command buttons, windows, and labels, but it doesn't. Instead, Visual Basic uses a unit called the *twip*. By definition, a twip is 1/20 of a printer's point, so 1440 twips equal one inch when printed. Because of the large number of possible screen resolutions, hardware display adapters, and monitors, it would be impossible to design a program using pixel measurements that would appear identical on every system. And the goal when you're writing a computer program is for every user to have a similar (if not nearly identical) experience. You don't want text disappearing under command buttons or running off the side of the window, for example, but this is exactly the type of thing that occurs if you don't plan accordingly. So, the designers of Visual Basic decided to use twips rather than pixels so that programs created with this language would have a better chance of appearing properly on the largest number of systems.

Therefore, properties such as *Width* and *Height* will have twip values, which can make them a little confusing to work with. Instead of setting the width and height properties to specific twip values, it's generally easier to simply make an eyeball judgment and then resize the dimensions with the mouse in the IDE. We'll take a look at both approaches.

TASK 2: TO RESIZE THE FORM WINDOW

1 Select the form window and examine the *Width* property in the Properties window. If you didn't change the width of the form, it should read 4770 (twips). You can change the width of the form by manually typing in a width value or by dragging the side of the form with the mouse.

2 Move the mouse cursor over to the right side of the form and note that the cursor changes into a double-sided arrow. This indicates that you can drag the side of the form to resize it.

3 Drag the side of the form left and right, noting how it resizes. For purposes of this example only, we will input an exact width.

4 Double-click the *Width* property of the form in the Properties window, type **4920**, and press (ENTER).
The screen should resemble Figure 3.2.

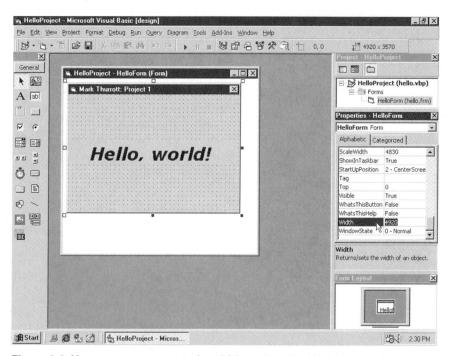

Figure 3.2 You can enter exact twip widths using the *Width* property.

Changing the lblHello Label Control

Next, you will need to move the lblHello label control to the top of the form. While looking at the form window you may notice that it has a grid of dots on it that allows you to precisely position controls on the surface of the form. The dots in this grid are 120 twips apart by default. One interesting behavior of this grid is that controls you place on the form will "snap to" the grid by default. If you need even more precise positioning, you can turn this feature off.

> **Tip** To change the behavior of the grid, choose *Options* from the *Tools* menu and navigate to the *General* tab, where you will find a *Form Grid Settings* section.

Using the grid dots, you will use the following steps to position the label control near the top of the form.

TASK 3: TO MOVE THE LABEL CONTROL TO THE TOP OF THE FORM

1   Position the mouse cursor over the center of the lblHello label control.

2   Using Figure 3.3 as a guide, drag the label toward the top of the form and release it so that the top of the label lines up with the first row of dots in the grid on the form.

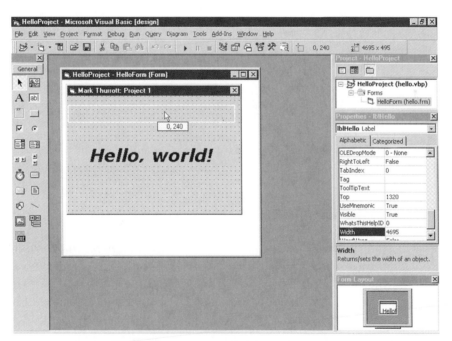

Figure 3.3 Position the label as shown here.

3   Release the mouse button.

You will also want to resize the label control so that it spans the width of the newly resized form.

TASK 4: CHANGE THE WIDTH OF THE LABEL

1 Select the label control so that the resizing rectangle appears around it.

2 Position the mouse over the right edge of the label.
You will see the mouse cursor change into the double-edged arrow.

3 Drag the right edge of the label to the right edge of the form and release the mouse button, as shown in Figure 3.4.

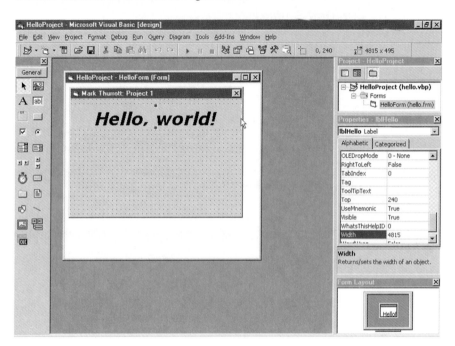

Figure 3.4 lblHello is now correctly positioned.

Using Command Buttons

Every Windows user is familiar with the **command button**, a rectangular button that appears in windows, dialog boxes, and even toolbars in numerous applications and the system itself. A command button is used when you want to give the user the option of causing an action to occur. Command buttons typically have captions such as Yes , No , OK , and Cancel .

Command buttons appear to visually push in when pressed with the mouse cursor and they fire events that you can handle with Visual Basic code. We'll soon be taking a closer look at events in general and command button events specifically.

Adding a Command Button to the Form

Adding a command button to your form is similar to adding the label control: Simply select the *CommandButton* control icon from the Toolbox window and double-click to add the button to the center of your form.

> **Tip** When you double-click a control in the Toolbox window, it will always appear in the center of the form and display in a preset, default size. You can also select a control in the Toolbox and then drag the mouse across an area of the form to draw it in a different place and size.

TASK 5: TO ADD A COMMAND BUTTON TO THE FORM

1   Locate the icon for the CommandButton control ▭ in the Visual Basic Toolbox window.

2   Double-click the CommandButton icon.
A command button called *Command1* will be added to the center of the form (Figure 3.5).

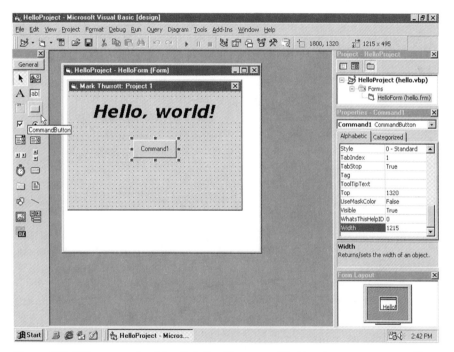

Figure 3.5 When you double-click the CommandButton icon, a command button is added to the center of the form window.

3   Using the control dragging skills you developed previously, drag *Command1* to the bottom of the form, as shown in Figure 3.6.

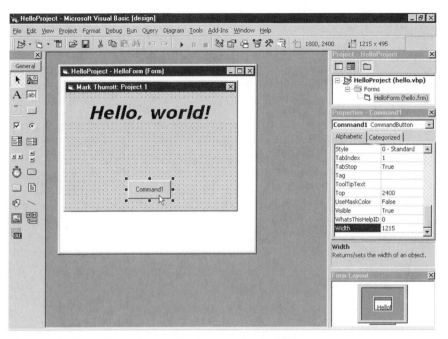

Figure 3.6 Move the command button to this location.

Setting Command Button Properties

The default caption of the command button is obviously inappropriate, so you will be changing that in the upcoming steps. Changing the *Caption* property of a command button is very similar to changing the caption of a form or label control: Simply locate the property in the Properties window, double-click it, and type the new caption. You will also need to rename the control.

TASK 6: TO CHANGE THE *CAPTION* PROPERTY

1. Select *Command1* by clicking it once with the mouse cursor.

2. In the Properties window, find the *Caption* property.

3. Double-click the *Caption* property, type **Greeting**, and then press (ENTER). The caption of the button will change as you type (Figure 3.7).

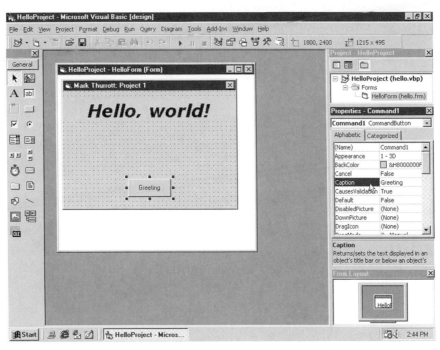

Figure 3.7 Change the caption of the command button to Greeting.

TASK 7: TO CHANGE THE *NAME* PROPERTY

1 Making sure the command button is still selected, locate the *(Name)* property at the top of the Properties window.

2 Double-click the property, type **cmdGreeting**, and then press (ENTER).
The name of the command button will change to *cmdGreeting* (Figure 3.8).

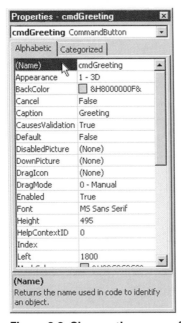

Figure 3.8 Change the name of the command button with the *Name* property.

If you were to run the program now (go ahead and try it), nothing will happen when you click the mouse button (Figure 3.9). That's because you haven't done anything to handle that event. In the following section, you will write your first event procedure.

Figure 3.9 Nothing happens when you click the command button because you haven't yet written the code to handle that event.

Writing Code to Handle Events

Until now, all of the code for your program has been generated by Visual Basic. You can't see the code, but behind the curtain (so to speak) Visual Basic is actually constructing the code needed to make your program work. For example, when you change the value of a property, Visual Basic writes the code to make that happen. When a user clicks the *Close Window* button in the title bar of your application, the program closes because Visual Basic provides the code to make it happen. But Visual Basic can't read your mind—for the controls you add to the form and for other tasks, Visual Basic has no way of knowing what you want to do. In these instances, you will have to write your own code.

Most of the code you write in Visual Basic will be entered into a procedure of some sort. A **procedure** is nothing more than a *block*, or *group*, of code that conveniently groups code that will always run together. One typical example of this is the **event-handler**, which is a procedure (remember, it's just a block of code) that runs every time a specific event occurs. All controls (and even your form window) support a list of events they can handle, and the list will be different for each control or form.

A command button, for example, can handle the event that occurs when the user clicks it. This is logically called the **Click** event. Even the form has a *Click* event, although you'd rarely need to handle it. (How many programs do you know of where you need to click the surface of a window to get something done?) In fact, the form has some interesting events that we'll also be looking at. For example, the form can handle the event that occurs when the form window first appears. This is called the **Form Load event**. The same is true when the form closes, or *unloads*: a **Form Unload event** fires at that point. If you think about it, Windows itself is nothing more than a user interface with a series of event-handlers. The mouse is clicked, objects are selected; even mouse movements and location are events.

Obviously, you can't respond to every single event that occurs. The goal is write a program that responds only to the events that directly affect it. Even then, the number of events can be enormous, but most of those events can be ignored: If you do not write an event-handler for events that happen to your program, nothing will happen. In most cases, this is the desirable result.

In the following subsections, you will create two event-handlers for your program.

Handling the *Form Load* Event

As mentioned previously, the form can handle the event that occurs when it is first started, or loaded. Because you will eventually be displaying a string of code in the label control, it doesn't make sense for that label to display anything until users enter their name. One way to make sure that the label control displays an empty string of text (that is, displays nothing at all) is to modify the value of the label control's *Caption* property, as you've done in the past. But you can also write code that will do this. In the following steps, you will erase the text in the label control using Visual Basic code.

TASK 8: TO CREATE A FORM EVENT-HANDLER

1   Select the form window by clicking on a blank area of the form (or by selecting *HelloForm* from the drop-down list at the top of the Properties window).

2   Double-click the label to open the code window.

3   Choose the form from the Object drop-down list at the top left of the code window (Figure 3.10).

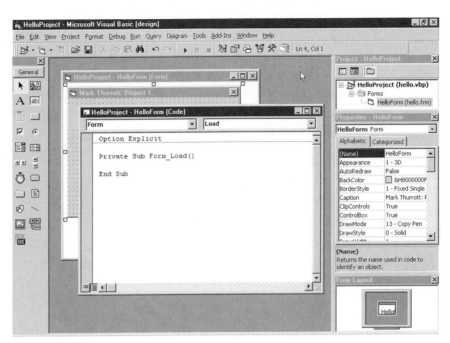

Figure 3.10 The Visual Basic code window lets you enter code.

Let's take a closer look at this window. The Visual Basic code window will appear any time you double-click a control or form. Visual Basic tries to guess which event you want to handle and loads the appropriate choice based on which type of control (or form) you double-clicked. If Visual Basic doesn't display the correct event-handler, you can always choose the correct one from the drop-down lists at the top of the window. On the left side, the ***Object drop-down list box*** displays a list of the objects for which you can write code (Figure 3.11). At this point in your work, this list will include *cmdGreeting*, *HelloForm*, and *lblHello*. There is also a general area for code that doesn't need to attach itself to a control or form. We will be investigating that later in this module.

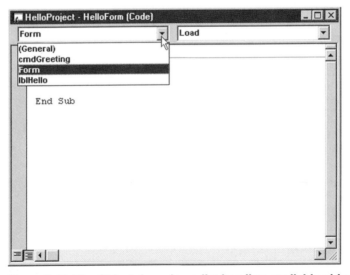

Figure 3.11 The Object drop-down list box lists available objects.

On the right side of the code window is the ***Procedure drop-down list box***. This will show you a list of the event-handlers you can use for the currently selected object. Obviously, this list will depend on which object is selected: Each object has a different set of events it can handle (Figure 3.12).

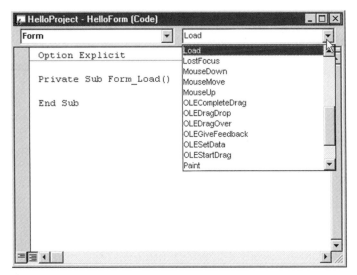

Figure 3.12 The Procedure drop-down list box provides a list of possible events to handle for the currently select object.

When you open the code window, the *shell* of a procedure is created for you. This is nice, because it saves you from having to write this code yourself. Each procedure starts with the keywords ***Private Sub*** (or ***Public Sub***) and is followed by an object name and then the event name and a pair of parentheses. You can see that the event-handler for the *Form Load* event is started with the following code:

```
Private Sub Form_Load()
```

A couple of notes here: The words *Private* or *Public* refer to the procedure's *visibility* or *scope*. We will discuss these terms in detail later in the module. Basically, when you write a "private" procedure, it simply means that only objects in this form can access that code. Also, the parentheses at the end of the procedure name may seem kind of strange, but some procedures actually place code in there. We will be looking at examples of that later in the module as well.

Any code following this line is considered to be part of the procedure, so any code that is contained there "runs" when the event that the procedure handles is triggered, or called. A procedure block ends with the following line:

```
End Sub
```

Given this information, you see why the complete procedure block shown in Figure 3.10 is empty. You will need to write code to handle this event to complete the procedure block.

Writing Code with AutoComplete

One last note before you write your first line of code: Visual Basic 6.0 includes an excellent example of Microsoft's *IntelliSense* technology called *AutoComplete*. **AutoComplete** is designed to provide the following features:

- **Automatically check syntax** This ensures that the code you write is grammatically correct, so to speak.

- **Auto Quick Info** As you type code, a small tooltip will appear to give you information about the options you add to complete the code you are writing.

- **Code completion** If you type in the name of an object, Visual Basic will provide a drop-down list of properties, methods, and event-handlers for that object. Rather than type in lengthy lines of code, you can simply choose the correct choice from the list to complete your code.

We will look at these features as you write your first line of code, as well as over the course of this module.

> **Web Tip** The AutoComplete feature comes from Microsoft Research, an advanced technology group at Microsoft. This technology is also used in Microsoft's Web browser, Internet Explorer, which can auto-complete Web addresses as you type. Microsoft Research is also responsible for the auto-spelling and grammar features in Microsoft Office. Visit http://www.microsoft.com/research for details.

TASK 9: TO WRITE CODE TO HANDLE AN EVENT

1. Make sure the code window is still open and that the input cursor is located inside the procedure.

2. Press (TAB) to indent the text you will type inside the procedure.

3. Type **lblHello.** inside the procedure.
   As soon as you type the period, a drop-down list will appear, as shown in Figure 3.13.

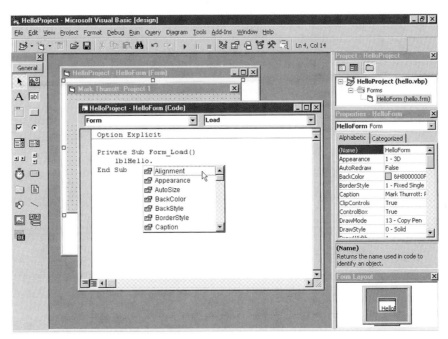

Figure 3.13 The AutoComplete feature presents you with a list of possible properties and methods for lblHello.

4   Scroll down the list and double-click *Caption*. Alternatively, you can simply type **Caption**.

5   Add the text = "" to the end of the line of code.
The complete line should read **lblHello.Caption** = "" (Figure 3.14).

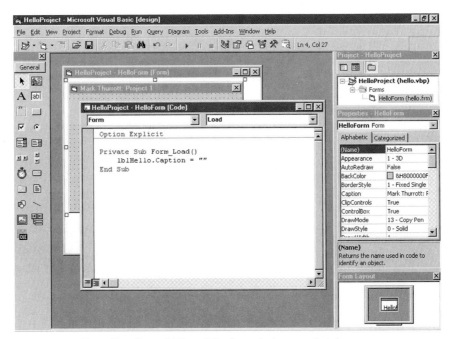

Figure 3.14 Your first line of Visual Basic code is complete!

6 Close the code window and run the program.

As you can see, the *Hello, world!* message is now missing (Figure 3.15), even though the *Caption* property for the label is set to that string.

Figure 3.15 The *Hello, world!* message is now missing because of the code you wrote.

7 Close the program and note that the label is still displaying the greeting string on the form inside the Visual Basic IDE (Figure 3.16).

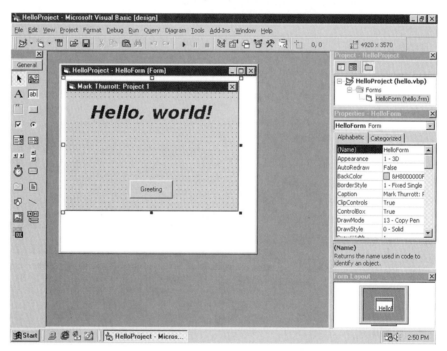

Figure 3.16 The default value of the label caption is still available before the form loads.

Understanding the Code

In the previous steps, you wrote code that affected the *Caption* property of the label control. Let's take a closer look at this code, which while simple, may not be obvious to the beginning Visual Basic coder. When you write code in Visual Basic to affect objects, you will often see the following syntax:

```
<object name>.<property name> = <value>
```

With the code you wrote, the object name was *lblHello* because you wanted to affect the label control. *Caption* is the property you are changing and "" represents a blank, or empty, string of text. If you wanted to change the caption of the label to "Howdy ho!" the following code would work:

```
lblHello.Caption = "Howdy Ho!"
```

This sort of coding, which is referred to as **dot notation** because of the period, or dot, that separates the object name and property name, is common in Visual Basic. You might read the previous line of code as "Set the *Caption* property of lblHello equal to 'Howdy Ho!'" if you wanted to translate it to English.

Handling the Command Button *Click* Event

Now you can handle the event that occurs when the user clicks the command button by displaying a greeting message. To handle this event, simply double-click the command button to display its *Click* event-handler and write the appropriate code.

TASK10: TO WRITE AN EVENT-HANDLER FOR THE COMMAND BUTTON

1 Select the *cmdGreeting* command button.

2 Double-click the *cmdGreeting* command button.
The code window will appear again with the command button's *Click* procedure ready; note that you can see the event-handler you wrote earlier as well (Figure 3.17).

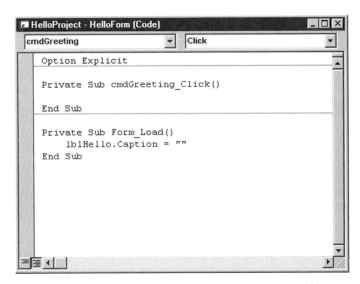

Figure 3.17 A new event-handler procedure appears, but you can still see the code you wrote to handle the *Form Load* event as well.

3 Press (TAB) and type **lblHello.Caption = "Hello, world!"** inside of the event-handler (Figure 3.18).

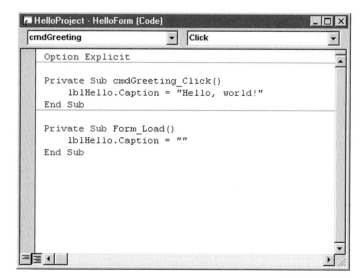

Figure 3.18 You should now have two event-handlers ready.

4 Close the code window and run your program.

5 Click the command button while your program is running.
Notice that the greeting appears when you do so, as shown in Figure 3.19.

Figure 3.19 You've come a long way, baby! With only two lines of code, you are handling two events that happen to your program.

6 Close your program.

The Conclusion

You have concluded the third part of your first Visual Basic project. In the fourth and final part, you will complete the specifications for the program by adding a text box that will allow users to enter their name. When the name has been entered, the user will be presented with a personalized greeting. You will also learn to write code that handles other controls and their events.

For now, you can either exit Visual Basic or go on to work the Study Questions.

Summary and Exercises

Summary

- You will need to write code to create a truly useful Visual Basic program.
- A command button provides the user with an obvious way to cause an event to occur.
- An event procedure is a block of code that executes in response to an event.
- Measurements in Visual Basic are computed in twips.
- The *Form Load* event occurs when the form first loads.
- Visual Basic's AutoComplete feature makes it easy to write code.

Key Terms and Operations

Key Terms
AutoComplete
Click event
Code window
command button
dot notation
event-handler
Form Load event
Object drop-down list box
pixel
procedure
Procedure drop-down list box
resolution
twip
Form Unload event

Operations
use AutoComplete
use dot notation
use the Code window
write event-handler procedures
write Visual Basic code

Study Questions

Multiple Choice

1. When you want the user to trigger an action, what control should you use?
   a. Form
   b. Text box
   c. Command button
   d. Label

2. Which of the following will trigger an event-handler?
   a. The user clicks the form window.
   b. The user clicks a command button.
   c. The form window opens.
   d. All of the above.

3. An event-handler procedure is
   a. an endless loop.
   b. a block of code that is triggered when an event occurs.
   c. coded with the Properties window.
   d. used in flowcharting only.

4. If you wanted to write code that changed the caption of a label named lblFooBar to "The Visual Basic Way," what code could you write?
   a. **lblFooBar.SetCaption = "The Visual Basic Way"**
   b. **Text.lblFooBar = "The Visual Basic Way"**
   c. **lblFooBar.Caption = "The Visual Basic Way"**
   d. **Caption.lblFooBar = "The Visual Basic Way"**

5. What does Visual Basic use to denote measurements?
   a. twicks
   b. pixels
   c. points
   d. twips

6. When positioning controls on the form, you can use the _____ to position the controls.
   a. grid
   b. twips
   c. points of light
   d. Project Explorer window

7. Which property sets the text on the face of a command button?
   a. *Text*
   b. *ButtonFace*
   c. *Alignment*
   d. *Caption*

8. A procedure is a
   a. block of code that executes together.
   b. block of code that provides online help.
   c. a list of functions you can perform.
   d. block of code that never executes.

9. When you want to execute code when the program starts, you could use the form's _____ event-handler.
   a. *Unload*
   b. *Start*
   c. *Begin*
   d. *Load*

10. A Private procedure is visible to
    a. the current form.
    b. all forms in the project.
    c. all forms and code modules in the project.
    d. the procedures that appear next to it in the Code window.

True/False

1. Visual Basic uses pixels to determine the height and width of controls.

2. 800 x 600 is a typical screen resolution.

3. Twips are designed to make programs look consistent on different systems.

4. A command button is typically rectangular.

5. Like other controls, the command button is available from the Visual Basic Toolbox window.

6. Events occur only when the user does something with the mouse or keyboard.

7. A procedure is a block of code that runs together.

8. Dot notation is used to write code for object properties.

9. The *Click* event occurs when the user clicks a control.

10. Event-handlers are procedures that execute in response to events.

Short Answer

1. What Hungarian Notation prefix do you use to name a command button?

2. When is a *Click* event-handler procedure triggered?

3. How do you typically access the code window?

4. How do you resize the form window?

5. How many twips are in an inch?

6. When might you use a command button in your programs?

7. What event occurs when the user clicks a command button?

8. What event occurs when a form window is closed?

9. What two drop-down list boxes appear in the code window?

10. What is dot notation?

Group Discussion

1. Describe the lifetime of a form.

2. How is the object-based dot notation used in Visual Basic code similar to English? How is it different?

3. Now that you understand events, how would you describe Windows and the way that it works with regard to events?

Hands-On

A dialog-box-like program

Write a program with two command buttons that have the captions *Yes* and *No*. When the user clicks the button labeled *Yes*, the caption of the form should change to read *You clicked Yes*. When the *No* button is clicked, the caption of the form should change to *You clicked No*.

On Your Own

1. Improved dialog box

Improve the dialog box you created above and add code that will respond to the form being clicked as well. This should change the caption of the form to *You clicked the form surface*.

2. Toggle program

Write a program that has two command buttons and a label. The label should be blank when the program starts. When the user clicks the first button, which should be labeled *On*, the label caption should change to display your name. When the user clicks the second command button, which should be labeled *Off*, the label should display no text.

3. Color picker

Create a Visual Basic program with a form and four command buttons labeled *Red, Green, Blue,* and *Yellow*. When the user clicks a button, the form background should change to that color (for example, if the *blue* button is pressed, the form window should change to a blue color). You can change the background color of the form in Visual Basic using this code:

Form1.BackColor = <color>

where <color> is a valid Visual Basic color. Use the color values shown in the table.

Table 3.1

Color	Color Value
Red	**VbRed**
Green	**VbGreen**
Blue	**VbBlue**
Yellow	**VbYellow**

Finishing the *Hello, world!* Program

Well, this is it! By the time you've finished this project, you will have completed the specifications for the *Hello, world!* program. This project expands on the additions you made in the previous project and adds new features, controls, and user input capabilities. Let's get started.

Objectives

After completing this project, you will be able to:

➤ **Add a text box**

➤ **Use the text box control in your programs**

➤ **Set control focus**

➤ **Understand the basics of error handling**

➤ **Enable and disable controls**

➤ **Make decisions in code with If-Then-Else**

➤ **Use more advanced procedures**

The Challenge

In the previous projects you created a program that displays the text *Hello, world!* when the user clicks a command button. The program was originally conceived as a simple text display but you enhanced it in Project 3 to include user interaction. In this final part of the project, you will further enhance the program so that users can enter their names and see a personalized greeting. The greeting should say *Hello,* followed by the name the user entered. If no user name is entered, the program should not display a message.

The Solution

The specifications for this project are as follows:

- The program will have a text box where users can enter their name.

- The message *Hello*, followed by the user's name and an exclamation point will appear when the *Greeting* button is clicked.

- A *Clear* command button will clear text from the edit box.

- A *Quit* command button will let the user quit the program

The Setup

As before, you will need to reload the project so that you may complete it.

TASK 1: TO RELOAD THE *HELLO, WORLD!* PROJECT

1. Start Visual Basic if it isn't already running.

2. Select the *Existing* tab in the New Project window.

3. In the *Existing* page of the dialog box, navigate to the location where you stored your project and load **hello.vbp**.

4. In the Project window, expand the *Forms* folder and double-click *HelloForm (hello.frm)* to display the form.

Adding User a Text Box

To enable the user to enter a name, you will need to add a **text box** control to the form. A text box is a Visual Basic control that, like the label control, can display text. Unlike the label control, however, the text box can also accept textual input from the user. You can provide a blank text box for user input, or you can supply text in the text box that the user can accept or modify.

> **Tip** You will sometimes see a text box referred to as an *edit box* or a *text edit box*. Text boxes are used only when user input is required. If you just want to output text, use a label control instead.

TASK 2: TO ADD A TEXT BOX CONTROL TO THE FORM

1 Select TextBox control icon [abl] in the ToolBox window.

2 Double-click the TextBox icon to add a text box control to the center of the form, as shown in Figure 4.1. By default, Visual Basic names the first text box you add *Text1*.

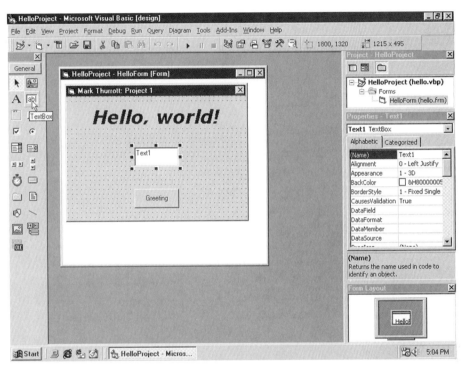

Figure 4.1 By default, the text box will appear in the center of the form, as do other controls.

3 Using Figure 4.2 as a guide, drag the left and right sides of the text box so that it is resized to occupy almost the full width of the form window.

Figure 4.2 Like the label control you added earlier, the text box should occupy most of the width of the form window.

Changing Text Box Properties

As with the other controls you've added, you will need to change some of the properties of the text box. Specifically, you will name the text box txtInputName, edit its font attributes, and change the default text that it displays. The text box control uses a *Text property* to determine what text it displays.

TASK 3: TO CHANGE TEXT BOX PROPERTIES

1 Select the text box to ensure that its properties are displayed in the Properties window.

2 Select the (*Name*) property at the top of the list and t ype **txtInputName**.

3 Double-click the *Font* property to bring up the Font dialog box. Change the *Font* to **Arial** and the *Font Size* to **16**.

4 Double-click the *Text* property, press (DELETE), and then press (ENTER) to change the text display to an empty string. We want the text box to be empty when the program starts.
Your screen should now resemble Figure 4.3.

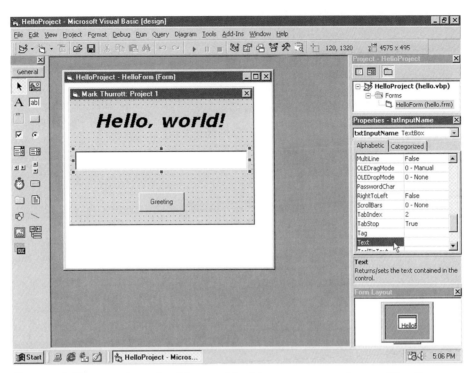

Figure 4.3   Your text box should resemble this once you are done setting its properties.

Setting Control Focus

When using Windows, you might have several application windows open, and thus programs running at a time—for example, one for Microsoft Word, one for Internet Explorer, and one for Visual Basic. Even though you can run as many programs as you want, only one window can have the *focus* at a given time; that is, only one window can be *selected* or *active*. The same is true of controls on a Visual Basic form window: Even though you could conceivably add as many controls as you'd like to a form, only one control can have the focus, or be selected, at any one time.

When you create a program and start adding controls to a form, Visual Basic sets up something called the ***tab order***. The tab order is simply a list of controls that can have the focus, arranged in a particular order. It's called a tab order because you can use the (TAB) key to move forward and backward between each visible and enabled control on a form while the program is running. Let's try it with the *Hello, world!* program.

TASK 4: TO LOOK AT THE TAB ORDER

1   Run your program by pressing (F5), or by choosing *Start* from the *Run* menu.
Notice that there are two controls visible on the window—the text box and

the command button. The command button will be selected, as noted by the dark shadow that can be seen on its surface. This is shown in Figure 4.4.

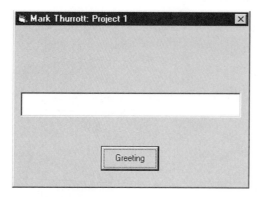

Figure 4.4 When your program runs, the command button gets the focus first.

2   Press (TAB).
The focus will switch to the text box, as shown in Figure 4.5.
The focus is indicated by the insertion pointer that appears in the text box and by the fact that the dark shadow disappears from the command button.

Figure 4.5 When you select the text box, the focus switches from the command button to the text box.

3   Tab back and forth a few times to see the effect.
Note that (SHIFT)+(TAB) lets you move backward through the tab order.

4   Close your program when you are done.

From this demonstration, we can conclude that the tab order for our program is the command button first, then the text box. However, since we want the user to enter a name, we prefer that the text box receives the focus first. Otherwise, the user will have to press (TAB) or manually select the text box with the mouse cursor before typing a name. And as you might expect, we can program this behavior using Visual Basic code.

Tip The tab order of controls is originally determined by the order you place controls on the form. Since the command button was added first, it was placed higher in the tab order. The label control does not appear in the tab order of the running program because it is not a control that the user can select.

Controls have a ***TabIndex property*** that determines the control's position in the tab order. The tab order, incidentally, is specific to the form or other container; in future projects you will see other types of containers that have their own internal tab order. For your current project, however, you only have to worry about two items in the tab order (for now, anyway): the text box and the command button. When you change the *TabIndex* property of a control, all of the other controls on the form will change accordingly.

Tip The TabIndex values for controls on a form begin with 0 and number up from there. That is, the first control you add to a form gets a TabIndex value of 0, the second gets a 1, and so on.

In the following steps, you will change the *TabIndex* property of the text box so that it has the focus when the program starts.

TASK 5: TO CHANGE THE *TABINDEX* PROPERTY OF THE TEXT BOX

1 Select *txtInputName*.

2 Double-click its *TabIndex* property in the Properties window.

3 Change the value to **0** and press (ENTER).

4 Run the program. Notice that the text box receives the focus as soon as you run the program (Figure 4.6).

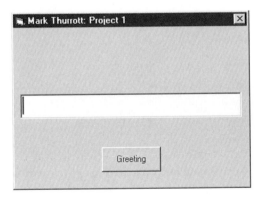

Figure 4.6 Now when the program begins, the text box gets the focus first.

5 Close the program.

Writing Code to Access the Text Box

If you press the *Greeting* button while your program is running, the label still displays the *Hello, world!* greeting. In the following steps, you will add code so that the label will display the *Hello* message using the name inputted into the text box. All it takes is a small edit to the command button's *Click* event-handler.

TASK 6: TO CHANGE THE CMDGREETING *CLICK* EVENT-HANDLER

1 Double-click *cmdGreeting* to open the code window.
The code for the cmdGreeting_Click() procedure currently reads

lblHello.Caption = "Hello, world!"

However, we want it to access the Text property of txtInputName.

2 Change the code inside the procedure to the following:

lblHello.Caption = "Hello, " & txtInputName.Text & "!"

The **&** character is used to create a string concatenation in Visual Basic. It basically "adds" the phrase "Hello, " to the name the user inputs and an exclamation point. Your screen should now resemble Figure 4.7.

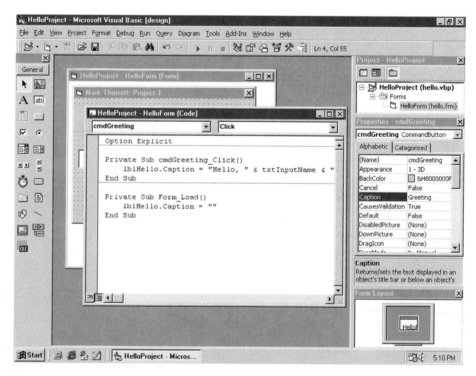

Figure 4.7 The code in the command button's *Click* event-handler will now grab the text in the text box.

3 Close the code window and run the program (Figure 4.8). The program does work, but there are two problems. Can you see them?

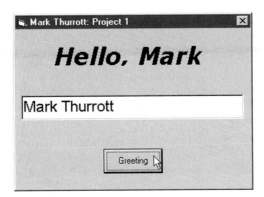

Figure 4.8 Technically this program works, but all is not well.

Handling Errors

Everyone makes mistakes. In Visual Basic, mistakes—or **bugs**, as they're called—can take the form of errors that cause your program to not run, crash horribly, or perhaps more subtly, not work properly. In many programs, most of the code is there specifically to make sure that bugs don't occur. These lines of code, sometimes called **error-handlers**, are even smart enough to keep your program running gracefully when a bug does occur. Over the course of this module, you will spend a lot of time examining these issues and the facilities that Visual Basic uses to make them occur less often. For now, however, we're going to take a quick look at some fairly simple bugs that are already present in this first program.

"Bugs?" you say. "But I only wrote two lines of code!" Well, that's how it goes sometimes. Let's take a quick look at the problems we've introduced at this stage of the program.

Investigating the Bugs in Hello, world!

The first bug will be particularly obvious if you enter a long name in the text box. When you press the *Greeting* button, the text of greeting is cut right off at the beginning and end, as shown in Figure 4.9. The solution is pretty simple: Just make the label control bigger. You can't handle any size string (something like *Mississippi Bernard Jones* will probably break almost any label control) but you can, at least, make it bigger.

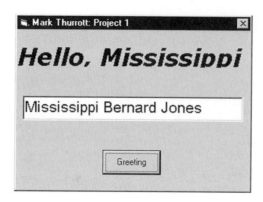

Figure 4.9 Long names can cause display problems.

The second bug is a little more subtle. It occurs when the user hasn't yet entered a name in the text box. In such a case, the nonsensical phrase *Hello, !* appears (Figure 4.10). The solution to this problem is not difficult either: You just need to prevent the user from clicking the *Greeting* button until some text has been entered in the text box. Then there will almost always be something to display. Why *almost*? Well, the user could simply enter a space character by pressing the (SPACE) bar, which would fool the program easily. The point here, however, isn't to figure out every possible combination of characters that could be entered, it's to provide answers to the most logical problems that could occur. If software developers didn't do this, they would never ship their programs at all.

Figure 4.10 Uh oh! Our program is easily fooled into displaying garbage text.

The key to preventing the user from clicking the *Greeting* button is to disable it. You will learn how to do this in the following section.

Disabling and Enabling Controls

The command button, like many other controls, has a property called **Enabled** that determines whether the control can respond to user events such as a mouse click. If the control is enabled (that is, the *Enabled* property is set to *True*), it can handle mouse clicks and other events. If the control is disabled (the *Enabled* property is set to false), it will ignore events and will be removed (temporarily) from the tab order of the form.

In the following steps, you will use Visual Basic code to disable the command button until there is text in the text edit box. The first step, disabling the control, is easy: You can set the *Enabled* property to *False* right in the Visual Basic IDE. But how do you change it back to *True* once text is entered in the text box? Fortunately, the text box control has an event called **Change** that is triggered when the text in the control is altered in some way. Simply typing a single character will cause this event to trigger. All you need to do is add code to enable the command button in the *Change* event-handler of the text box.

TASK 7: TO DISABLE THE COMMAND BUTTON UNTIL TEXT IS ENTERED

1 Select *cmdGreeting* and locate its *Enabled* property in the Properties window.

2 Change the property to *False* by double-clicking it.

3 Double-click *txtInputName*.
The code window will open with a new event procedure, txtInputName_Change.

4 Add the following code inside the procedure (Figure 4.11):

```
cmdGreeting.Enabled = True
```

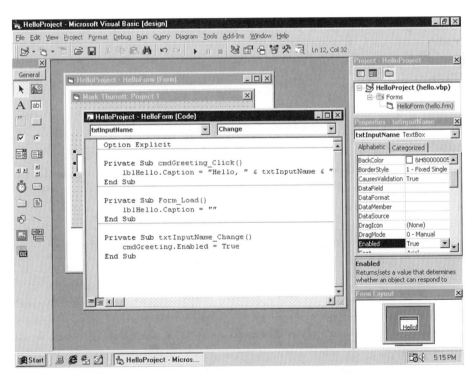

Figure 4.11 Now the command button will be enabled when the user types something in the text box.

5 Close the code window.

You also need to resize the label so that it can handle larger names.

TASK 8: TO CHANGE THE HEIGHT OF THE LABEL CONTROL

1 Select *txtInput* and drag it down a few rows on the grid, as shown in Figure 4.12.

Figure 4.12 Move the text box lower in the form.

2 Select *lblHello* and drag its lower edge down so that it is one or two grid rows above txtInput, as shown in Figure 4.13.

Figure 4.13. Resize the label control so that it can display two lines of text.

3 Run the program (Figure 4.14) and input some names to see if they fit. Resize the label again if needed.
Notice that the command button is not enabled until you type something in the text box.

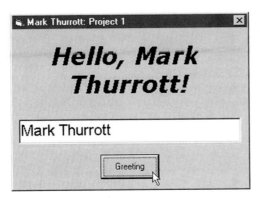

Figure 4.14 Not bad! The program now handles some subtle errors.

Adding an Instruction Label

Another nice feature you can add to the program is a short line of text on the form that will explain to users what they are supposed to do. This instructional text can be created by adding a label control to the form.

TASK 9: TO ADD AN INSTRUCTION LABEL

1 Double-click the label control icon in the Toolbox window to add a new label control to the center of the form.

2 Using Figure 4.15 as a guide, resize the new label so that it sits right above lblHello and occupies only one row of dots on the form's grid.

Figure 4.15 The instructional label should sit right on top of lblHello.

3 Change the *Caption* property of the label to **Please type your name**.

There is no need to change the name of the label since you will never access it from Visual Basic code. Your screen should now resemble Figure 4.16.

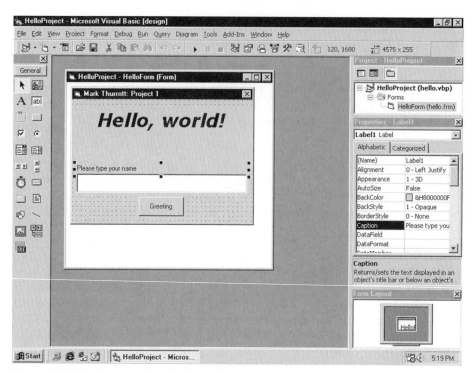

Figure 4.16 The instructional label will make the program more usable.

Adding More Command Buttons

If you look at the specifications for this project, you will realize that there are only a few more steps to complete. The specs call for two more command buttons, one to clear the text in both the label control and the text box, and one to quit the program. In the following steps, you will add these command buttons.

TASK 10: TO ADD THE *CLEAR* COMMAND BUTTON

1 Double-click the CommandButton icon in the Toolbox window to add a new command button to the center of your form.

2 Drag this button to the lower-left corner of the form window, as shown in Figure 4.17.

Figure 4.17 A second command button is added to the form.

3 Rename the command button **cmdClear**.

4 Change the caption of cmdClear to **Clear**.

5 Change the *Enabled* property to *False*.

6 Double-click *txtInputName* to bring up the code window. You must add code to enable the *Clear* button when text is entered.

7 Below the existing line of code, add the following text and then close the code window:

cmdClear.Enabled = True

TASK 11: TO WRITE CODE FOR CMDCLEAR

1 Double-click *cmdClear* to bring up the code window.

2 In the *Click* event-handler, add the following code:

lblHello.Caption = ""

txtInputName.Text = ""

cmdGreeting.Enabled = False

cmdClear.Enabled = False

txtInputName.SetFocus

The *SetFocus* method will return focus to the text box. Your screen should now resemble Figure 4.18.

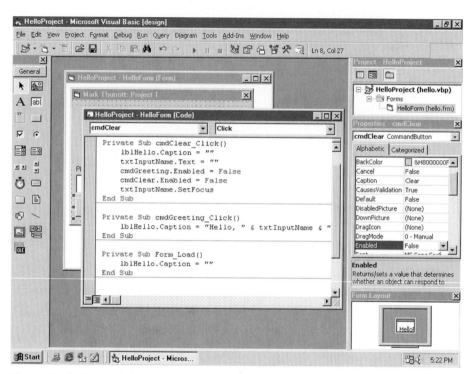

Figure 4.18 **The code in this event-handler will reset the program to resemble the way it looks when it first runs.**

3   Close the code window, save the project, and run the program. Observe how cmdClear works (Figure 4.19).

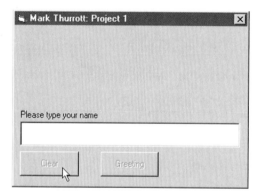

Figure 4.19 **When you press the *Clear* button, the text in both the label and text box is erased and the *Greeting* button is disabled.**

4   Close your program and return to the Visual Basic IDE.

TASK 12: TO WRITE CODE FOR CMDQUIT

1   Double-click the CommandButton icon in the Toolbox window to add a third command button to your form.

2   Drag the command button to the lower-right corner of the form, as shown in Figure 4.20.

Figure 4.20 The third command button will be used to quit the program.

3   Change the (*Name*) property of this command button to **cmdQuit**.

4   Change the *Caption* property of cmdQuit to **Quit**.

5   Double-click *cmdQuit* and add the following code to its *Click* event-handler:

End

This Visual Basic statement will cause the program to quit.

6   Run the program (Figure 4.21) and test all of its features.

Figure 4.21 We're just about done! At this point, the program will meet the basic specification requirements.

Finishing Touches

Sometimes when you develop a program you discover a needed feature that isn't spelled out in the specifications but is faithful to the meaning of the specifications and would increase the usability of the program dramatically. In your program, it would be nice if users could type a name and then press (ENTER) to see the greeting rather than having to tab over to the *Greeting* command button (or click it with the mouse). This type of feature is pretty easy to add, thanks to Visual Basic. For example, if the key pressed to enter the user's name is (ENTER), you could tell the program to execute the code in the *Greeting* command button's *Click* event-handler.

Using the If-Then-Else Statement

Visual Basic has a decision-making statement that is ideally suited for this job. Known as **If-Then-Else**, this statement tells your program to execute certain lines of code if a particular condition is true. For the feature described above, you would write code that checks to see *If* the (ENTER) key was pressed; *If* it was, *Then* the code would execute in cmdGreeting_Click(). A pseudocode representation of this code might look like this:

```
If the key press is (ENTER) Then
    Execute the code in cmdGreeting_Click()
End If
```

Sometimes, you'll see an **Else** clause as well; we will be looking at more advanced examples of this statement later in the module.

Using a Procedure with a Parameter

For now, let's add the code to make this happen. All you need to do is add the right code to the **KeyPress event-handler** for txtInputName. This event occurs every time a key is pressed while the text box has the focus. The default event-handler procedure for this event looks like this:

```
Private Sub txtInputName_KeyPress(KeyAscii As Integer)

End Sub
```

The first thing you might notice about this procedure is that there is something inside the parentheses. Don't panic! This is normal and, in this case, desirable. What you're seeing is a **parameter**, or **argument**, which is a value that is passed to a procedure. Although this particular procedure has a single parameter, some have more than one. The KeyAscii parameter, in this case, sends the ASCII code value for the key that is pressed to the procedure; this is equivalent to telling the procedure that (ENTER) has been pressed. Looking at an ASCII chart (you carry one in your pocket at all times, right?), you will see that the ASCII code for (ENTER) (also known as a *Carriage Return*, or *CR*) is 13. So, all you have to do is tell your program to check for a KeyAscii value of 13.

Troubleshooting Tip What in the world is an ASCII chart, you ask? The most commonly used characters (letters, numbers, punctuation marks, and other characters) in the English language are represented in a chart of characters called the ASCII chart. Each character in this chart is given a unique code value numbered from 0 to 255. That way, the actual character value is separated from the eventual rendering of the character in the display.

You can view the ASCII charts in MSDN Library, but you'll have to tell it to display the topics for all of Visual Studio first (the topic is called "ASCII codes" in the Index).

TASK 13: TO CHECK WHETHER (ENTER) IS PRESSED

1 Double-click *txtInputName* to display the code window. This time, you will need to access a different procedure than the default.

2 Open the Procedure drop-down list box and choose *KeyPress*.
The shell of the txtInputName_KeyPress procedure will appear, as shown in Figure 4.22.

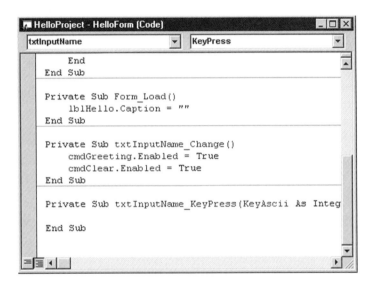

```
HelloProject - HelloForm (Code)

txtInputName          ▼    KeyPress          ▼

        End
End Sub


Private Sub Form_Load()
      lblHello.Caption = ""
End Sub


Private Sub txtInputName_Change()
      cmdGreeting.Enabled = True
      cmdClear.Enabled = True
End Sub


Private Sub txtInputName_KeyPress(KeyAscii As Integ


End Sub
```

Figure 4.22 The *KeyPress* event-handler lets you find out which keys are pressed by the user.

3 Enter the following code inside this procedure:

If KeyAscii = 13 Then

    If txtInputName <> "" Then

        cmdGreeting.SetFocus

        cmdGreeting_Click

    End If

End If

This code may look complex at first, but after you look at it closely, you should be able to understand it. There are two If-Then loops, one of which is embedded, or ***nested***, inside the other. The first, or outer, loop checks for the (ENTER) key press and then, if it was pressed, executes the inner loop. If the (ENTER) key wasn't pressed, then the test in the inner loop won't execute. If the (ENTER) key was pressed, the inner loop first makes sure the text box isn't blank. If it isn't, the loop then sets the focus on cmdGreeting as if that button had been pressed, and finally executes the *Click* event-handler for cmdGreeting. Note that you can **call**, or execute, a procedure simply by stating its full name as we did here, preceded by the **Call** statement.

4   Save the project, close the code window, and execute the program. Test the (ENTER) key to see if it works. Success!

The Conclusion

You have concluded Project 4 and thus your work with the *Hello, world!* program. Over the course of these four projects, you honed this program into a relatively sophisticated application that interacts with the user and handles simple problems. In Part Two, you will examine more features of Visual Basic, including variables and constants, menus, About Boxes, and other user interface elements as well as the way that Visual Basic handles calculations. These concepts will be presented within the scope of an energy calculation program that you will create.

For now, you can either exit Visual Basic or go on to work the Study Questions.

Summary and Exercises

Summary

- A text box control displays text that the user can edit.
- The *TabIndex* property determines a control's position in the list of controls that can get the focus while your program is running.
- Logic errors are often very subtle.
- Controls can be enabled and disabled.
- The End statement ends a Visual Basic program.
- You can use the If-Then-Else statement to make decisions with Visual Basic code.

Key Terms and Operations

Key Terms
& (concatenate)
argument
bug
call
Change event
Enabled property
error-handler
focus
If-Then-Else statement
KeyPress event-handler
nested loop
parameter
tab order
TabIndex property
text box
Text property

Operations
add a text box
enable and disable controls
end a running program
get user input
handle key presses
make decisions with code
perform simple error handling
set control focus

Study Questions

Multiple Choice

1. How is a text box different from a label control?
   a. A text box does not allow the user to change its text display.
   b. A text box is faster, but larger, than a label control.
   c. A text box allows the user to change its text display.
   d. They are the same control with different names.

2. Which of the following statements can be used to make a decision?
   a. If-Than-Else
   b. If-Then-Else
   c. If-Else
   d. None of the above

3. Which of the following is the correct statement to stop execution of your program?
   a. Stop
   b. Quit
   c. End
   d. Exit

4. Which symbol is used to concatenate two text strings into a single text string?
   a. $
   b. %
   c. #
   d. &

5. A text box is used to
   a. get user input.
   b. display text that will never change.
   c. provide a label for other controls.
   d. change the focus from a label.

6. You can change the focus by calling which method?
   a. *GetFocus*
   b. *SetFocus*
   c. *Focus*
   d. *Focused*

7. You can enable and disable controls with which property?
   a. *Enable*
   b. *Disable*
   c. *Enabled*
   d. *Disabled*

8. An If-Then-Else statement can check to see if certain conditions are
   a. A or B.
   b. True or False.
   c. 1 or 2.
   d. enabled or disabled.

9. Which event would you handle if you wanted to know which key was pressed?
   a. *KeyType*
   b. *KeyEntered*
   c. *Keyed*
   d. *KeyPress*

10. When one If-Then loop is found within another, they are said to be
    a. nested.
    b. compounded.
    c. complicated.
    d. duplexed.

True/False

1. A text box is sometimes called a caption box.

2. The Text property of the text box control sets the text displayed by the control.

3. You can determine the tab order of the controls in your program by using the ⸢TAB⸥ key to navigate from control to control while the program is running.

4. A control's position in the tab order is determined by its *TabOrder* property.

5. Programming mistakes are called bugs.

6. You can disable a control with its *Disabled* property.

7. The *Change* event occurs when the size of the text box is changed.

8. The Hungarian Notation prefix for a command button is btn.

9. The *SetFocus* method is used to manually change the focus to the current control.

10. If-Then-Else is used to make decisions and execute code based on those decisions.

Short Answer

1. What prefix is used for a text box?

2. How did the *TabIndex* property get its name?

3. Which control would you use to display text that can't be changed by the user?

4. How do you change the focus in your programs?

5. What property of the text box is used to determine the text it displays?

6. How does the user change control focus while using a program?

7. What are bugs?

8. How do you disable a control using VB code?

9. Is it important to name a label that will only be used for instructional output?

10. Are ASCII codes fun, or are they just for geeks?

Group Discussion

1. Bugs can be very subtle. What do you think is the best way to ensure that your program has no bugs?

2. Describe when a label control would be more appropriate than a text box.

3. How can you terminate a program you've written in Visual Basic?

4. Why would you want to disable a control while the program is running?

Hands-On

Write pseudocode for a password protection window

Write pseudocode for a program that will prompt the user to enter a password. If the correct password is entered, the program should display a message indicating success. Otherwise, an error message should display. The program should use a label to prompt the user and a second label to display the confirmation message.

On Your Own

1. Designing a password protection window
Using the pseudocode for the Hands-On exercise as a guide, develop a program that will prompt a user for a password.

2. ASCII code program
Write a program that has a text box for user input and a label control to output results. Allow the user to input any letter or number in the text box and display the ASCII number for that letter on the label.

3. Using If-Then-Else
Create a Visual Basic program that contains a single command button. The caption for the form should read *It was the best of times, it was the worst of times* when the program starts. When the command button is pressed, the program should check to see whether the caption of the form matches the initial value (the *It was the best of times, it was the worst of times* text). If it doesn't match, then change the caption of the form to *In a hole in the ground there lived a hobbit*. You will need to use an If-Then-Else block to accomplish this.

The following pseudocode should help you with this exercise:

```
If the form caption is not "It was the best of times, it was the worst of
times" Then

    change the form caption to "It was the best of times, it was the
    worst of times"
Else

    change the form caption to "In a hole in the ground there lived a
    hobbit"
End If
```

4. Working with fonts
Write a program that has a text box for user input and a label control to output results. The label should be fairly large and display text in 24-point Arial. Four command buttons, labeled "Normal," "Bold," "Italic," and "Underlined" should be added as well. A fifth command button, labeled "Go," should be added next to the text box. When the user types text in the text box and clicks the *Go* button, the text should be displayed in the label control. Clicking the *Normal*, *Bold*, *Italic*, and *Underlined* buttons should apply those effects on the text using the *FontBold*, *FontItalic*, and *FontUnderline* properties. For example, the *Click* event-handler for the *Bold* button will resemble the following code:

```
If Label1.FontBold = True Then

    Label1.FontBold = False
Else

    Label1.FontBold = True
End If
```

To set the text to "Normal," change the *FontBold*, *FontItalic*, and *FontUnderline* properties to *False*.

PART TWO

Energy Calculator

PROJECT

Performing Calculations with Visual Basic

Back when computers were nothing more than wishful thinking on the part of over-worked engineers and accountants, people believed that someday there would exist intelligent machines that would make mundane but important calculations easier. Of course, the reality of this dream is even better than they imagined: Today's computers are nothing short of amazing in their ability to quickly and accurately perform complex calculations. In this project, you will examine Visual Basic's prowess as a computing engine.

Objectives

After completing this project, you will be able to:

➤ **Declare and use variables and constants**

➤ **Perform simple calculations**

➤ **Use Visual Basic functions**

➤ **Format output with the Format function**

The Challenge

Electric power companies perform complex calculations that determine the correct billing for each customer. These calculations, which are based on energy consumption, time of consumption, and the season, vary from state to state. For example, in warmer climates such as Arizona and Florida, energy is more expensive in the summer months because the load on power generators increases as air conditioning use rises dramatically. In colder climates such as New England and the upper Midwest, the opposite is true due to the rise in heater use during the winter. Beyond this simple fact, most people don't really understand how their electric bills are determined and why electricity is more expensive on certain days, hours, and times of the year.

You may be hard-pressed to sympathize with power companies and the calculations they must perform on a daily basis. However, your exploration of the process will introduce you to simple systems analysis and at the same time will shed light on some new features of Visual Basic.

You will build a program in Visual Basic (Figure 5.1) that will be used by customer service representatives (CSRs) at your local power company. It is designed to estimate monthly electric bills, based on the number of kilowatt-hours used, a fuel cost adjustment, and the current tax rate. The program will be improved over the course of the next two projects as well.

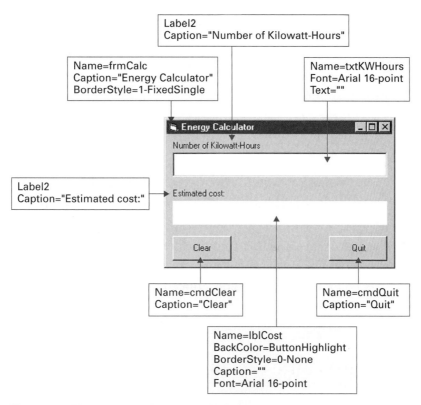

Figure 5.1 The completed energy calculator

The Solution

The specifications for this first part of the program are as follows:

- The program should have a simple interface.
- The user will type in the number of kilowatt-hours used to find the cost of that usage.

- The program will eventually handle different billing rates, based on the time of year and the area of the country. For this project, however, the cost will be estimated using a simpler, nonseasonal, nonregional formula (see below).

- The usage rate is $0.00942 per kilowatt-hour.

- The cost is reduced by a fuel factor of $0.001403 per kilowatt-hour used.

- Taxes are 8.20%.

- The raw cost is calculated by multiplying the number of kilowatt-hours used by the usage rate. Then, the fuel factor adjustment is subtracted (this is determined by multiplying the number of kilowatt-hours used by the fuel factor). Finally, this figure is multiplied by a tax muliplier, 1.082 (1 + tax rate), to arrive at the total estimated cost.

The Setup

Because this is a new project, you will need to create a new project in Visual Basic.

TASK 1: TO START A NEW PROJECT

1 Start Visual Basic and create a new Standard EXE project.

2 Save the Project: Name the form **calc.frm** and the project **calc.vbp**. Make sure you create a new directory for this project as well.

3 In the Visual Basic IDE, change the name of the form to frmCalc and the name of the project to Calc.

4 Using Figure 5.1 as a guide, create the objects listed and assign only their properties.

Using Constants and Variables

In the previous project, you worked solely with the properties and events of objects, such as the form window and its controls. This works well with the visual nature of Visual Basic, but there are times when you have to write code that doesn't necessarily correspond to any visual object that the user will see. Specifically, you will sometimes want to store values that your program can use over and over again. These values can be stored using constants and variables.

Simply stated, variables and constants are containers that can hold values. *Constants* are used to hold values that will never change during the "life" of the program. For example, the value of pi or the number of days in a week would be good candidates for constants because those values are set in stone and never change. *Variables*, on the other hand, are used to hold values that can—and often do—change.

Just like objects you place on a form, variables and constants have ***names*** that must be set before you can use them. You access a variable or constant in Visual Basic code by using its name. Variables and constants also have an associated ***data type*** that describes the kind of value they contain. For example, a variable that is designed to hold a string of text would have a data type of ***String***. A constant created to hold a whole number, such as the number of days in a week, would have a data type of ***Integer***.

Declaring Constants and Variables

Before you use a constant or variable in your program, you must *declare* them. The ***declaration*** tells Visual Basic to set aside memory for the variable or constant. In fact, this is the reason why you must use a data type: Different data types have different memory requirements.

Technically, you don't *have* to declare variables or constants, because Visual Basic is (perhaps foolishly) lenient in this particular area. Other programming languages, such as Java and C++, *force* you to declare variables and constants and, frankly, there's no good reason not to do it. Fortunately, there is a way to make Visual Basic force declarations. In the following steps, you will add this capability to Visual Basic.

TASK 2: TO ENABLE THE FEATURE THAT REQUIRES DECLARATIONS

1   Choose *Options* from the *Tools* menu.
    The Options dialog box appears.

2   In the *Editor* page, check the option for *Require Variable Declaration* in the *Code Settings* area, as shown in Figure 5.2.

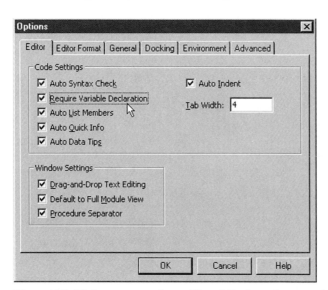

Figure 5.2 Make sure you force Visual Basic to force variable declarations.

3   Click   OK   to close the dialog box.

> **Tip** Every time you begin a new project, you should enable this set-
> ting. Otherwise, all kinds of coding errors can be introduced because
> of spelling mistakes. With this option on, Visual Basic will catch such
> errors before your program runs.

To declare variables in Visual Basic code, you generally use the **Dim** statement. Dim, which is short for *Dimension*, is used like this:

```
Dim Count As Integer
```

```
Dim MyMessage As String
```

The first example reserves enough memory for an Integer, and you can
read that as "Dimension a variable named Count, which is an Integer."
The second example sets aside memory for a string of text. String variables, of course, can vary in size, but Visual Basic handles that automatically.

Declaring constants is very similar, except that the **Const** statement is used
instead. The As clause in constant declarations is actually optional (there
goes Visual Basic again, being too lenient on the programmers!), but we
will always use it here. Examples of typical constant declarations are:

```
Const DaysInWeek As Integer = 7
```

```
Const Pi As Single = 3.14
```

Notice that the constant declaration includes an *assignment* of value.
When you declare a constant, you must tell Visual Basic what value it will
contain. For variables, this can be done in code following the declaration,
at any time. Indeed, once you've declared a variable, you can set its value
again and again if you'd like:

```
Count = 6
```

```
MyMessage "Welcome to my second Visual Basic program!"
```

```
Count = 300
```

A Quick Introduction to Data Types

You will be encountering more data types as you work through this module. Table 5.1 provides a quick reference to the Visual Basic data types.

Table 5.1 Visual Basic Data Types

Data Type Name	Type of Data It Contains
Byte	Positive integer numbers ranging from 0 to 255
Boolean	Can be True (–1) or False (0)
Integer	Whole numbers from –32,768 to 32,767
Long	Whole numbers from –2,147,483,648 to 2,147,483,647
Currency	Used for currency values and calculations
Single	Floating-point numbers (numbers with a decimal point)
Double	Large floating-point numbers
Date	Date and time values
String	A variable-length string of text characters
Variant	A special data type that can hold almost any kind of data. If you don't declare a data type, Variant is used.
Object	A special data type that refers to an object exposed by DLLs in Windows.

Naming Conventions for Constants and Variables

Remember our earlier discussion of Hungarian Notation? You could apply the same naming convention to Visual Basic constants and variables if you'd like, and many programmers do just that. In this module, however, we're going to use simple, descriptive names. It should be obvious, for example, that a variable named *Count* is some kind of number, probably an integer. Calling it *intCount* wouldn't really make the program easier to read.

However, Visual Basic does have a few rules for naming variables and constants.

- They must begin with a letter.
- They must contain only letters, numbers, and the underscore character. No punctuation marks or spaces are allowed.
- They must be 40 or fewer characters in length.
- They cannot be *reserved words*. (A reserved word is any word used by the Visual Basic language, such as If, Then, Else, and Dim.)

Performing Calculations

Visual Basic allows you to perform mathematical operations such as addition, subtraction, multiplication, and division. Table 5.2 shows the symbols Visual Basic uses for the allowable operations. Some may seem a little strange at first (especially if you've never used a programming language before), although they will probably be familiar to Excel and Access users.

The following table describes the arithmetic operators:

Table 5.2 Visual Basic Symbols for Mathematical Operations

VB Symbol	Operation
+	Addition
−	Subtraction
*	Multiplication
/	Division (floating-point)
\	Division (integer, no remainder)
Mod	Modulus (the remainder from an integer division)
^	Exponentiation

You can use these symbols right in your Visual Basic code. For example, the following code applies the value of a multiplication to a variable:

```
Dim Total As Integer
Total = 12 * 12
```

Using Code to Perform Calculations

In your energy calculator program, the cost of electricity will be calculated any time a change is made to the txtKWHour text box. In the following steps, you will add this code, which is loosely based on similar code you wrote earlier.

TASK 3: TO CODE THE TXTKWHOURS CHANGE EVENT-HANDLER

1 Double-click *txtKWHours* to open the code window.

2 Enter the following code in the *Change* event-handler for KWHours:

```
Private Sub txtKWHours_Change()
    Dim Cost As Single
    Dim KWHours As Single
    Const CostPerKWH As Single = 0.0942
    Const FuelFactor As Single = 0.001403
    Const TaxMultiplier As Single = 1.082

    If IsNumeric(txtKWHours.Text) Then
        KWHours = Val(txtKWHours.Text)

        Cost = KWHours * CostPerKWH
```

```
        Cost = Cost - KWHours * FuelFactor
        Cost = Cost * TaxMultiplier


        lblCost.Caption = Format(Cost, "$ ##, ##0.00")
    Else
        txtKWHours.Text = ""
    End If
End Sub
```

3 Close the code window, then save and run the program. The estimated cost will change as you type numeric values in the text box (Figure 5.3).

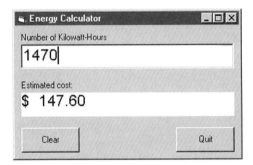

Figure 5.3 It's a lot of code, but your program already is pretty functional.

4 Close the program when you are done.

As you can probably tell, there is a lot going on here. Let's take a look at this block of code and examine each line. The first two lines declare, or dimension, two variables: Cost and KWHours. The value of Cost will, after a lot of computation, display in the label control. The variable KWHours is used to store the numeric *value* contained in txtKWHours. In fact, we use a *function* called **Val** to convert the string of numbers in txtKWHours to numbers we can use (otherwise, there would be a conversion problem, because the text box can only hold strings). *Functions* are described in the next subsection, but you can think of them as procedures that return a value: The Val function returns the numeric equivalent of a string of text.

> **Troubleshooting Tip** There is also a function called **CInt** that will convert a value to an integer (think of it as "Convert Integer"). The difference between CInt and Val in this context is subtle. In general, CInt should be used instead of Val when developing software that will run in multiple languages. Check out the MSDN Library for the lurid details.

After the variables were declared three constants were declared, as described in the specifications for this program. The constants are used later, in a series of computations, to determine the value of Cost.

Then, an If-Then-Else loop executes. This loop determines whether the text that is entered in txtKWHours is, indeed, numeric. If the text is *not* numeric, the Else clause runs and the text in txtKWHours is erased. If the text *is* numeric, the calculations commence. Finally, the formatted cost is displayed, in lblCost. The formatting occurs courtesy of the **Format** function, which takes two arguments: The number you want to format (which is stored in Cost) and a bizarre string that determines how the formatting will look. Check out the Format function in MSDN Library if you want more information (hey, it's good reading!).

> **Tip** You may have wondered why we're not using the Currency data type even though we are dealing with currency values here. We could use Currency, but then we'd have to do a lot of data type conversions with the variables and constants that are declared as Single. Since the numbers we're using fit within the range for Single, it just makes sense to always use that data type and keep the code simple.

Using Functions

A quick look at functions is now in order. You've already worked with procedures—blocks of code that execute together. A *function* is just like a procedure except that it can potentially return a value. In other words, you call a function and it returns *something* back, something you can use in an expression perhaps. For example, the Format function returns a text string formatted in a certain way and the Val function returns the numerical equivalent of the text string.

Functions can also be thought of as methods that aren't attached to an object. A method, you'll recall, describes something an object can *do*. A function is really the same thing except its functionality isn't tied to a particular kind of object. The Val function, for example, will work with any kind of text—variable, constant, or text from the caption of a label. It isn't associated with an object but is rather just part of the Visual Basic language because it provides a specific functionality.

> **Tip** For more information on functions, visit the MSDN Library and go to the entry for *functions* in the Index.

Finishing Up

Before we can wrap this up and move on to the next phase of this program, code needs to be written to handle the cmdClear and cmdQuit command buttons. In the following steps, you will add that code.

TASK 4: TO ADD CODE TO CMDCLEAR

1. Double-click *cmdClear* to bring up the code window.

2 Add the following code to the *Click* event-handler for cmdClear:

txtKWHours.Text = ""

lblCost.Caption – ""

txtKWHours.SetFocus

The *Click* event-handler should resemble Figure 5.4.

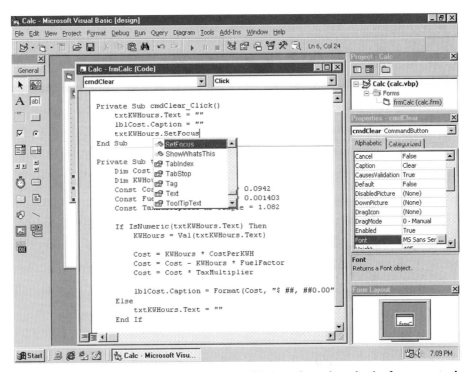

Figure 5.4 The code in this event-handler will clear the values in the form controls.

3 Close the code window.

TASK 5: TO ADD CODE TO CMDQUIT

1 Double-click *cmdQuit* to bring up the code window.

2 Add the following line of code to the *Click* event-handler for cmdQuit:

End

3 Close the code window, save the project, and test the program (Figure 5.5)

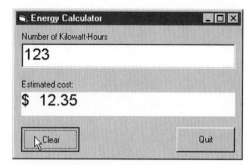

Figure 5.5 This first stab at the energy calculator is simple yet powerful.

The Conclusion

You have completed your first step in your energy calculator program. While this project included a lot of theory, the code you wrote demonstrates how powerful Visual Basic code can be for performing calculations. In the next project, you will expand the energy calculator to handle the cost calculations for two seasons while adding new Visual Basic controls and learning new concepts.

You can either exit Visual Basic now or go on to work the Study Questions. If Visual Basic asks you to save any files when you exit, choose [Yes] from the dialog box.

Summary and Exercises

Summary

- Variables are used to store temporary values that can change.
- Constants are used to store values that do not change.
- Constants are declared with the Const statement.
- Variables are generally declared with the Dim statement.
- Variables and constants have names and data types.
- Functions are procedures that return a value.

Key Terms and Operations

Key Terms	Operations
CInt Function	declare a constant
Const statement	declare a variable
constant	perform calculations
data type	use data types
declaration	use functions
Dim statement	
Format function	
function	
Integer data type	
name	
reserved word	
String data type	
Val function	
variable	

Study Questions

Multiple Choice

1. A variable is used to hold a value that
   a. never changes.
   b. can move.
   c. changes.
   d. is not typed.

2. A constant is used to hold a value that
   a. never changes.
   b. can move.
   c. changes.
   d. is not typed.

3. Variables and constants should always be
   a. numbers.
   b. letters.
   c. reserved words.
   d. declared.

4. Variables and constants have data types so that
   a. the language is more confusing.
   b. the requirements for object-oriented programming are satisfied.
   c. the proper amount of memory can be allocated.
   d. they will be correctly formatted when printed.

5. Dim is short for
   a. dimentia.
   b. dementia.
   c. dimension.
   d. dim sum.

6. Which of the following symbols does Visual Basic use to denote multiplication?
   a. *
   b. %
   c. /
   d. =

7. A function is like a procedure that
   a. cannot be written by the programmer.
   b. can return a value.
   c. does not accept any arguments.
   d. is not typed.

8. Which function is used to format output?
   a. Form
   b. TextDisplay
   c. Caption
   d. Format

9. Which data type is used to handle date and time values?
   a. Time
   b. Date
   c. DateTime
   d. Season

10. Which keyword appears in the declaration for both a constant and a variable?
   a. As
   b. Dim
   c. Const
   d. For

True/False

1. The value of a constant will never change.

2. The value of a variable will never change.

3. A data type determines the kind of value contained by a constant or variable.

4. By default, Visual Basic forces you to declare variables and constants.

5. Once you set the value of a variable, you must never change it again.

6. 7Count is a valid variable name.

7. The Format function allows you to format numeric values in a variety of ways.

8. A function is a procedure that returns a value.

9. A function, like a method, is tied to an object.

10. You must give a name to a constant or a variable.

Short Answer

1. What is the difference between a constant and a variable?

2. Why do variables and constants have data types?

3. Can you change the value of a constant?

4. What statement is generally used to declare a variable?

5. How do you force Visual Basic to require variable declarations?

6. What is the keyword Const used for?

7. What is the symbol for integer division?

8. Would Visual Basic allow you to create a variable named Caption? Why or why not?

9. What does the Val function do?

10. Based on the code used in this project, what does the equal sign (=) do?

Group Discussion

1. Why is it important for you to declare variables if Visual Basic doesn't force you to do so?

2. Write code to multiply the three numbers 45, 4, and 6 together and assign the result to a variable named **x**.

3. What do you know about a variable that is declared as being of type Short?

4. In algebra, the expression X = X + 1 is always false. Why do you think this statement is valid in Visual Basic?

Hands-On

Write a simple function
Just as the Visual Basic language provides functions you can use, you can also write your own functions. Use your Visual Basic coding skills to write a pseudocode function that will accept two numbers and return the value of the larger number. For example, if you pass the function the numbers 10 and 78, it will return 78.

On Your Own

1. Writing an addition calculator
Write a program that will function as an addition calculator. It should have a text box to accept numerical input, an Add command button that will take the number in the text box and add it to the total, and a label that will constantly display a running tally. The program should also feature two other command buttons: One that will clear the text box and set the running total to zero, and one that will quit the program.

2. Writing your own function
Write a Visual Basic program that implements the function whose pseudocode you created in the Hands-On exercise. The form should contain two text boxes, a

label, and a command button. When the command button is clicked, you should call your function, passing it the values from the text boxes. The larger of the two values should then be displayed as the caption of the label.

Here are some tips to get you started:

- The function body should be added to the (*General*) section in the code window.

- The empty function will look like this:

```
Public Function Greater(x, y As Integer) As Integer

End Function
```

- To return a value from a function, you assign the value to the name of the function. For example, if you wanted to return the value 13 from the Greater function, you could write a line of code like the following:

```
Greater = 13
```

- You can assume that the user will always enter valid integer values and that the text boxes will always contain a value. (In other words, you don't have to perform any complicated error checking: The goal here is to work through your first function.)

3. Formatting output

Write a Visual Basic program that allows the use to enter numerical text into a text box and press a command button to cause the text to be displayed in three separate labels. Each label should be assigned a unique formatting style using the Format function. View the MSDN Library for information about Format and pick three distinct formatting styles. Assume that the user will always enter a number and not text.

Improving the Energy Calculator

In Project 5, you created a simple energy calculator program that you will now enhance so that it can handle the correct billing for different seasons in different parts of the country. This version of the energy calculator will also feature an enhanced user interface with new Visual Basic controls.

Objectives

After completing this project, you will be able to:

➤ **Understand the scope of variables and constants**

➤ **Create global variables and constants**

➤ **Create forms and option buttons**

➤ **Write code that depends on the value of a group of option buttons**

➤ **Use the Select Case statement**

The Challenge

The program that you created in Project 5 is powerful but simple-minded. Predictably, the customer service representatives using your energy calculator have returned with some requests. In most parts of the country, charges for energy consumption are based on the time of the year, or season, and the CSRs would like to see that capability added to your calculator. In this project, you will comply with their request by adding a pair of seasonal options—peak and off-peak—that will determine how the calculation occurs. Peak season cost estimates will be based on the calculation you used in Project 5. Off-peak cost estimates will use a new, more complex computation.

The Solution

You will need to redesign the form slightly to accommodate the new features. The specifications for this part of the program are as follows:

- The program will include a pair of option buttons, surrounded by a frame. These options will determine whether the calculation is for peak or off-peak consumption.

- The user will select the season and then type in the number of kilowatt-hours used to find out the cost of that usage.

- The program will handle different billing rates, based on the season.

- Peak season cost estimates will use the same calculation performed in Project 5.

- Off-peak cost estimates will be calculated on a sliding scale. This will include a basic charge of $10.99, regardless of the number of kilowatt-hours used. Off-peak electrical usage will then be billed using the following rate scale: $0.0834 per kilowatt-hour for the first 400 kilowatt-hours used, $0.0635 per kilowatt-hour for the next 400 kilowatt-hours used, and $0.0396 for 801 kilowatt-hours and above.

- The fuel factor adjustments and taxes for off-peak costs will be applied as they were in Project 5.

When this project is complete, it should resemble Figure 6.1.

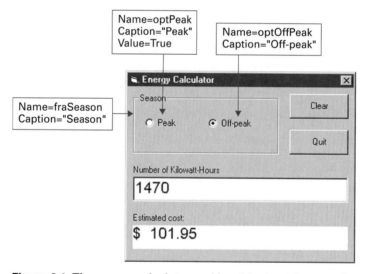

Figure 6.1 The energy calculator and its objects and properties.

The Setup

To continue working on the energy calculator program, you will need to load it into the Visual Basic IDE. Looking at the specifications for this phase of the project, you can see that the visual design of the form is changing a bit. Thus you will need to reorganize the location of some controls to match the design for this second phase.

TASK 1: TO RELOAD THE ENERGY CALCULATOR PROJECT

1 Start Visual Basic.

2 Using the Open Project dialog box, open the calc project.

3 Open the form *frmCalc*.

TASK 2: TO REARRANGE CONTROLS ON THE FORM

1 Drag the lower edge of the form down to make more room on its surface, as shown in Figure 6.2. Don't worry about an exact height; that will change some as controls are added.

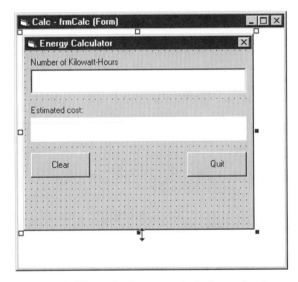

Figure 6.2 First, the form needs to be resized.

2 Move lblCost and its descriptive label to the bottom of the form, as shown in Figure 6.3.

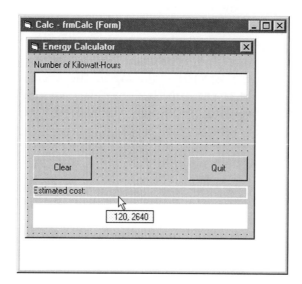

Figure 6.3 Next, the label control should be moved down.

3 Move txtKWHours and its descriptive label so that it appears right above lblCost, as shown in Figure 6.4.

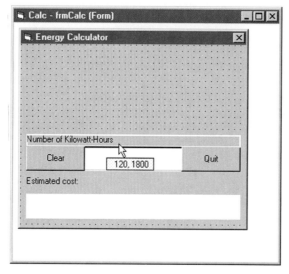

Figure 6.4 The text box should be placed above the label control.

4 Move cmdClear and cmdQuit to the top right of the form, as shown in Figure 6.5.

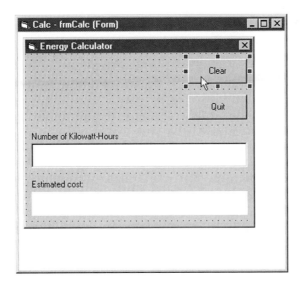

Figure 6.5 Both command buttons should be realigned near the top-right corner of the form window.

5 Run the program (Figure 6.6).
Now the form layout will accommodate the new controls you'll be adding, and the code you wrote will work as before.

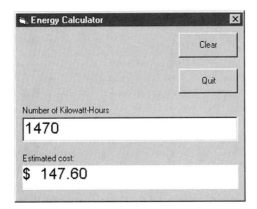

Figure 6.6 It may look a little strange, but it still works. We now have room to add some new controls.

6 Exit the program when you're done.

Another Look at Variables and Constants

Where constant and variable declarations are placed is very important. In Project 5, the constants and variables you used appeared in one of the event-handling procedures—the *Change* event-handler for the txtK-WHours text box. You were using these variables and constants only within that procedure, so the code worked fine: You declared the variables, used them in your code, and then the procedure ended.

But what happens when the procedure ends? And what if you wanted to use these variables and constants in other parts of your program? In this project, for example, you *will* need to access some of these values from other event-handler procedures. In the following section, we will look at some of these issues.

Understanding Variable Scope

The **scope** of a variable or constant determines *where* that value can be accessed in your program. For example, if you declare a variable in a procedure, the variable is only available, or *visible*, during the *lifetime* of the procedure. While the procedure is running, you can work with the variable, change its value, and use it as you see fit. Once the procedure ends and control returns to the code that called the procedure, the variable "dies" along with the procedure. These two attributes of scope—lifetime and visibility—are important. If you need to use a variable or constant throughout your program (or even throughout a single form), you will need to declare them differently; you won't be able to declare them in a procedure as you've done before.

Local and Global Variables

Variables that are declared within a procedure are *local* to that procedure and are, thus, **local variables**. The scope of these variables—that is, their visibility and lifetime—is the same as the scope of the procedure within which they are declared. If you need to access variables or constants in more than one procedure (or even in more than one form), you must declare them *globally*. **Global variables** are declared in a special declaration section for a form or code module (we will cover code modules in a later project) and can be used from any procedure in that form. Their scope is the same as the scope of the form itself, so they retain their values while the form window is available.

> **Tip** The MDSN Library has great information about scope.

Given this knowledge, you will now change the declarations for your variables and constants so that they have global scope.

1

TASK 3: TO CREATE GLOBAL VARIABLES AND CONSTANTS

1 Double-click on the form window to open the code window.

2 In the *Change* event-handler for txtKWHours, select and cut the following block of code to remove it from the procedure:

Dim Cost As Single

   Dim KWHours As Single

   Const CostPerKWH As Single = 0.0942

   Const FuelFactor As Single = 0.001403

   Const TaxMultiplier As Single = 1.082

3 In the Object drop-down list box of the code window, select (*General*). The Procedure drop-down list box will automatically change to (*Declarations*), as shown in Figure 6.7.

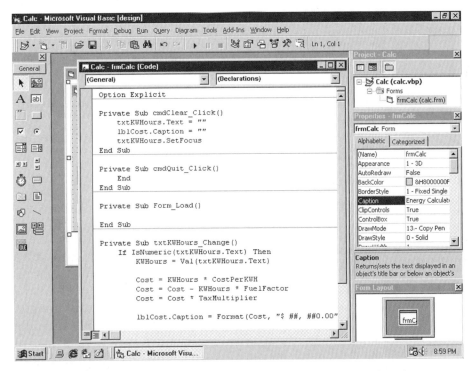

Figure 6.7 The *Declarations* section is used for global variable declaration.

4 Paste the code into the code window (Figure 6.8).

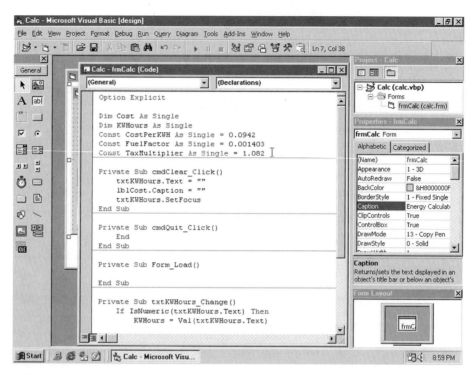

Figure 6.8 Now the local declarations you made in Project 5 are global.

5   Save and run the program. Notice that it still works as before.

6   Close the program when you are done testing it.

Using the Private and Public Keywords

In addition to giving your variables scope by placing their declarations in certain places, you can also explicitly set their scope by using two keywords, **Private** and **Public**. You should remember seeing the keyword *Private* before the event-handler procedures you've been writing. Just as Private procedures belong to the form in which they're used, Private variables are private to the form module (or code module) within which they're declared. So far, you've been creating single-form projects (though that will change in the next part of this project), but you can declare variables as *Public* that will be available to any form (or code) module in your project.

You may be wondering whether the constants and variables you've just moved to the declarations section of the form are Public or Private, since you didn't specifically declare them as either. They are private; Visual Basic will, by default, make these values Private to the form unless you specify otherwise. This means that the following two declarations are functionally identical:

```
Dim Cost As Single
Private Cost As Single
```

Note that when you do explicitly use the keywords *Private* or *Public*, the *Dim* keyword is unnecessary. A Public variable declaration, then, might look like this:

```
Public MyCost As Single
```

This variable would be available to any form module (or code module) in the project, so its scope would be the scope of the project. Regardless of which forms were available, the MyCost variable would be available for use as long as the program is running. Incidentally, the same is true of procedures. If you wanted to be able to call a procedure in a form from another form, you could declare that procedure as Public. We'll be taking a look at this in an upcoming project.

Frames and Option Buttons

Looking at the specifications for this phase of the project, we can see that some additions need to be made to the user interface. Two *option buttons* need to be added so that the user can determine whether the current rates are for peak or off-peak usage. Peak usage will depend on the area of the country: In colder climes, peak usage occurs in the winter when more electricity is used for heating. In warmer climes, peak usage occurs in the summer when air conditioning use skyrockets. Peak and off-peak usage will be billed at separate rates per the specifications for this project.

To add these new user interface elements to the program, you will need to add a few new controls.

Using the Frame Control

As shown in Figure 6.1, a labeled frame should enclose the option buttons. This effect is created by adding a frame control to the form and adding the option buttons directly onto the frame rather than the form. A frame is used to create logical groups of related controls, such as the option buttons we will use. For example, if you select *Options* from the *Tools* menu in the Visual Basic IDE, you will see a dialog box (shown in Figure 6.9) that uses two frame controls to offset related options. We will be using a frame in a similar manner.

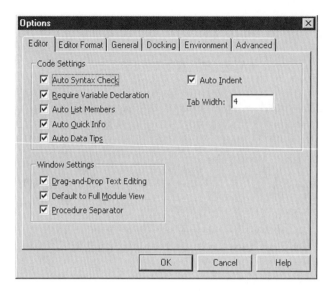

Figure 6.9 The Options dialog box in Visual Basic makes good use of the frame.

TASK 4: TO ADD A FRAME CONTROL TO THE FORM

1 Locate the frame control icon on the Toolbox window.

2 Double-click the frame control icon to add a frame to the center of the form, as shown in Figure 6.10.

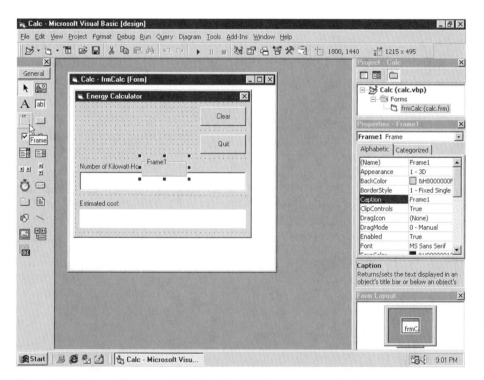

Figure 6.10 A new frame control is added to the energy calculator.

3   Drag the frame to the upper-left corner of the form and resize it to occupy the available space, as shown in Figure 6.11.

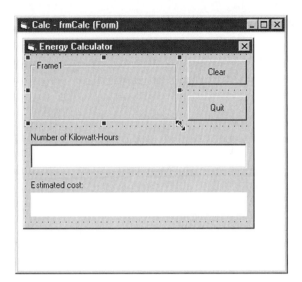

Figure 6.11 Resize the frame control per the specifications.

4   Change the name of the frame to **fraSeason**.

5   Change the frame caption to **Season**.

Now you will need to add option buttons to the frame.

Using Option Buttons

You are probably familiar with **option buttons** from your use of Windows or other Windows applications. They are used to provide a list of choices where only one option can be chosen. Option buttons turn up in all kinds of dialog boxes. They are only used when the list of choices is short, usually two or three choices. If there are more than three choices, other controls such as the drop-down list box would be more appropriate.

The list of option buttons is arranged in a row, either vertically or horizontally. If the list is vertical, then the top option is the default choice. In a horizontal list of choices, the leftmost choice is the default. We will be creating a horizontal list of two option buttons to the frame control.

TASK 5: TO ADD AN OPTION BUTTONS TO THE SEASON FRAME

1   Locate the OptionButton icon ⊙ on the Toolbox window.

2   Double-click the icon to add an option button to the form and drag it to the location inside the frame shown in Figure 6.12.

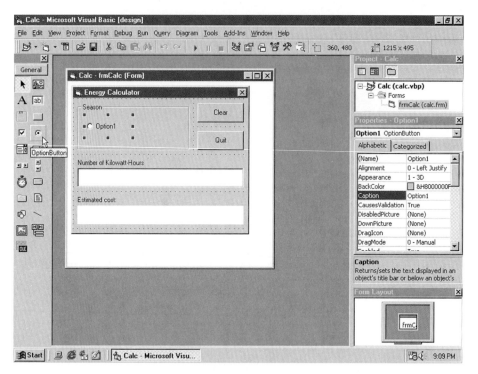

Figure 6.12 An option button is added to the form.

3 Change the name of the option button to **optPeak** and its caption to **Peak**.

4 Change the value of its *Value* property to *True*.

5 Add the second option button as shown in Figure 6.13.

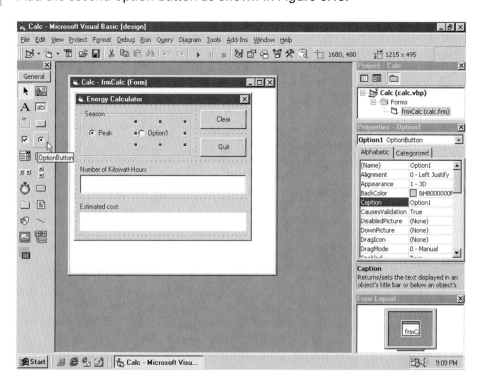

Figure 6.13 With both option buttons in place, the program is beginning to more closely meet the specifications.

6   Change the second option button's name to **optOffPeak** and its caption to **Off-peak**.

7   Test the program (Figure 6.14).
Notice that the *Peak* option button is selected when the program starts. If you select the other option, the *Peak* option is deselected and vice versa. In other words, only one option can be selected at a time.

8   Quit the program when you are done.

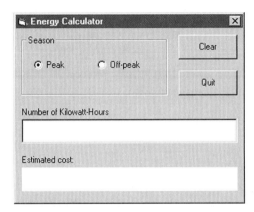

Figure 6.14 Only one option button can be selected at a time.

Programming the Option Buttons

Now that we have the two option buttons in place, we'll have to change the code that determines how the cost is estimated. You'll recall from Projedt 5 that the cost is calculated in the *Change* event-handler for KWHours using the following lines of code:

Cost = KWHours * CostPerKWH

Cost = Cost - KWHours * FuelFactor

Cost = Cost * TaxMultiplier

The first line of this code will have to change dramatically. If the *Peak* option is chosen, the calculation is the same as before (the Project 5 version of the calculator only estimated peak season costs). If the *Off-peak* option is chosen, however, a different (and complex) computation will be needed to figure the cost.

Off-peak costs are calculated on a sliding scale in conformance with the specifications. Although an If-Then-Else loop could be used for this calculation, it would quickly get out of hand. Consider the following pseudocode:

If Peak Option = True Then

    Cost = Calculation we used before

Else

    If KWHours > 0 And KWHours <= 400 Then

        Compute Cost using sliding scale

```
    Else
        If KWHours > 400 And KWHours <= 800 Then
            Compute Cost using sliding scale
        Else
            Compute Cost using sliding scale
        End If
    End If
End If
```

As you can see, this quickly gets quite ugly. A more elegant and more readable alternative to the use of so many nested If-Then-Else clauses is the Select Case statement. Let's take a look.

Using Select Case

Visual Basic's **Select Case** statement makes your program easier to read, debug, and understand. The Select Case statement takes the following form:

```
Select Case <expression>
    Case <test>
        <instruction block>
    Case <test>
        <instruction block>
    ..
    Case Else
        <instruction block>
End Select
```

where **expression** is any standard Visual Basic expression, **test** is one or more test ranges, and **instruction block** is one or more lines of Visual Basic code. The *Case Else* section is optional; if present, it executes when none of the preceding cases match the test (it's just like the Else clause in an If-Then-Else). The example above shows three test cases (two explicit and one implicit in the Else clause), but the Select Case could have almost any number of test cases.

Select Case vs. If-Then-Else

The Select Case statement differs from If-Then-Else in that it tests whether an expression falls within a range of values; If-Then-Else only tests whether certain conditions are true or false. Furthermore, the range of values the Select Case statement can test for is far more powerful than the true or false tests performed in If-Then-Else. Table 6.1 lists the possibilities.

Table 6.1 Select Case Range Tests

Range Type	Example
Equality	Case Is = 50 or Case 50
Explicit Range	Case 10 to 20
Multiple	Case Is > 10, Is < 20
Relational	Case Is <= 20

Coding the Calculator with Select Case

With this understanding of how Select Case works, you can now improve the energy calculator to match the specifications. The first step will be to add code to handle the events that occur when either option button is selected, which will require a separate event-handler for each option button. Then the appropriate constants will need to be added to the form's declaration section. And finally, the simple computation code in the *Change* event-handler for txtKWHours will need to be changed dramatically so that it calculates correctly based on the season that is selected.

TASK 6: TO WRITE CODE FOR THE OPTIONS BUTTONS

1   Double-click *optPeak* and add the following two lines of code to its *Click* event-handler:

txtKWHours_Change

txtKWHours.SetFocus

This will trigger the *Change* event-handler for txtKWHours and set the focus to the text control.

2   Add the same two lines of code to the optOffPeak *Click* event-handler (Figure 6.15).

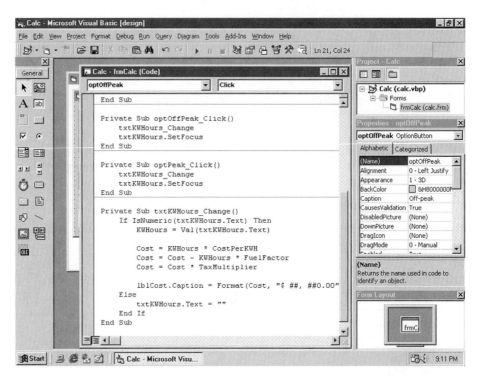

Figure 6.15 The event-handler for optOffPeak will execute the same code as the event-handler for optPeak.

3 Keep the code window open, but save the project.

TASK 7: TO ADD NEW CONSTANT DECLARATIONS

1 Scroll up to the top of the code window. You will see the constant and variable declarations you created earlier.

2 Change the line of code that reads
Const CostPerKWH As Single = 0.0942
to

Const PeakCostPerKWH As Single = 0.0942

3 Below that, and above the declaration for FuelFactor, add the following lines of code:

Const OffPeakCost1st400 As Single = 0.0834

Const OffPeakCost2nd400 As Single = 0.0635

Const OffPeakCostOver800 As Single = 0.0396

Const OffPeakBasicFee As Single = 10.99

Your declaration section should now resemble Figure 6.16.

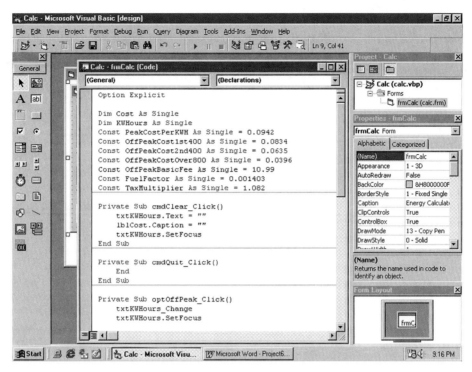

Figure 6.16 The global declarations now reflect the season requirements of the specifications.

4   Close the code window and save the project.

TASK 8: TO CHANGE THE WAY COST IS CALCULATED

1   Double-click *txtKWHours* to display the code window with the *Change* event-handler for the text box centered.

2   Replace the code in this event-handler with the following:

```
If IsNumeric(txtKWHours.Text) Then
    KWHours = Val(txtKWHours.Text)
    If optPeak.Value = True Then
        Cost = KWHours * PeakCostPerKWH
    Else
        Select Case KWHours
        Case 0 To 400
            Cost = OffPeakBasicFee + KWHours * OffPeak
            Cost1st400
        Case 401 To 800
            Cost = OffPeakBasicFee + 400 *
            OffPeakCost1st400
            Cost = Cost + (KWHours - 400) *
            OffPeakCost2nd400
```

```
    Case Else
        Cost = OffPeakBasicFee + 400 *
        OffPeakCost1st400
        Cost = Cost + 400 * OffPeakCost2nd400
        Cost = Cost + (KWHours - 800) *
        OffPeakCostOver800
    End Select
End If
Cost = Cost - KWHours * FuelFactor
Cost = Cost * TaxMultiplier
lblCost.Caption = Format(Cost, "$ ##, ##0.00")
Else
    txtKWHours.Text = ""
End If
```

3 Close the code window and save the project.

4 Run and test the program. Notice that selecting the option buttons changes the estimated cost immediately (Figure 6.17).

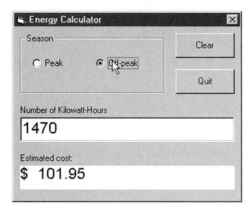

Figure 6.17 Your new and improved energy calculator computes cost according to specs.

5 Quit the program when you are done testing.

The Conclusion

You have completed Project 6. In the next project, you will enhance the energy calculator so that it more closely adheres to the Windows look and feel by adding such features as a menu bar with cascading menus, an About Box dialog, and access keys (once known as hot keys) that allow the user to more easily navigate the controls in the program.

You can either exit Visual Basic now or go on to work the Study Questions. If Visual Basic asks you to save any files when you exit, choose Yes from the dialog box.

Summary and Exercises

Summary

- Variables and constants can have local or global scope.
- The keywords *Private* and *Public* are sometimes used to explicitly set scope.
- Frame controls are used to visually arrange other controls.
- Option buttons, arranged in a group, are used for picking one choice from a short list.
- Option buttons are arranged in a row, either horizontally or vertically, and are typically found inside of a frame.
- The standard event associated with option buttons is the *Click* event.
- The Select Case is an excellent replacement for multiple nested If-Then-Else statements.

Key Terms and Operations

Key Terms	Operations
frame control	add a frame control to the form
global variable	calculate on a sliding scale
local variable	create global variables and constants
option button	group controls inside a frame
Private	set option button properties
Public	use option buttons
scope	use the Select Case statement as a replacement
Select Case	for nested If-Then-Else statements
	write code for option buttons

Study Questions

Multiple Choice

1. How many option buttons in a group can be selected at one time?
   a. all of them
   b. one
   c. two
   d. none

2. The default option button in a group is the one
   a. on the left or top.
   b. on the right or top.
   c. on the far left or right.
   d. chosen by the programmer with the *Default* property.

3. Frame controls are used
   a. to group frames.
   b. to group Form windows.
   c. to connect text.
   d. to group option buttons.

4. The prefix used for an option button is
   a. option.
   b. optn.
   c. opt.
   d. onion.

5. The Select Case statement
   a. replaces the GOTO statement.
   b. replaces nested If-Then-Else statements.
   c. replaces the need to code decisions.
   d. replaces lateral If-Then-Else statements.

6. The Select Case statement tests whether an expression
   a. falls within a range of values.
   b. is true or false only.
   c. evaluates to a nonzero value.
   d. can be selected.

7. The two keywords that explicitly set scope are
   a. *Dim* and *Dimmer*
   b. *Project* and *Program*
   c. *Private* and *Public*
   d. *Protected* and *Private*

8. A variable that is global to the form should be declared in
   a. the form's *OnLoad* event-handler.
   b. the *Declarations* section for the form.
   c. any event-handler.
   d. another module.

9. A global variable is a variable that is available
   a. anywhere in that form (or code module).
   b. only in that specific event-handler.
   c. anywhere in the world.
   d. only in the *Declarations* section for the module.

10. The prefix for a frame is
    a. fra.
    b. frm.
    c. frame.
    d. france.

True/False

1. Variables declared within a procedure are local to that procedure.

2. The scope of a variable determines where that value can be accessed in a program.

3. Global variables can be used by any procedure in the current form (or code module).

4. Local variables can be used by any procedure in the current form (or code module).

5. A frame control is used to group related controls together.

6. Option buttons provide a list of choices to the user, where only one choice can be selected at a time.

7. The Select Case statement is harder to read than multiple nested If-Then-Else statements.

8. The Case Else block in a Select Case statement is used to handle any case that isn't explicitly handled elsewhere in the statement.

9. The code Case Is = 50 and Case 50 have the same effect when used in a Select Case statement.

10. A Public variable is available to objects in other forms and code modules.

Short Answer

1. Can two option buttons in a group be selected at the same time?

2. What is the shape of an option button?

3. Is the frame control something the user might click to cause an action to occur?

4. Why would one or more frames be useful on a form that had two groups of option buttons?

5. How is Select Case different from If-Then-Else?

6. Why is Select Case preferable to several nested If-Then-Else statements?

7. When would you declare a global variable?

8. When would you declare a local variable?

9. Can you create Public procedures?

10. Where can you access Public variables?

Group Discussion

1. The Select Case statement is far more versatile than the If-Then-Else statement, but when would If-Then-Else be more appropriate?

2. Tool around Windows a bit and examine the way frame controls are used. In what ways do you see these controls used in Windows?

3. Why would you not want to use option buttons if there were 100 options to choose from?

4. The concept of scope can be confusing to new programmers, especially given the number of keywords there are to learn. Compare a Private variable with a global form variable.

Hands-On

Color combinations
Create a Visual Basic program that has two frames. Each frame should include four option buttons, each labeled with a color of your choice. The first frame should be labeled "Foreground" and the second frame should be labeled "Background." Add a blank label control that occupies a good portion of the free area of the form. When the user selects a color in the foreground group, the *BackColor* property of the label should change to the corresponding color. Likewise, when a color in the background group is chosen, the *BackColor* property of the form should change appropriately.

The first color in each group is the default and should be chosen when the program starts. In the form's *Load* event-handler, make sure you set the two colors correctly so that the form and label color match the default colors.

On Your Own

1. Using Select Case

Convert the following convoluted If-Then-Else into a Select Case block.

```
Dim X As Integer
Dim S As String
If X < 21 Then
    S = "Not old enough to vote."
Else
    If X >= 21 And X <= 30 Then
        S = "Old enough to know better."
    Else
        If X < 60 Then
            S = "Old enough to wonder why."
        Else
            S = "Old enough to not care less."
        End If
    End If
End If
```

2. Having fun with option buttons

Write a program that includes a group of four option buttons labeled *Chocolate*, *Vanilla*, *Strawberry*, and *Pistachio*. *Chocolate* should be selected by default and the form caption should be set to the caption of the selected option button. When the selected flavor is changed, the caption of the flavor should display as the form caption.

3. Creating an astro scale

The weight of an object on the surface of a planet depends on the gravitational attraction between that object and the planet, which in turn depends on the mass and radius of each. Your weight on another planet may be more or less than your weight on Earth. If you know your weight on Earth, you can calculate your weight on other planets by multiplying your Earth weight by a conversion factor appropriate for the other planet. For example, the moon's conversion factor is 0.16; this means that your weight on the moon is only 16% of your weight on Earth. If you weigh 100 pounds on Earth, you would weigh only 16 pounds on the moon.

Write a program featuring a group of four option buttons labeled *Moon*, *Mars*, *Jupiter*, and *Pluto*. There should be a text box for users to enter their Earth weight and a label that will display their weight on the selected planet. The weight conversion factors (where Earth = 1.0) are shown in Table 6.2.

Table 6.2 Weight Converion Factors

Planet	Conversion Factor
Moon	0.16
Mars	0.39
Jupiter	2.54
Pluto	0.06

4. Creating a postal calculator

Create an express mail cost calculator that includes two frames. In one frame, place a text box where the user can enter the weight of a package. The frame caption should read *Weight in Pounds*. Inside the second frame, place a label control that will display the correct cost as the weight is inputted. The cost of sending a package is calculated using Table 6.3.

Table 6.3 Cost of Sending a Package

Total Cost	Weight Range (in pounds)
$10.75	Weight > 0 and Weight <= 0.5
$15.00	Weight > 0.5 and Weight <= 2.0
$17.25	Weight > 2.0 and Weight <= 3.0
$19.40	Weight > 3.0 and Weight <= 4.0
$21.55	Weight > 4.0 and Weight <= 5.0

Weights above 5.0 pounds should display the text *Too heavy* in the label.

7

PROJECT

Making a Better Windows Application

In the previous two projects, you constructed an energy calculator that features some pretty serious calculation abilities. But you also need to learn to create applications that can coexist peacefully with other Windows applications. This project will focus on that goal: Using Visual Basic's strengths—ease of use and full compatibility with a wealth of Windows controls—you will mold your energy calculator into a better Windows citizen.

Objectives

After completing this project, you will be able to:

➤ **Build applications that will conform to the Windows user interface guidelines**

➤ **Add access key support to your applications**

➤ **Create a menu bar**

➤ **Add cascading submenu items to a menu bar**

➤ **Create an About Box dialog**

➤ **Write code that will open a second window in your application**

The Challenge

Well, your update to the energy calculator was a big hit! Except for one thing: Many of the CSRs complained that the program doesn't have the look and feel of their other Windows applications. In some ways, this is easy to fix because Visual Basic supplies you with a toolbox full of standard Windows controls. On the other hand, it's easy to abuse these controls and use them unwisely. Also, your program needs to conform to the basic user interface features that other Windows applications use, such as menus and an About Box dialog.

The Solution

The specifications for this part of the program are as follows:

- The existing energy calculator program will be enhanced.

- Access key support will be added for easier navigation.

- A menu bar with *File* and *Help* menu items will be added. The *File* menu item will have *Clear* and *Exit* subitems. The *Help* menu item will have an *About* subitem that will launch an About Box dialog.

- A new, second form will be used as an About Box dialog that will supply basic information about the program.

The Setup

One of the original goals for Windows was for the operating system to provide a consistent look and feel for all applications. This makes it easier for the user to learn *any* program because *all* programs should work the same way. And certainly, even your energy calculator has a basic Windows look and feel, even though you didn't do anything specific to make that happen. This is because Visual Basic supplies a standard set of controls that match those of other Windows applications. But compliance with the standard Windows look and feel goes a little deeper than that.

> **Tip** Microsoft has developed a set of guidelines for programmers to use to ensure that their programs conform to this standard. Called *The User Interface Guidelines for Windows*, this guide was even published as a book titled *The Windows Interface: An Application Design Guide*. The book is a little out-of-date, however, since it was published when Windows 95 first came out and many of the design elements in Windows have been updated since then.

It's not difficult to tell a good Windows program from a poor one. Properly designed Windows applications have menu bars, toolbars (when needed), and other consistent interface elements that, when used correctly, do not cause the user to pause and wonder how to complete a task. An excellent example of consistent user interface design is Microsoft Office, whose many applications share similar, if not virtually identical, menu bars and toolbars. Consequently, the applications in Microsoft Office are easy to use because they are so familiar and because they work in a manner similar to each other.

As an interesting historical note, when Visual Basic first came out it was common to see horribly designed applications with enormous command buttons and illogical control placement, such as the monstrocity shown in Figure 7.1. These programs were widely distributed by Visual Basic users giddy with their newfound power of easily and quickly creating programs. This somewhat sullied the Visual Basic name among serious C and C++ programmers, who are quick to point out such programs and identify them as the product of a Visual Basic user. Don't fall into this power trap: Just because Visual Basic makes it easy to create programs doesn't mean you shouldn't take the extra step to make your creations good Windows citizens. You owe your users at least that much.

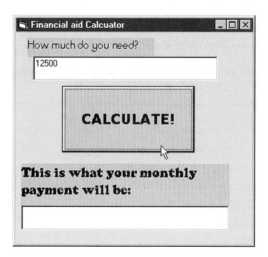

Figure 7.1 Haven't we all seen a program like this? Don't do this to your users!

Improving the Energy Calculator

While the energy calculator can't possibly encompass all of the features used by powerful Windows applications such as Microsoft Word, there are some features we could add to make it more consistent with other applications. As mentioned in the specifications, these features include a *menu bar* and an *About Box dialog*. You will also add *access key support* so that your users can more easily navigate the program. In the following sections, you will add these features and turn the energy calculator into a compliant Windows citizen.

Adding Access Key Support

Your current version of the energy calculator offers two simple methods of navigating its user interface: The user can simply click on the controls they wish to access or use the ⌈TAB⌋ key to move from control to control. Most Windows programs, however, offer a third navigation method—the *access keys*. An **access key**—also known as a *hot key*—is a single letter that will cause the focus to shift to a particular control. For example, command buttons may have an underline under the letter "O": In such cases, pressing (ALT)+o on your keyboard causes that button to be selected and activated.

You can add access key support to many of your own controls by selecting a letter in the control's label to be underlined. In the energy calculator there are two command buttons and a frame that would benefit from this addition.

Adding an access key to most controls is as simple as adding the ampersand character (&) to the appropriate place in that control's caption. You type the ampersand into the caption directly in front of the letter that should act as the access key. For example, if the *Caption* property is set to Exit, you would type **E&xit** and it would appear as Exit on the control. While the program is running, pressing (ALT)+x would select that control. Let's add this functionality to our command buttons and frame.

TASK 1: TO ADD ACCESS KEY SUPPORT TO THE ENERGY CALCULATOR

1 Load the calc project into Visual Basic and display the form.

2 Select the *Clear* button and double-click its *Caption* property in the Properties window.

3 Type **&Clear** and press (ENTER).
The caption will change to Clear, as shown in Figure 7.2.

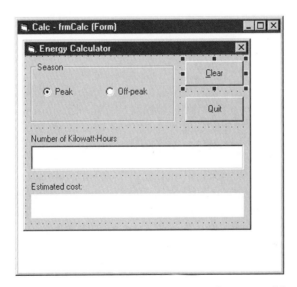

Figure 7.2 The ampersand character lets you add access key support.

4 Change the caption of cmdQuit to Quit.

5 Change the caption of fraSeason to Season.

6   Change the caption of optPeak to Peak and the caption of optOffPeak to Off-Peak.

7   Run the program (Figure 7.3) and test this functionality by typing (ALT) with the **q**, **s**, **c**, **p**, and **o** keys to see that doing so causes the appropriate control to become focused.

8   Quit the program when you are done.

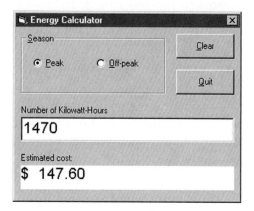

Figure 7.3 Now that your calculator sports access keys, navigation is easier for keyboard users.

Tip   Access keys are only available to those controls that have a *Caption* property.

Adding a Menu Bar

Almost every Windows program has a ***menu bar***, a strip of text-based choices directly below the title bar. A menu bar gives a cascading list of options under each heading. Menus are pervasive throughout Windows, so you should have no problem using them. Adding menus to your Visual Basic programs is also a snap thanks to the Menu Editor.

The Visual Basic ***Menu Editor*** (Figure 7.4) allows you to create new menus; add, delete, and modify menu items; and modify existing menus. Since a menu is far more complex than a typical control, it is accessed in the Visual Basic IDE from the *Tools* menu, not the Toolbox window. And, unlike controls you used in the past, most of the properties for the menus you create can be set from this window. The Properties window can also be used, but while you're in the IDE, it is hard to select the menu you need and then access its properties from the Properties window.

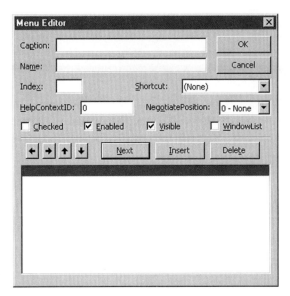

Figure 7.4 The Visual Basic Menu Editor gives you easy access to menu creation.

Creating a menu system requires a few steps. First, you will create the actual menu itself, which in this case will feature two top-level items, *File* and *Help*. Then you will create the actual cascading menus themselves. The File menu will have two menu items separated by a ***separator bar***: *Clear* and *Exit*. The Help menu will have one item, *About . . .* , which will launch the About Box dialog that you will soon create. OK, let's make some menus.

TASK 2: TO ADD A MENU TO THE PROGRAM

1 Select *Menu Editor* from the *Tools* menu to display the Menu Editor.

2 To add the first menu item, type **&File** in the Caption text box.

3 Press (TAB) and type **mnuFile** in the Name text box.
Your screen should resemble Figure 7.5.

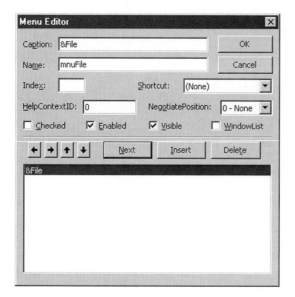

Figure 7.5 By typing the ampersand, you added the access key feature to the control as you created it. You will do this from now on.

4 Press (ENTER) to begin a new item and type **&Help** as the caption of the second top-level menu item.

5 Press (TAB) and type **mnuHelp** in the Name text box (Figure 7.6).

Figure 7.6 A second menu item, labeled Help, appears at the same level as File in the Menu Editor.

6 Click ___OK___ to close the Menu Editor.
The menu will be added to your program and the form resized automatically. Your controls will also be correctly moved down to accommodate the menu.

When you run the program (Figure 7.7) you will see that even though your menu is visible, clicking the items doesn't yet do anything. You will need to add your submenu items first.

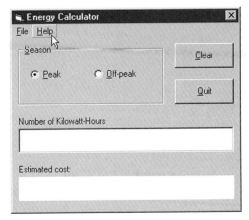

Figure 7.7 When you add a menu, you don't have to move controls on the form; they are automatically moved down for you.

TASK 3: TO ADD A SUBMENU ITEM TO THE *FILE* MENU

1 Open the Menu Editor again (*Tools→Menu Editor*) and select your second menu item, Help, from the list box at the bottom of the window.

2 Click [Insert] (Figure 7.8) to add an item between File and Help. This will be the first submenu item below File.

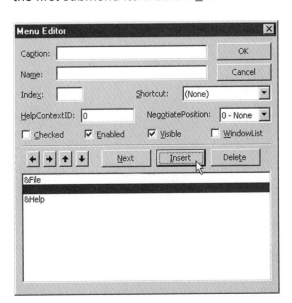

Figure 7.8 Use [Insert] in the Menu Editor to add a new item between other items.

3 In the Caption text box, type **&Clear**.

4 Press ⟨TAB⟩ and type **mnuClear** in the Name text box.

5 Because this is a submenu item below File, you will need to indent it within the menu editor. Press → (Figure 7.9).
In the bottom list box, the view will change to show that Clear is a subitem of File and not a top-level menu item.

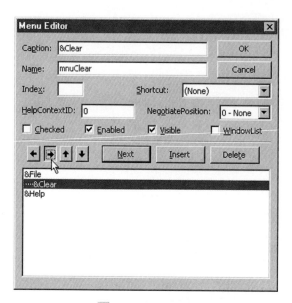

Figure 7.9 The ➡ button indents a menu item, indicating that it is a subitem of the item above it.

TASK 4: TO ADD A SEPARATOR BAR

1 Click Next and then Insert .
The focus will shift automatically to the Caption text box.

2 Type a hyphen (**-**) as the caption and press (ENTER).
The hyphen is used in the Menu Editor to denote a separator bar.

3 Type **mnuSep** as the name.

4 Click ➡ to indent the separator bar into the submenu (Figure 7.10).

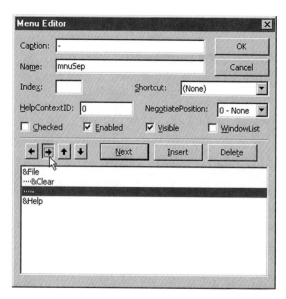

Figure 7.10 A separator bar visually separates items in a menu.

TASK 5: TO ADD THE OTHER SUBMENU ITEMS

1 Click Next .

2 Add a submenu item below File whose caption is **E&xit** and whose name is **mnuExit**. Remember to indent properly so that it is a submenu item (Figure 7.11).

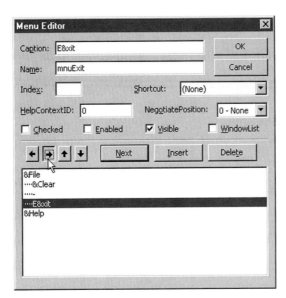

Figure 7.11 The Exit item should also be a submenu item of File.

3 Select Help in the list box and press Next to add a submenu item for the Help menu.

4 Add a submenu item below Help whose caption is **&About** and whose name is **mnuAbout**. This should be indented as well.

5 Close the Menu Editor when you are done and run the program. The menus do not perform any actions yet, but they do display properly (Figure 7.12).

6 Quit the program when you are done.

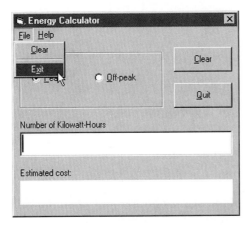

Figure 7.12 Wasn't that easy? A full menuing system done the visual way!

Writing Code for the Menu

As you will recall, to write code for a control on the form you simply double-click the control to bring up the code window, make sure the correct event-handler procedure is chosen, and start writing. As you might expect, writing code for menus is very similar. Simply select the menu item you want to write code for and the code window will open. Since you will typically want to handle the *Click* event with menu items, that is the event-handler that will appear by default when you select a menu item.

You currently have three submenu items to write code for in your energy calculator. The Clear submenu item should duplicate the functionality of the *Clear* button, so the *Click* handler for mnuClear can simply call the *Click* event-handler for cmdClear. The Exit submenu item will quit the program, which duplicates the functionality of the *Quit* button. And the About submenu item, which will display an About Box dialog. We will handle that in the next section.

In the following steps, you will write code for the submenu items you've added.

TASK 6: TO ADD CODE FOR THE FILE MENU ITEMS

1 In the Visual Basic IDE, open the File menu on the form by clicking it once. The File menu will open.

2 As shown in Figure 7.13, select the Clear submenu item.
The code window will open with a blank *Click* event-handler ready and waiting.

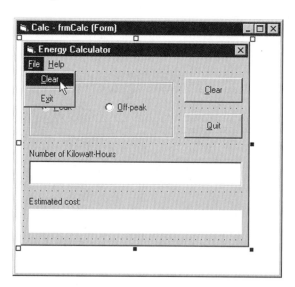

Figure 7.13 When you select a menu item in the IDE, the code window opens with that item's blank *Click* event-handler.

3 Type **cmdClear_Click** in the event-handler and close the code window.
This calls the *Click* event-handler. There is no need to write the code twice, just call the procedure that already performs the action you want to perform.

4 Select the Exit submenu item to reopen the code window, which is now displaying the *Click* event-handler for mnuExit.

5 Type **cmdQuit_Click** in the event-handler and close the code window.

6 Save the project and run your program. Test the submenu items under the File menu (Figure 7.14).

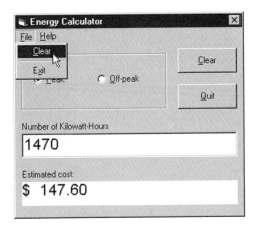

Figure 7.14 The submenu items under File should now work properly.

Creating an About Box Dialog

Up until now, you've worked solely with single-form projects. While this is fine in a learning environment, most Windows applications have at least two windows. At the least, an ***About Box dialog*** will be avaialable to provide some information about the program and its author(s). Adding a second form to Visual Basic projects is straightforward. Microsoft even provides default templates for a variety of form window types—blank forms, About dialogs, standard dialogs, Log-in dialogs, Splash screens, and more.

Adding a Second Form to Your Project

Adding a second form to your project is as simple as clicking a menu item and choosing the kind of form you'd like to add. In the following steps, you will add a blank About Box dialog to your project.

TASK 7: TO ADD AN ABOUT BOX DIALOG

1 Choose *Add Form* from the *Projects* menu in the Visual Basic IDE, as shown in Figure 7.15

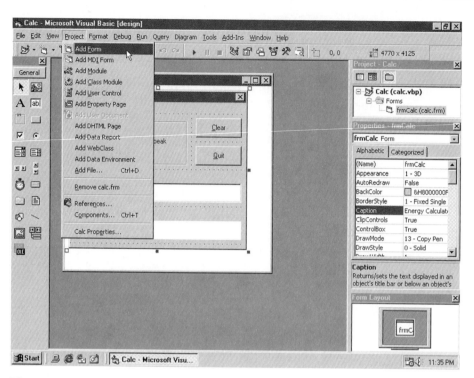

Figure 7.15 Adding a second form is as easy as selecting a menu item.

2   In the Add Form dialog, select *About Dialog* and click `Open` .
A second form window will open in the IDE, as shown in Figure 7.16.

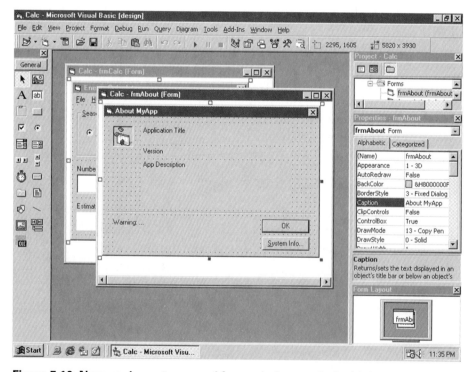

Figure 7.16. Now you've got a second form window to deal with in your solution.

3   Save the project.
    A dialog box will appear asking you to save the new form.

4   Navigate to the folder where you are storing the calc project.

5   Save the About Box form as **about.frm** (Figure 7.17).

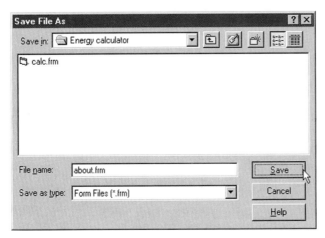

Figure 7.17 Make sure you save the new form in the same folder as the other files in your project.

Editing the About Box Dialog

Because Microsoft has provided a nice template for the About Box dialog, the default form we got is already feature-rich with space to type in our application name, version number, and other features. On the other hand, some of the features that Microsoft gives us are overkill for the energy calculator. So we will actually need to delete some of the controls on the About Box, such as the Warning label and the system information button. We will also want to provide the correct information for the other labels.

TASK 8: TO DELETE UNNEEDED CONTROLS IN THE ABOUT BOX

1   Select *lblDisclaimer*, which has the caption of *Warning*, and delete it by pressing the (DELETE) key.

1   Select the *System Info* button and delete it.

2   Drag the bottom edge of the form up so that it more closely lines up with the bottom of cmdOK, as shown in Figure 7.18.

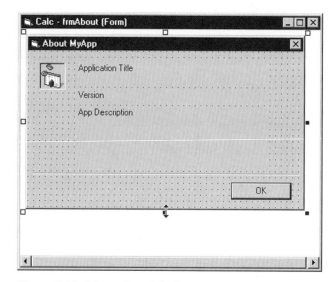

Figure 7.18 After a few deletions, the About Box is looking better.

TASK 9: TO MODIFY THE ABOUT BOX

1 Select the label for *Application title* and replace the value in its *Caption* property with **Energy Calculator**.

2 Select the *Version* label and change its caption to **Version 1.0**.

3 Select the *App Description* label and change its caption to **Calculate electricity consumption in peak and off-peak seasons.**
Your About Box dialog should now resemble Figure 7.19.

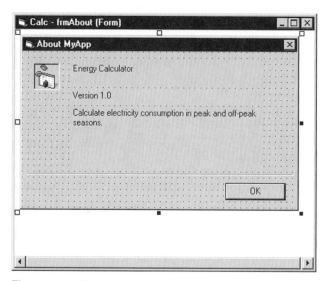

Figure 7.19 Here is our kinder, gentler About Box.

Displaying the About Box Dialog

Now that the About Box dialog is set up for your application, you will need to write code to display the dialog. This will be tied to the *Click* event of frmCalc's About menu item.

Visual Basic lets you open new windows programmatically with the form's **Show method**. The *Show* method can be called without arguments if you'd like to accept its default style, like so:

frmAbout.Show

However, you can also call *Show* with an optional argument called *style*. The *style* option determines whether the window you are opening—in this case frmAbout—will open *modally* or *nonmodally* (the default is non-modally). A **nonmodal** window is one that opens normally, and it allows the user to go back and select other windows in the program. A **modal** form is one that grabs all of the user input when it is opened: The user will not be able to access any of the other windows in the program until the modal form window is closed. Typically, you want an About Box to open modally.

To show a window modally, you need to write the following code:

frmAbout.Show vbModal

Let's do that now.

TASK 10: TO WRITE CODE TO OPEN THE ABOUT BOX DIALOG

1   In the Visual Basic IDE, select *frmCalc* to bring that window to the front and select the About menu item under Help.
The code window will open.

2   Type the following line of code in the *Click* event-handler for mnuAbout:

frmAbout.Show vbModal

3   Close the code window, save the project, and run the program as shown in Figure 7.20.

4   Open the About Box dialog box.
Wait! Two of the labels are displaying text that don't match the captions we've chosen. Let's take a look at this: Close the program and return to the Visual Basic IDE.

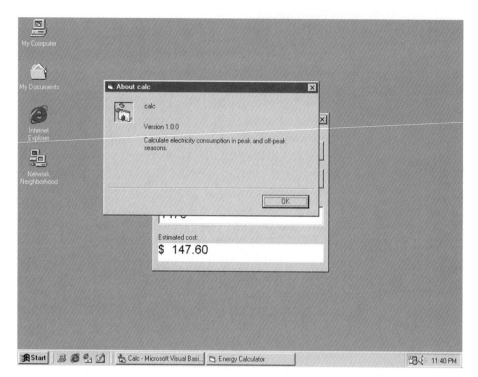

Figure 7.20. What's this? You didn't type those values into the About Box!

Using Project Properties

Two of the labels on the About Box, the application name and version number, seem to be getting their values from somewhere other than the label captions we created. And they are: When Microsoft built its About Box dialog template, it decided to code it so that the dialog box could grab information from the internal structure of the project itself. We could just delete those labels and create new ones without much problem, but it's also possible to modify the actual properties of the project. Like objects in the project, the project itself has properties you can set and get. These properties are available from a menu in the Visual Basic IDE.

TASK 11: TO CHANGE PROJECT PROPERTIES

1   In the Visual Basic IDE, choose *Calc Properties* from the *Project* menu. The Project Properties dialog will appear, as shown in Figure 7.21.

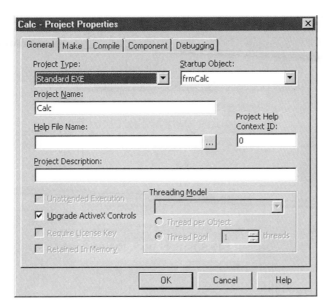

Figure 7.21 The Project Properties dialog box offers an extensive collection of project attributes.

2   Navigate to the *Make* tab.

3   Select the Title text box in the *Application* section and change the name to **Energy Calculator** (Figure 7.22).

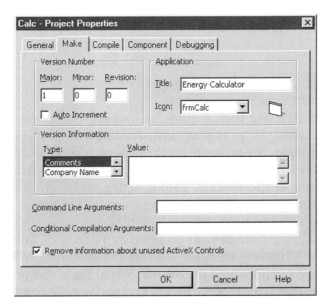

Figure 7.22 Change the project's title in the Project Properties dialog box.

4   Since the version number is acceptable, click [OK] to close the dialog box.

5   Save the project and run the program again (Figure 7.23).
    Success!

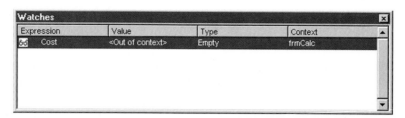

Figure 7.25 The Watches window contains a list of all current watch variables.

TASK 13: TO STEP THROUGH THE CODE

1 Open the Debug toolbar (if it is not already present) by right-clicking the toolbar and choosing *Debug*.
The Debug toolbar is shown in Figure 7.26; you may want to dock it to the other Visual Basic toolbars.

Figure 7.26 The Debug toolbar offers debugging options.

2 Click the *Step Into* button 🗐.
The energy calculator program will begin running.

3 Type **7** into the text box of the running program.
The focus will shift suddenly to the Visual Basic IDE, and the beginning of the txtKWHours *Change* event-handler will be highlighted, as shown in Figure 7.27.

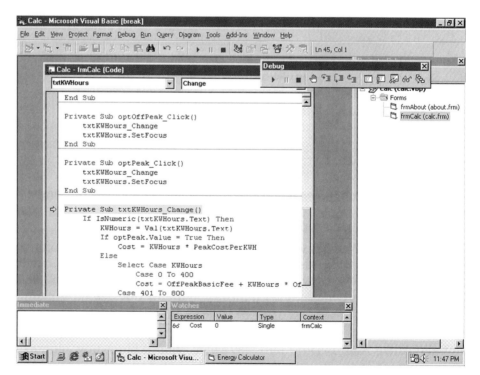

Figure 7.27 When the debugger is running, you can step through your code one line at a time.

4 Click the *Step Into* button to step through the code. Repeat this until you get to the line that reads:

Cost = KWHours * PeakCostPerKWH

5 Step past this line.
Notice that the value of Cost in the Watches window has changed to 0.6594 (Figure 7.28).

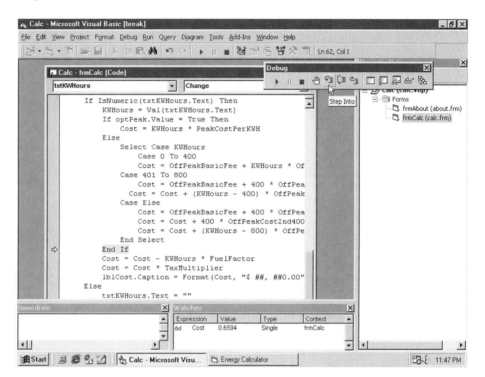

Figure 7.28 The values of any watched variables you have set up will change in the Watches window as the program executes.

6 Step through to the end of the procedure, noticing that the value of Cost changes in the Watches window each time you encounter a line of code that modifies this value.

7 When the highlighting disappears, switch out of the Visual Basic IDE and return to the program.

8 Click the *Off-peak* option button and step through the code until the highlighting disappears, noting that this time the calculation for an off-peak season occurs.

9 Quit the program.
You will have to step through the code for cmdQuit_Click as well.

TASK 14: TO TURN OFF THE WATCH

1 From the *Debug* menu, choose *Edit Watches*.

2 Click Delete .
The window will close automatically.

3 Close the Watches window in the IDE.

A Note on Debugging

As this module progresses, you will be spending more time in the debugger. It's a great tool for finding problems. In the energy calculator, for example, you might want to figure out some peak and off-peak costs with a handheld calculator and then compare them with the values you get in the program itself. If your test values and the values given by the program do not match, you could step through the code and see what happens. Often the debugger will show you that while the code you wrote does, indeed, run properly, the code you wrote isn't quite the code you meant to write. We will explore the debugger more in the future.

The Conclusion

Congratulations! You have completed Project 7, as well as Part Two of this module and the work you will do with the energy calculator program. Over the course of the past several projects, you've learned a lot about Visual Basic, its language, and the tools it offers to the programmer. In the next and future projects, you will expand this knowledge with programs that work with databases and the Internet.

You can either exit Visual Basic now or go on to work the Study Questions. If Visual Basic asks you to save any files when you exit, click ⬚ Yes ⬚ in the dialog box.

Summary and Exercises

Summary

- It is important to build applications that are consistent with Windows user interface guidelines.
- Access keys provide a quick way for keyboard users to navigate around the controls in your applications.
- Menus are added to Visual Basic programs with the Menu Editor.
- The main interface to menu items is through their *Click* event.
- An About Box dialog can be added to your application to display information about your program to the user.
- You can display a second form window modally or non-modally.
- The Visual Basic debugger lets you step through your code and view the values held by variables during program execution.

Key Terms and Operations

Key Terms	Operations
About Box dialog	add a second form to your solution
access key support	add a separator bar
breakpoint	add access key support
debugger	add menu items
menu bar	add submenu items
Menu Editor	display a window
modal	navigate with access keys
nonmodal	set a watch on a variable
separator bar	set Project Properties
Show method	step through code in the debugger
step	use the About Box dialog template
watch window	use the debugger
	use the Menu Editor
	write code for menu items

Study Questions

Multiple Choice

1. Microsoft's set of guidelines for application user interface standards is called
   a. *User Interface Guidelines for Windows*.
   b. *Programming Windows*.
   c. *Introduction to Microsoft Windows*.
   d. *Inside Microsoft Windows*.

2. Access keys are also called
   a. nav keys.
   b. hot keys.
   c. tab keys.
   d. action keys.

3. What character appears *under* the letter that is designated an access key?
   a. &
   b. +
   c. =
   d. _

4. A menu system is added to your programs using the
   a. Toolbox window.
   b. Properties window.
   c. Menu Editor.
   d. Resource Kit.

5. The prefix used for menu items is
   a. mnu
   b. menu
   c. mn
   d. item

6. A separator bar is added to a menu by typing what character(s) as its caption?
   a. =
   b. ...
   c. (-)
   d. -

7. The primary interface to a menu item is
   a. its *Click* event.
   b. its *Load* event.
   c. its *Action* method.
   d. its *Selected* method.

8. An About Box dialog is
   a. a special kind of window.
   b. a form window.
   c. a message box.
   d. a control.

9. The Visual Basic debugger lets you _____ through code.
   a. step
   b. jump
   c. skip
   d. run

10. If you want to see the values held by a variable change during run-time, what must you set on that variable?
   a. a tag
   b. a swatch
   c. a watcher
   d. a watch

True/False

1. An access key is also known as a hot key.

2. Access keys let the user focus a control with the keyboard.

3. The Visual Basic Menu Editor is used to add menus to your programs.

4. The Hungarian Notation prefix for a menu item is `menu`.

5. If you want a menu item to display as Cut, you would give it a label of &Cut.

6. When you want to add an About Box dialog to a Visual Basic project, you can simply add a new form to the project.

7. The *Show* method displays a form.

8. A modal form allows you to switch to other windows in the program.

9. Projects have properties just like forms and controls.

10. You can step through your code with the Visual Basic debugger.

Short Answer
1. How do you set properties for the Project?

2. What method displays a form window?

3. What is the difference between modal and nonmodal?

4. What does setting a watch accomplish?

5. Why are consistent user interface standards important?

6. How do you determine the access key for a menu item?

7. What does the Menu Editor do?

8. Where does a menu bar normally reside in your program?

9. How do you add a second form to your solution?

10. If you open a form modally, will you be able to access the calling form while the new form is open?

Group Discussion
1. User interface guidelines such as those used by Windows programmers are desirable for a number of reasons. What is the most important reason in your opinion? Why?

2. What other features might be desirable in an About Box dialog?

3. In the future, we will be considering Windows user interface issues for each project ahead of time. What benefits will this have over the current approach of tacking them on later?

Hands-On

Using a second nonmodal form
Create a project with two form windows and place a command button on the first window that will cause the second window to appear when clicked. The second window should open nonmodally. Run the program and observe how the two windows can be selected and how the second window can be hidden behind the first and vice versa.

On Your Own

1. Create a complex menuing system

Create a new application that features a single form with a menu bar. The menu bar should have three top-level items: *File*, *Edit*, and *Help*. The File menu should have the following submenu items: *New*, *Open*, *Close*, a separator bar, and then *Exit*. The Edit menu should have the following submenu items: *Cut*, *Copy*, and *Paste*. The Help menu should have the following submenu items: *Help*, a separator bar, and then *About this program*.

2. Improving the complex menu program

Using the previous exercise as a starting point, write code to handle each of the menu *Click* events. Use a label in the center of the form to record which menu item is selected. For example, when the Cut menu item is selected, the label should display the text "The Cut menu item was selected." The label should be blank by default when the form loads.

3. Complete the complex menu program

Complete the complex menu program used in the previous two exercises by displaying an About Box dialog when the About menu item is clicked. Also, the program should quit when the Exit item is selected. Add a text box that allows the user to simulate the cut, copy, and paste functionality: When the user selects Copy, the text in the text box should be copied into a global variable. When Cut is selected, the text should be copied into the same variable, but the text in the text box should also be erased. When Paste is selected, the text in the global variable should replace the text in the text box.

4. Working with checked menu items

You might have seen menu items somewhere in Windows that contained a check mark. For example, the *View* menu in My Computer has a submenu item called *Status Bar*. If the status bar in the My Computer window is visible, the *Status Bar* option is checked (that is, there is a check mark next to that option). If you then select the *Status Bar* option, the status bar disappears and the option becomes unchecked.

Write a program that includes a form whose background color is green (set the form's *BackColor* property to vbGreen in the *Form_Load* event-handler). It will have a menu with a single menu item labeled Color. Under the Color menu item is a single submenu item labeled *Blue*. This option should be unchecked by default (that is, its *Checked* property is set to *False*). When the *Blue* option is selected, the code should check to see if it is checked. If it is checked, uncheck the option (set its *Checked* property to *False*) and change the color of the form to vbGreen. Otherwise, check the option and change the color of the form background to vbBlue.

5. More checked menu items

Improve on the previous exercise so that there are four menu items under Color: *Blue*, *Green*, *Yellow*, and *Red*. When the items are selected, change the background color of the form to the right color and check the correct option (remembering to uncheck the other options).

PART THREE

Slot Machine

8

PROJECT

Creating a Computer Slot Machine

Objectives

After completing this project, you will be able to:

- ➤ Use image controls to display graphic images
- ➤ Use shape controls to display borders
- ➤ Use the timer control to cause periodic code execution
- ➤ Update another control's display because of timer events
- ➤ Use static variables

The Challenge

Computers are used for business calculations and other number-crunching applications, but it's an established fact that computers are most often used to play games. Games and other multimedia programs dominate the software best-seller charts. In keeping with this trend, you will create the basis for a computer slot machine in this project and will improve on this game in the following projects in Part Three. The program you will create is a first tentative step into the waters of entertainment software design that will offer a glimpse into the depths of Visual Basic's graphics manipulation capabilities. No, Nintendo and Sega have nothing to fear (at least not yet), but the slot machine you will create will provide a suitable introduction to this exciting and dynamic field of software development.

The Solution

The program will use bitmapped graphics to display items on a slot machine reel. These images will be changed over a period of time to simulate the spinning of the slot machine reels. As each reel stops "spinning," a border shape will appear around the image in the reel to indicate that it is done.

This program will form the basis of the next three projects, in which you will fine-tune and enhance the slot machine's performance, give it new features, and make it easier to use.

The specifications for this program are as follows:

- The user will be presented with the window shown in Figure 8.1.

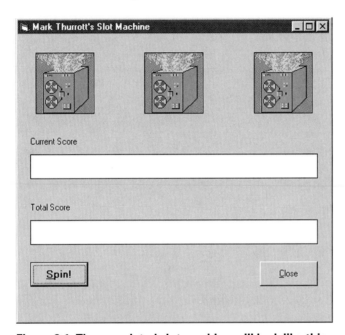

Figure 8.1 The completed slot machine will look like this.

- The window will consist of three reels: a [Spin!] button, labels for the current spin's score and the total score, and a [Close] button that will allow the user to exit the program.

- The three reels should display images of a sparking mainframe computer when the program is first run.

- When the user clicks the [Spin!] button, each reel should show an image randomly. The applicable images include the following:

Table 8.1 Images and Values for the Slot Machine

Image	Bitmap File	Point Value
Banana	banana.bmp	0
Cherry	cherry.bmp	1
Computer	computer.bmp	2
Lemon	lemon.bmp	3

Your instructor will make the images available to you.

- New images for each reel should be selected randomly by the program and displayed after a brief time interval.

- A moment-to-moment point value should appear in the current score label as the images change. This is computed by summing the point values for the image currently displayed in each reel and then multiplying the result by 100.

- The Spin! and Close buttons should be disabled while the reels are spinning.

- Eventually, the images in each reel should stop spinning and freeze, starting with the leftmost reel, then the middle reel, and finally the right reel.

- As each image freezes, a bright green border will appear around the reel.

- When all three reels have stopped spinning, the session total score should be incremented by the final value in the current score label. The Spin! and Close buttons should be enabled.

- When the user clicks the Close button, the program should stop.

The Setup

Figure 8.1 shows the basic layout of the slot machine and the controls you will need to add to the form to create this program.

Building the Basic Form

Now that you are more experienced with Visual Basic, the steps presented for the basic form and the controls to be added will be somewhat abbreviated.

TASK 1: TO BUILD THE FORM AND BASIC CONTROLS

1. Start Visual Basic and create a new Standard EXE project.

2. Save the form as **slot.frm** and the project as **slot.prj** in a new folder.

3. Using Table 8.2 and Figure 8.1 as a guide, create the objects listed and assign only their properties.

Table 8.2 Objects for the Slot Machine

Object	Purpose
frmSlot	The form window
lblCurrentScore	Displays the current score
lblTotalScore	Displays the total score for the current session
lblCurrentDescription	Heading for the current score
lblSessionDescription	Heading for the total score
cmdSpin	Command button that will spin the reels
cmdClose	Command button to end the program

When you are finished, the screen should resemble Figure 8.2.

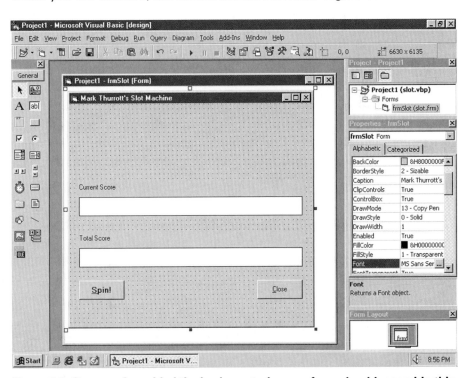

Figure 8.2 Once you've added the basic controls, your form should resemble this.

You will probably have to resize the form and controls as you add new features to your program. Don't worry if they aren't perfectly sized and located yet; the important thing right now is to get the basic controls on the form. You can always fiddle with placement and sizing as the program comes together.

Working with Images

Visual Basic makes it easy to work with graphic images such as bitmapped graphics. Although you can use images with various Visual Basic controls and forms, you will typically use the *image control*, which has a *Picture property* to which you can assign the image file. Visual Basic also has an *image list control* that allows you to contain numerous images inside a single control. We will take a look at the image list in Part Four.

Your instructor will have the four images used by this program; you should copy them to the folder you created to hold this project. The filenames are **banana.bmp**, **cherry.bmp**, **lemon.bmp**, and **computer.bmp**. The .bmp extension indicates that the images are *bitmapped graphics*.

Creating the Image Control

For the slot machine program to display each of the four images easily, you must create a separate image control for each picture. This makes the images available for later use in the reels at the top of the window. In the steps that follow, you will create four image controls and assign them to the four bitmapped graphics. The *Visible property* on each control will be set to *False* so that the controls don't appear when the program is first run.

TASK 2: TO CREATE AN IMAGE CONTROL

 Select the image control ⬚ from the Visual Basic toolbox by double-clicking it.

A blank image control will appear in the center of the form, as shown in Figure 8.3.

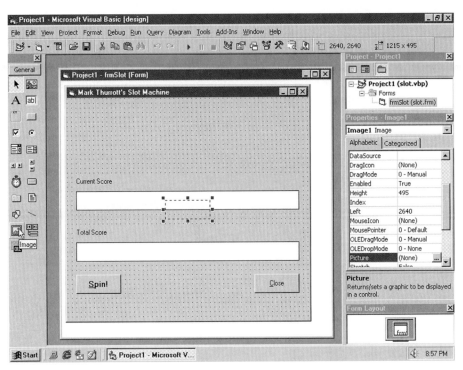

Figure 8.3 The image control appears as a blank rectangle by default.

Tip Don't choose the picture box control by mistake: its icon in the toolbox looks very similar to the image control.

2 Drag the image control over to the left side of the form.
It doesn't matter exactly where you place it because it will not display when the program runs.

3 Making sure the image control is selected, double-click the *Picture* property in the Properties window.
The Load Picture dialog will appear, as shown in Figure 8.4.

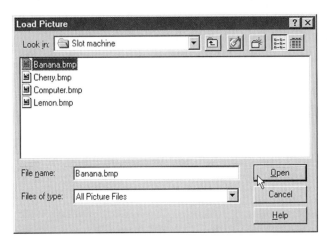

Figure 8.4 The Load Picture dialog allows you to navigate to the image you'd like to display.

4 Navigate to the folder where you've stored the image files for this project (usually the same folder you've saved the project to) and select *banana.bmp*.
The image of the banana will fill the image control (Figure 8.5). Notice that the size of the image control automatically changes so that the image displays correctly.

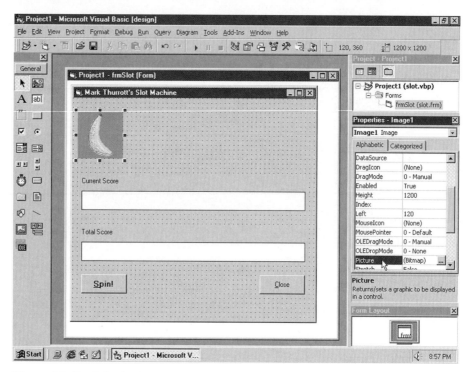

Figure 8.5 By default, the image control will resize to correctly display the image.

5 Change the *Name* property of the image control to **imgBanana** and set the *Visible* property to *False*.

6 Save the project and run the program to confirm that the image property is not visible (Figure 8.6).

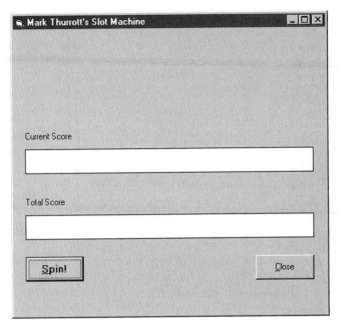

Figure 8.6 Because the image control's *Visible* property is *False*, you can't see it when the program runs.

7 Stop the program and return to the Visual Basic IDE.

TASK 3: TO CREATE THE REMAINING IMAGE CONTROLS

1 Using Figure 8.1 and the steps in the previous task as a guide, create the following three image controls:

imgCherry	**cherry.bmp**
imgComputer	**computer.bmp**
imgLemon	**lemon.bmp**

Make sure the *Visible* property of each is set to *False*.
When you're done, the screen should resemble Figure 8.7.

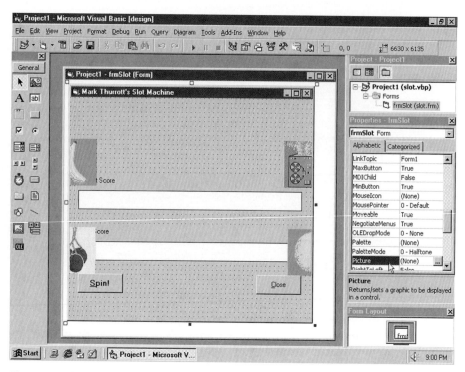

Figure 8.7 It doesn't matter where the image controls are placed because they won't be seen when the program runs.

2 Run the program to ensure that none of the images appear.

3 Stop the program and return to the Visual Basic IDE.

Creating the Reels

The three reels at the top of the window will initially display the computer image, but they will eventually be programmed to display the other images randomly as they spin. Since we will need to display bitmapped graphics, it makes sense to use image controls for the reels.

TASK 4: TO ADD THE THREE REEL IMAGES

1 Create three image controls named **imgReel1**, **imgReel2**, and **imgReel3**. Place them in a row along the top of the form, as shown in Figure 8.8.

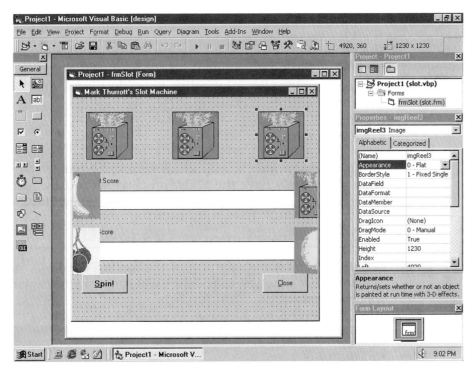

Figure 8.8 Three image controls will be used to simulate slot machine reels.

2   Assign the *Picture* property of each to **computer.bmp**.

3   Set the *BorderStyle* property of each to *1 - Fixed Single*.

4   Set the *Appearance* property of each to *0 - Flat* to remove the 3D look. When you're done, the screen should resemble Figure 8.9.

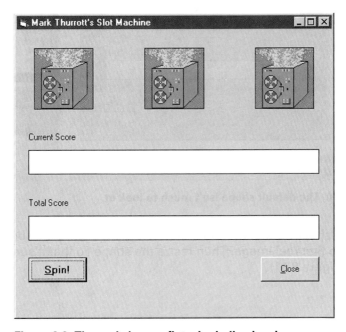

Figure 8.9. The reels have a flat, single-line border.

5   Close the form.

VB-194

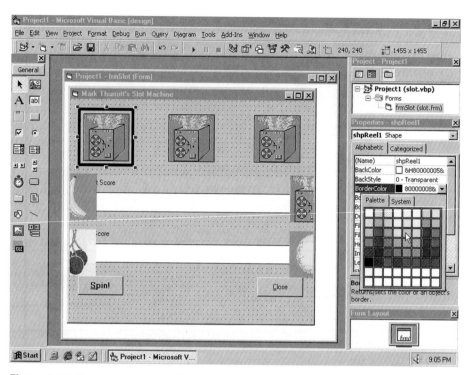

Figure 8.12 Use the color palette to select a bright green color for the shape.

7   Following the preceding steps, create two more shapes named **shpReel2** and **shpReel3**; other than the name, give these shapes the same properties as the first shape.

When you are done, the screen should resemble Figure 8.13.

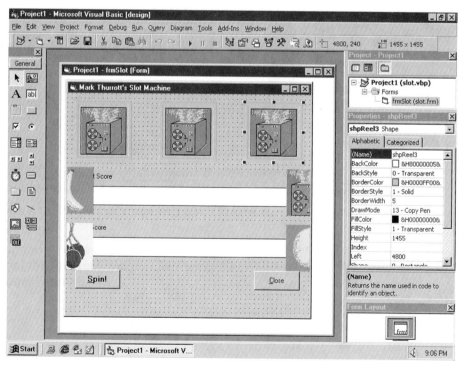

Figure 8.13 The three shapes are now complete, forming borders for the reel images.

Using the Timer Control

Occasionally, you may want to write code that responds to the passage of time. Because this is an event like any other you might handle with Visual Basic code, you can do this by using a control. You will use the *timer control*, which unlike the controls you've used up until now, is a *nonvisual control*; that is, the user will never see the control while the program is running. But the timer control offers a unique type of functionality by supplying *timer events* that occur at definable intervals. In other words, you could program the timer control to fire timer events every 5 seconds or every 50 seconds. As with any other event, you handle a timer event with an event procedure.

The timer control uses its *Interval property* to specify the number of milliseconds (one millisecond is equivalent to $1/1000$ or 0.0001 seconds) that pass between one timer event and the next. The *Interval* property can be set to any value between 0 and 65,535, where 65,535 milliseconds represents just over one minute (1000 milliseconds is roughly 1 second in real time). The *Interval* property is not very accurate and shouldn't be used for anything critical. However, it will work nicely for our purposes.

In the following steps, you will add to your program a timer control that fires a timer event every fifth of a second.

TASK 6: TO ADD A TIMER CONTROL TO YOUR PROGRAM

1   Locate the timer control in the Visual Basic Toolbox window and double-click it to add it to the center of the form. You may want to move it off to the side, as shown in Figure 8.14.

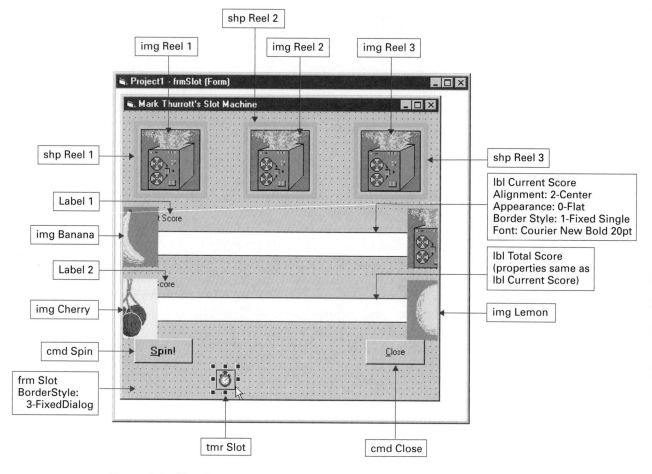

shp Reel 2

img Reel 1   img Reel 2   img Reel 3

shp Reel 1

Label 1

img Banana

Label 2

img Cherry

cmd Spin

frm Slot
BorderStyle:
   3-FixedDialog

shp Reel 3

lbl Current Score
Alignment: 2-Center
Appearance: 0-Flat
Border Style: 1-Fixed Single
Font: Courier New Bold 20pt

lbl Total Score
(properties same as
lbl Current Score)

img Lemon

tmr Slot

cmd Close

Figure 8.14 The timer control will not display when you run the program.

2   Change the name of the timer to **tmrSlot**.

3   Change the timer's *Interval* property to **200**.

4   Change the *Enabled* property to *False*.

5   Save the project.

Testing the Timer

The code you write within the timer event procedure will execute once every 200 milliseconds, or roughly five times a second. To better understand how this works, it may be helpful to write some code that will increment the current score. In the following steps, you will increment the current score display every time the timer event fires.

TASK 7: TO TEST THE TIMER CONTROL

1   Double-click *tmrSlot* to bring up the Code window with the timer event procedure, tmrSlot_Timer(), ready.

2   Add the following code within this procedure:

Static Counter As Integer

lblCurrentScore.Caption = Counter

Counter = Counter + 1

3 Close the Code window and double-click the [Spin!] button (cmdSpin) to handle the event that occurs when this button is clicked.

4 Add the following code to this procedure:

tmrSlot.Enabled = True

cmdSpin.Enabled = False

cmdClose.Enabled = False

Your screen should now resemble Figure 8.15.

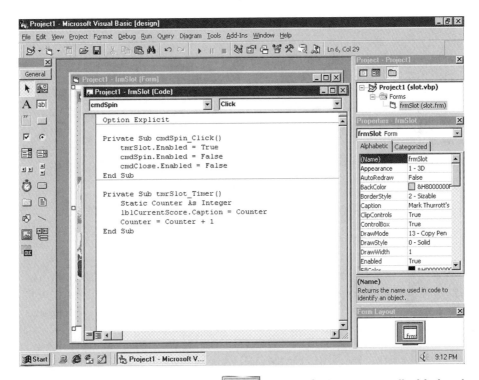

Figure 8.15 When the user clicks the [Spin!] button, the buttons are disabled and the current score begins updating.

5 Close the Code window, save the project, and run the program.
When you click the [Spin!] button, notice that the current score label updates quickly (Figure 8.16).

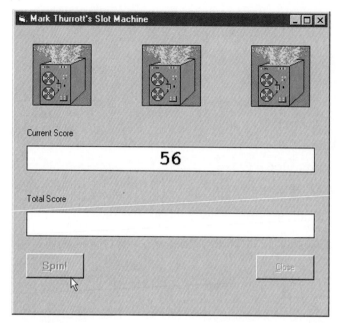

Figure 8.16 Once you've tied the display of the label to the timer event, it will update continuously.

6   Stop the program by clicking the ☒ button in the toolbar.

Static? What's Static?

You might recall from our discussion of variable scope and lifetime (in Part Two) that many factors affect the behavior of a variable. Like *Dim*, the **Static keyword** can be used to declare a variable within a procedure, as we did in the previous section. There is one difference, however: **static variables** (as they are called) retain their values after the procedure ends. This way, if the procedure is executed again and again, the static variable will not be reinitialized every time. Using *Static* is one of the key ways you can affect the lifetime of a variable.

The Conclusion

You can see that your program is starting to come together, but much work needs to be completed before it functions as a true slot machine. In the next project, you will enhance the slot machine by writing the code that will spin the reels and update the current score and total score properly. Along the way, you will discover how to create random numbers in Visual Basic.

Summary and Exercises

Summary

- Image controls are used to hold single images.
- The *Picture* property of the image control determines which image it contains.
- Shape controls can be used to add decorative elements such as borders.
- The timer control is a nonvisual control that triggers events at specific time intervals.
- Static variables retain their values after the procedure ends.

Key Terms and Operations

Key Terms	Operations
image control	respond to timer events
image list control	use image controls
Interval property	use shape controls
nonvisual control	use static variables
Picture property	use timer controls
shape control	
Static keyword	
static variables	
timer control	
timer events	
Visible property	

Study Questions

Multiple Choice

1. Which control is typically used to display a bitmap image?
   a. timer
   b. bitmap
   c. frame
   d. image

2. Which control is used to display simple shapes such as rectangles?
   a. timer
   b. image
   c. frame
   d. shape

3. The timer control responds to what event?
   a. time
   b. date
   c. right-clicking
   d. selection

4. Which timer property is used to specify the amount of time that passes between one timer event and the next?
   a. time
   b. timer
   c. interval
   d. mSec

5. The timer control is
   a. not very accurate.
   b. extremely accurate.
   c. accurate for nongraphical uses only.
   d. accurate enough to be used for critical purposes.

6. If you set the *Interval* property to 300, how often would the timer event fire?
   a. every 3 seconds
   b. every 30 seconds
   c. every 1/3 of a second
   d. every 1/30th of a second

7. If you want to hide a control, which property would you set?
   a. *Invisible*
   b. *Visible*
   c. *Seen*
   d. *Hidden*

8. Which property would you set to change the width of a shape control's border?
   a. *Width*
   b. *Thickness*
   c. *BorderStyle*
   d. *BorderWidth*

True/False

1. The *Picture* property determines which image is displayed by an image control.

2. Numerous images can be stored in an image control.

3. The *Visible* property is Boolean (can be set to True or False).

4. The picture box control is easily confused with the image control.

5. The shape control includes a way to make a star shape.

6. You can control the width of a shape control's border.

7. A timer control responds to the passage of time.

8. The user can see a timer control you add to a form.

Short Answer

1. What can you display with an image control?

2. To what would you set the *Visible* property of a control if you want to make the control visible?

3. Can the shape control display three-dimensional objects?

4. Name the shapes that can be displayed by the shape control.

5. What type of event fires at specific intervals?

6. What is the longest timer event you can set?

7. How can you make a variable retain its value after the procedure it is declared in has ended?

Group Discussion

1. Causing periodic code execution is one of the most powerful ways to use the timer control. Can you think of other situations where this control might be useful?

2. Static variables retain their values even when the procedure they are declared within is ended. How would you reset a Static integer variable to 0 every time that procedure executed?

Hands-On

Shapes, shapes, and more shapes

Work up a simple Visual Basic program that displays a shape in the center of the form. Each time the form is clicked, the shape control should change its shape to the next possible shape (where the list of shapes includes rectangle, square, oval, circle, rounded rectangle, and rounded square). When the last shape (rounded square) is encountered and the form is clicked, cycle back to the first shape. A Select Case statement would be ideal for this. Be sure to use a large, thick, colorful shape.

On Your Own

1. Creating a timer

Create a simple program with a label, a text box, a command button, and a timer control. The user will enter a numeric value into the text box representing the number of seconds the timer should run. At the start of the program, the label should be empty. When the command button is clicked, start the timer and make the text box and command button disabled. The label should also be set to an empty string. When the timer reaches the allotted amount of time, display a message in the label indicating the amount of time that has elapsed. Also, make the button and text button enabled again.

2. Working with the Image control

Create a form with an image control. Load a bitmap image into the image control and then write Visual Basic code that will size the image to occupy the entire surface of the form as the form is resized. (*Hint*: Look at the properties of the image control to determine which ones need to be set to pull this off.)

9

PROJECT

Improving the Slot Machine

Objectives

After completing this project, you will be able to:

➤ **Use the Rnd function to create random numbers**

➤ **Use the Randomize statement to seed the random number generator**

➤ **Change the image displayed by an image control based on the results of random number generation**

➤ **Work with advanced timer control features**

The Challenge

In the previous project, you created the foundation of the slot machine program, adding the basic user interface controls and a timer, which you tested by displaying a value in the current score label. Now it's time to add more functionality to your program; you will have a working slot machine by the time this project is complete.

The Solution

You will use the specifications from Project 8 to determine where to go from here. Specifically, the following goals remain:

• When the user clicks the [Spin!] button, each reel should randomly show an image.

• New images for each reel should be selected randomly by the program and displayed after a brief time interval.

- A moment-to-moment point value should appear in the current score label as the images change. This is computed by summing the point values for the image currently displayed in each reel and then multiplying the result by 100.

- The [Spin!] and [Close] buttons should be disabled while the reels are spinning.

- Eventually, the images in each reel should stop spinning and freeze, starting with the leftmost reel, and then the middle reel, and finally the right reel.

- As each image freezes, a bright green border should appear around the reel.

- When all three reels have stopped spinning, the session total score should be incremented by the final value in the current score label. The [Spin!] and [Close] buttons should be enabled.

- When the user clicks the [Close] button, the program should stop.

The Setup

Looking over these goals, we can see that the first step will be to figure out a way to display a random image in each reel when the user clicks the [Spin!] button. This can be accomplished by having Visual Basic generate random numbers. Let's take a look.

Creating Random Numbers

The slot machine program can use randomly generated numbers to decide which image will display in each reel. Random numbers are chosen with the **Rnd function**, which produces a random number between 0 and 1—0.7055475, for example. Your program needs to generate integers that fall between and include 0 and 3 because 0, 1, 2, and 3 are four numbers and we have four images to choose among.

To use Rnd to generate random integers between 0 and 3, you will use the following expression:

Int(Rnd * 4)

Here's what's happening: Inside the parentheses, the Rnd function is used to find a random number between 0 and 1. This number is multiplied by four. The **Int function** then is used to return the integer portion of the number (that is, the portion of the number before the decimal point). For example, let's say the Rnd function returned the value 0.7055475. This number multiplied by 4 is 2.88219. When you run the Int function on 2.88219, the number 2 is returned. Thus, 2 would be the random number returned by this expression.

There's one catch to using Rnd, however. If you don't initialize Visual Basic's random number generator every time your program is run, the same sequence of "random" numbers will occur every time you run the program. To avoid this, Visual Basic supplies a **_Randomize statement_** that initializes the random number generator; this statement should be placed somewhere near the beginning of any code utilizing Rnd.

Let's test the expression. In the following steps, you will replace the code in tmrSlot's *Timer* event-handler so that only the numbers 0, 1, 2, or 3 will be displayed in the current score label.

TASK 1: TO CREATE AND DISPLAY RANDOM NUMBERS

1. Start Visual Basic and load the slot machine project.

2. Display the Form window and double-click *tmrSlot* to display the code window.

3. In the event-handler for tmrSlot_Timer(), change the code so that it matches the following:

Static Counter As Integer

Randomize

lblCurrentScore.Caption = Int(Rnd * 4)

Counter = Counter + 1

4. Save the project and run the program.
   When you click the *Code* button, notice that the only numbers that display are 0, 1, 2, and 3, as shown in Figure 9.1.

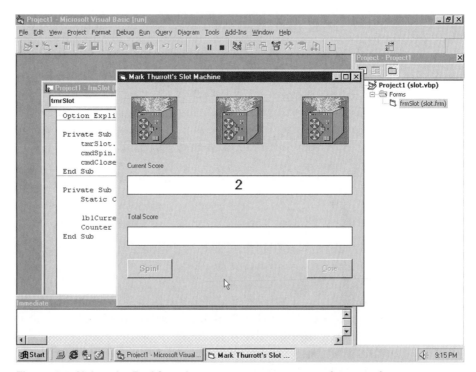

Figure 9.1 Using the Rnd function, you can generate random numbers.

5 Stop the program after a few moments.

Notice that the constantly changing numbers appear to "pause" sometimes rather than change. That's because the random number generator generated the same number that was there previously, so it didn't appear to change.

While this is interesting as an example, it doesn't really get us any closer to our goal of spinning the reels. In the following steps, we'll change this code once again to actually "spin" the first reel.

TASK 2: TO CHANGE A REEL IMAGE WITH THE TIMER

1 In the Visual Basic IDE, open the Code window again by double-clicking *tmrSlot* if necessary.

2 Modify the code in the *Timer* event-handler so that it matches the following:

```
Static Counter As Integer
Static Reel1Stop As Integer


Randomize
Reel1Stop = Int(Rnd * 4)
Select Case Reel1Stop
    Case 0
        imgReel1.Picture = imgBanana.Picture
    Case 1
        imgReel1.Picture = imgCherry.Picture
    Case 2
        imgReel1.Picture = imgComputer.Picture
    Case 3
        imgReel1.Picture = imgLemon.Picture
End Select


Counter = Counter + 1
```

3 Close the Code window, run the program, and click the [Spin!] button. The picture in reel 1 should change continuously, as shown in Figure 9.2.

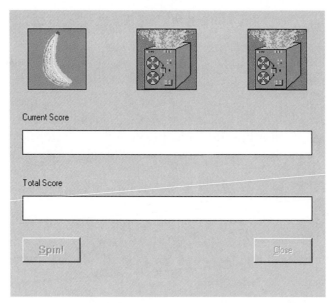

Figure 9.2 Now the first reel spins continuously.

4   Stop the program and return to the Visual Basic IDE.

Stopping the Spinning Reel

The reel images aren't supposed to change indefinitely. You need to add code so that imgReel1 stops spinning after 15 timer ticks, imgReel2 after 30, and imgReel3 after 45. You will use the Counter variable, which increments each time the *Timer* event triggers, to determine when to stop each reel. Once a reel stops, the rectangular border shape will appear around the reel image.

TASK 3: TO STOP THE FIRST REEL FROM SPINNING

1   Open the Code window for tmrSlot and modify the code as follows. The new code is presented in bold text.

```
Static Counter As Integer
Static Reel1Stop As Integer

If Counter < 15 Then
    Randomize
    Reel1Stop = Int(Rnd * 4)
    Select Case Reel1Stop
        Case 0
            imgReel1.Picture = imgBanana.Picture
        Case 1
            imgReel1.Picture = imgCherry.Picture
```

```
        Case 2
            imgReel1.Picture = imgComputer.Picture
        Case 3
            imgReel1.Picture = imgLemon.Picture
    End Select
```

Else

    shpReel1.Visible = True

End If

Counter = Counter + 1

2   Close the Code window, save the project, and test the program. After changing the image 15 times, the first reel should stop spinning and a bright green border should appear around it (Figure 9.3).

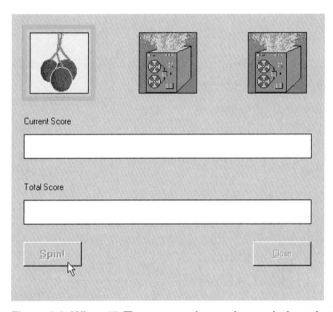

Current Score

Total Score

Spin!   Close

Figure 9.3 When 15 *Timer* events have triggered, the spinning stops and a border appears.

3   Stop the program and return to the Visual Basic IDE.

Controlling the Other Reels

Now that you've gotten the first reel to cycle correctly, you need to add code for the other two reels. You can do this with some simple copy and paste: You just need to copy everything from the If statement down to the End If in Task 3 and paste it twice more into the code, replacing all of the references to Reel1Stop, imgReel1, and shpReel1 as appropriate.

> **Troubleshooting Tip** There's a lot of code here, so the chance of an error happening is greater than ever. Remember to save the project periodically as you work through the code and double-check everything you've added against the code shown in the book.

TASK 4: TO SPIN THE OTHER TWO REELS

1 Using your copy and paste skills, change the *Timer* event-handler to match the following code. Note the addition of new variable declarations and two new If-Then-Else statements. New code appears bold.

```
Static Counter As Integer
Static Reel1Stop, Reel2Stop, Reel3Stop As Integer
Randomize

If Counter < 15 Then
    ' note that the Randomize statement was removed here
    Reel1Stop = Int(Rnd * 4)
    Select Case Reel1Stop
        Case 0
            imgReel1.Picture = imgBanana.Picture
        Case 1
            imgReel1.Picture = imgCherry.Picture
        Case 2
            imgReel1.Picture = imgComputer.Picture
        Case 3
            imgReel1.Picture = imgLemon.Picture
    End Select
Else
    shpReel1.Visible = True
End If

If Counter < 30 Then
    Reel2Stop = Int(Rnd * 4)
    Select Case Reel2Stop
        Case 0
            imgReel2.Picture = imgBanana.Picture
        Case 1
            imgReel2.Picture = imgCherry.Picture
        Case 2
            imgReel2.Picture = imgComputer.Picture
        Case 3
```

```
            imgReel2.Picture = imgLemon.Picture
        End Select
    Else
        shpReel2.Visible = True
    End If


    If Counter < 45 Then
        Reel3Stop = Int(Rnd * 4)
        Select Case Reel3Stop
            Case 0
                imgReel3.Picture = imgBanana.Picture
            Case 1
                imgReel3.Picture = imgCherry.Picture
            Case 2
                imgReel3.Picture = imgComputer.Picture
            Case 3
                imgReel3.Picture = imgLemon.Picture
        End Select
    Else
        shpReel3.Visible = True
    End If


Counter = Counter + 1
```

> **Tip**   There is a more elegant Visual Basic programming construct
> called a *control array* that would produce similar results while reduc-
> ing the amount of repetitive code here. The use of control arrays is
> somewhat complex and is beyond the scope of a beginning Visual Ba-
> sic project such as this. An image list could also be used. Image lists
> are covered in Part Four.

2   Close the Code window, save the project, and run the program.
When you click the `Spin!` button, all three reels should spin and then, in
order from left to right, each should stop and green borders should appear
around each. Figure 9.4 shows this progress.

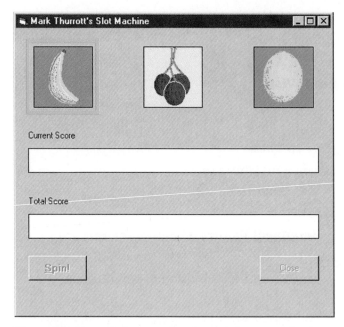

Figure 9.4 Now all three reels spin and then stop, in the proper order.

3   When the reels are done spinning, stop the program and return to the Visual Basic IDE.

Clearly, the slot machine is coming along, but there are a few things that need to be completed. The score needs to be displayed, and the command buttons will need to be enabled when the reels are done spinning. In the following sections, we will address these needs.

Displaying the Current Score

As the reels spin, the current score should display, changing continuously, in the current score label. You will add code for this near the bottom of the *Timer* event-handler that will calculate and display this score.

TASK 5: TO DISPLAY THE CURRENT SCORE

1   Open the Code window and navigate to the tmrSlot *Timer* event-handler.

2   Enter the following line of code near the top of the event-handler, with the other variable declarations:

Static CurrentScore As Integer

3   Enter the following line of code after the last End If statement in the event-handler and before the line that increments Counter:

CurrentScore = (Reel1Stop + Reel2Stop + Reel3Stop) * 100

lblCurrentScore.Caption = Format(CurrentScore, "##,##0")

The screen should resemble Figure 9.5 when you are done.

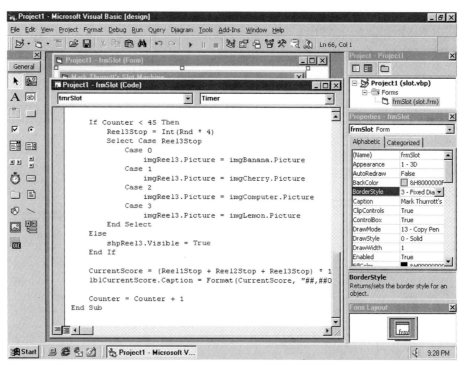

Figure 9.5 Only a few lines of code need to be added in the *Timer* event-handler to display the current score.

4   Close the Code window and run the program a few times, noting how the current score updates (Figure 9.6).
The current score should change continuously until all three reels are done spinning.

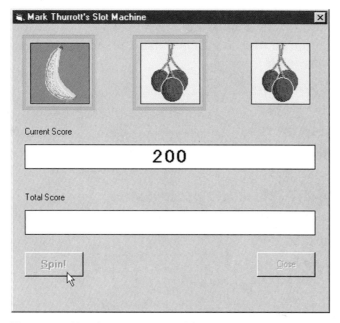

Figure 9.6 Here's your slot machine in action!

5   When you're done, quit the program.

What Happens When the Reels Stop Spinning

When all three reels have finished spinning, the following things should happen:

- The timer should stop ticking (or, in Visual Basic terminology, it should stop firing *Timer* events) because it is no longer needed.
- The total score should be updated.
- The Counter variable should be set to zero again.
- The [Spin!] and [Close] buttons should be enabled again.

All of these things should occur when the final reel is done spinning. That happens when Counter reaches 45, which we can test for inside the *Timer* event-handler (we already do check for this, as you may recall, using an If-Then-Else statement).

TASK 6: TO WRITE CODE TO EXECUTE WHEN THE REELS ARE DONE SPINNING

1 Open the Code window and navigate to the top of tmrSlot's *Timer* event-handler.

2 Modify the line of code that reads

Static CurrentScore As Integer

so that it matches the following (in other words, add a declaration for a new static variable named TotalScore):

Static CurrentScore, TotalScore As Integer

You will need a TotalScore variable to store the value of the total score.

3 Navigate to the bottom of the event-handler and *replace* the line of code that currently reads

Counter = Counter + 1

with the following:

If Counter >= 45 Then

    tmrSlot.Enabled = False

    Counter = 0

    TotalScore = TotalScore + CurrentScore

    lblTotalScore.Caption = Format(TotalScore, "##,##0")

    CurrentScore = 0

    cmdSpin.Enabled = True

    cmdClose.Enabled = True

Else

    Counter = Counter + 1

End If

4 Close the Code window, save the project, and run and test the program by spinning the reels a few times as shown in Figure 9.7.

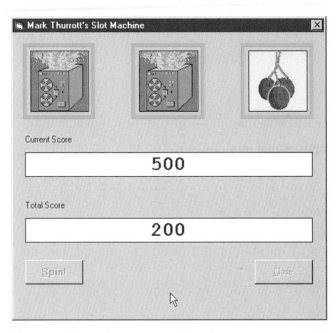

Figure 9.7 Now the current and total scores are updated.

There's one little problem; can you see what it is? The user can click the [Spin!] button again when the reels stop spinning, but the green border shapes around the reels don't ever disappear. To solve this problem, you'll need to add code to the cmdSpin's *Click* event-handler to disable the border shapes.

TASK 7: TO DISABLE THE BORDER SHAPES WHEN THE [Spin!] BUTTON IS CLICKED

1 Open the code window by double-clicking *cmdSpin*.

2 Add the following lines of code to the event-handler:

shpReel1.Visible = False

shpReel2.Visible = False

shpReel3.Visible = False

When you're done, the screen should resemble Figure 9.8.

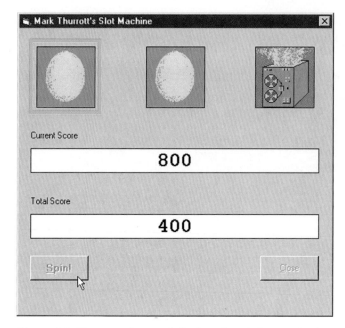

Figure 9.8 Now you have a fully functional electronic slot machine, courtesy of Visual Basic!

3 Save the project and run the program. Test it thoroughly (and have fun).

Quitting the Program

You might have noticed that the [Close] button doesn't do anything yet. Let's add the single line of code that will allow this button to function correctly.

TASK 8: TO QUIT THE PROGRAM WITH THE [Close] BUTTON

1 Open the Code window by double-clicking *cmdClose*

2 Add the following line of code to the event-procedure:

End

3 Save the project.

The Conclusion

The slot machine program you are developing is nearly complete. After using the image, shape, and timer controls to manipulate graphic images, you should have developed an appreciation of the way Visual Basic makes this kind of development easier. Visual Basic is often used as a multimedia development tool because of its effortless interaction with various graphics elements, sounds, and music.

In the next project, you will complete the slot machine by adding the ability to save and view high scores in a database.

Summary and Exercises

Summary

- The Rnd function is used to generate random numbers.
- The Int function can be used in conjunction with Rnd to generate random integers.
- The Randomize statement is used to initialize the Visual Basic random number generator.

Key Terms and Operations

Key Terms
Int function
Randomize statement
Rnd function

Operations
change images randomly in response to timer events
create random numbers
trim the integer portion of a number

Study Questions

Multiple Choice

1. Random numbers are created with which function?
   a. Random
   b. Rand
   c. Rnd
   d. Seed

2. Which statement is used to initialize the random number generator?
   a. Seed
   b. Init
   c. Randomize
   d. Rnd

3. Rnd produces random numbers between _____.
   a. 0 and 9
   b. 0 and 1
   c. 1 and 100
   d. two previously determined numbers

4. When you want to retrieve the integer portion of a number, which function do you use?
   a. IntPortion
   b. Integer
   c. CInt
   d. Int

5. How do you stop timer events from firing?
   a. Change the timer's *Enabled* property to *False*.
   b. Change the timer's *FireEvent* property to *False*.
   c. Change the timer's *Visible* property to *False*.
   d. Call Reel1Stop.

True/False

1. The Rnd function generates random numbers.

2. You can generate random numbers between 1 and 10 with the code
   Int(Rnd * 9) + 1

3. The Int function returns the numbers to the right of the decimal point.

4. The Randomize statement initializes the Visual Basic random number generator.

5. You should always use Randomize with Rnd.

6. You must use a control array when working with a group of similar controls.

7. The Rand function is functionally equivalent to Rnd.

Short Answer

1. Can a computer generate truly random numbers?

2. Why do you need to use Randomize before calling Rnd?

3. How would you generate random whole numbers between 1 and 100?

4. How would you generate random years between 1950 and 2050?

5. How do you stop *Timer* events from firing?

Group Discussion

1. The Abs function returns the absolute value of a number. How is this different from Int? (*Hint*: Use the MSDN Library.)

2. John Von Neumann asserted that generating truly random numbers using arithmetical methods was impossible. Was he right? Why or why not?

Hands-On

Creating a PIN generator

Banks typically assign a randomly generated Personal Identification Number (PIN) to each new customer. Write a Visual Basic PIN generator program that uses a label and two command buttons. The first command button will be labeled "Generate": When clicked, this will generate a random four-digit PIN and display it in the label. (*Hint*: Generate four random numbers and concatenate them.) The second command button will exit the program.

On Your Own

1. Upgrading your PIN generator

Modify the PIN generator from the Hands-On exercise so that each number cycles through a randomly generated list of numbers. To do this, you will need to use four labels and display each cycling number in its own label. Use a large font to display the numbers as they cycle. The numbers should be generated one at a time: When the *Generate* button is clicked, the first number should cycle, then the second, and so on.

2. Creating a more realistic slot machine

Using the slot machine files you have created for this project, change the scoring system so that each spin involves an automatic bet of one dollar and so that only certain combinations of images (for example, three cherries) yields a payoff. It will therefore be possible for the total score to become a negative number. You can assume that the user has infinitely deep pockets. (Hey, it's a computer game, not the real thing!) Here is the suggested payoff system:

- 3 cherries pays $50.

- 2 cherries pays $5.

- 3 of a kind (lemon, banana, computer) pays $25.

- 2 of a kind (lemon, banana, computer) pays $1.

- All other combinations cause the total score to be reduced by $1.

10 PROJECT

Saving High Scores in a Database

Objectives

After completing this project, you will be able to:

➤ **Add database functionality to your Visual Basic programs**

➤ **Use the Visual Data Manager (VisData) to create new Access databases**

➤ **Add data to a database with VisData**

➤ **Use objects in the ActiveX Data Objects (ADO) Object Model to access databases from Visual Basic code**

➤ **Read data from a database with ADO**

➤ **Write data to a database with ADO**

The Challenge

The slot machine program you've developed over the past two projects is now fully functioning, in that it offers the user a fully working slot machine with animated reels and a scoring system. But any game with a score deserves some method of storing high scores. In this project, you will add the ability to write scores into a database and then display them from a High Scores dialog.

The Solution

The specifications for this part of the program are:

- A simple menu system will be added to the slot machine.

- The *Game* menu will have three items: *New Game, High Scores,* and *Quit.* The *New Game* option will reset the score and start a new game. The *High Scores* option will display a dialog box that shows the high scores, as stored in the high score database. The *Quit* option will end the program.

- When a new game is started or the game is exited, the program will ask users whether they would like to save their score.

- If the score is saved, users will enter their name, and this information will be written to the high score database.

- The *Help* menu will have one item, *About Slot Machin*e, which will display an About Box dialog.

The Setup

Before you can begin adding the database-backed high score system, it's important to understand some database basics. In the following sections, we'll take a look at databases and how you can work with them in Visual Basic.

Database Concepts

One of the oldest structures of computers is the **database**, which is used to store and ultimately retrieve data in a logical format. Many database applications exist today, including Microsoft Access, SQL Server, and Visual FoxPro. These products are all designed to store data—be it text, numbers, graphics, whatever—in files on a computer. But databases aren't just about storing data. They are also designed to make organizing data easy, so that the user can quickly get at just the information needed. For example, a database of people living in the Phoenix, Arizona, area might include the following information: first name, last name, street address, city, and ZIP code. Someone accessing this information could sort the data (by last name or city, for example) or display a subset of the data (such as only those people that are in the 85016 ZIP code).

Although Visual Basic was designed from the beginning to work with databases, improvements over the past few versions have, in many ways, made Visual Basic the easiest way to get at data in a variety of databases. Also, through various technology initiatives, Microsoft has made the concept of **Universal Data Access** a reality: Using this new technology, it is now possible to access different databases from different manufacturers using the same objects, properties, methods, and events. We will examine the most recent implementation of this technology—called ActiveX Data Objects—later in the project.

Relational Databases

Most databases you will work with in Visual Basic are *relational databases*, meaning that information is stored in *tables*, which are collections of columns and rows (like you'd see in a spreadsheet). Each column in a table is called a *field*, which is a single piece of information. For example, in the preceding address example, fields would include first name, last name, and so on. The rows in a table, known as *records*, represent the actual data. Each record consists of a collection of field data. So in our example, we might have an address table like the one in Table 10.1.

Table 10.1 A Database Address Table

FirstName	LastName	StreetAddress	City	ZIPCode
Paul	Thurrott	9705 E Mountain View Rd.	Scottsdale	85111
Steph	Thurrott	9705 E Mountain View Rd.	Scottsdale	85111
Brian	Kelley	1311 N. 34th Place	Phoenix	85018
Kip	Dean	3109 W Miraballis Ave.	Phoenix	85017
Gary	Brent	3709 W Carefree Ave.	Peoria	85708

Microsoft Access and Visual Basic

The most popular relational database is Microsoft Access and, as you might expect, Visual Basic works very nicely with Access databases. In fact, you can create Access databases from Visual Basic without even owning a copy of Microsoft Access. For this reason, we will be working with an Access database in this project. The Access database you will create will store the high scores generated by the slot machine.

Using the Visual Data Manager

Using Visual Basic, we can create a database with its integrated Visual Data Manager. But before we jump into the creation of the database, let's consider its design.

Designing the Database

The database will need only one table, which we will call tblScore (the tbl prefix identifies it as a table). This table will have two fields, Name and Score. Like Visual Basic variables, fields have associated data types. The Name field will be a String and the Score field will be a Number (a Long Integer, to be exact).

Creating the Database

The **Visual Data Manager (VisData)** is an add-in to Visual Basic in that it is a separate application. You can run VisData from the Visual Basic IDE, however, as it is available from the *Add-ins* menu. The Visual Data Manager window, shown in Figure 10.1, is pretty Spartan in its initial appearance. When the window first appears, your only real options are to open an existing database or create a new database. In the following steps, you will use VisData to create a new database.

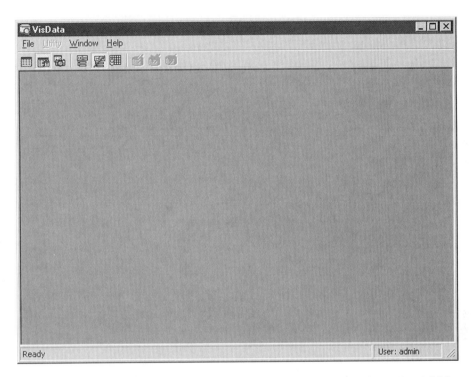

Figure 10.1 The Visual Data Manager window can be accessed from the *Add-ins* menu.

TASK 1: TO CREATE A NEW DATABASE WITH VISDATA

1 Start Visual Basic, and load the slot machine project.

2 Select *Visual Data Manager* from the *Add-ins* menu.
   The VisData window will appear. You may want to resize the window a bit to make it larger.

3 Select *File*, *New*, *Microsoft Access*, and then *Version 7.0 MDB*. The Select Microsoft Access Database to Create dialog box will appear, as shown in Figure 10.2.

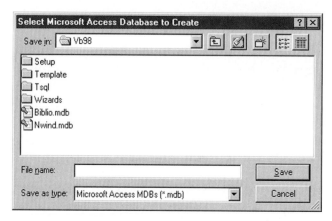

Figure 10.2 Navigate to the location where you'd like to create a new database.

Tip "MDB" refers to the file extension for Access databases, which is .MDB. This means, of course, "Microsoft DataBase."

4 Navigate to the folder where your slot machine project is stored.

5 Type **scores** and click Save to create a new Access database.
Two new child windows will appear in VisData, Database Window and SQL Statement (Figure 10.3).

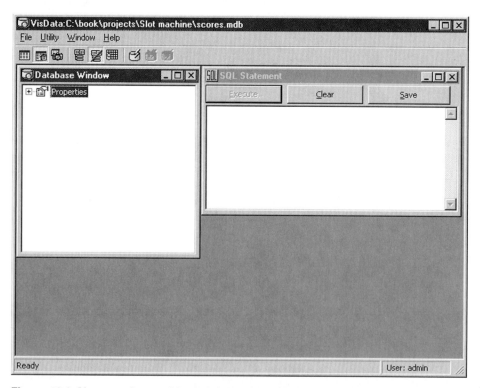

Figure 10.3 Now you have a blank database ready for a new table.

Adding a Table to the Database

The Database Window in VisData is used to add a new table to the database. The SQL Statements window, however, will not be needed for this example. It is used to type in commands in a language called ***SQL (Structured Query Language)***, which is the *lingua franca* of relational databases. Everything you can do with Access, can be done with SQL statements, which resemble Visual Basic statements in many ways. But for this project, we'll focus on other ways to work with databases.

TASK 2: TO CREATE THE TBLSCORE TABLE

1   Right-click the Database Window and choose *New Table*.
    The Table Structure dialog box will appear, as shown in Figure 10.4. You will use this dialog to give your table a name (tblScore) and two fields (Name and Score).

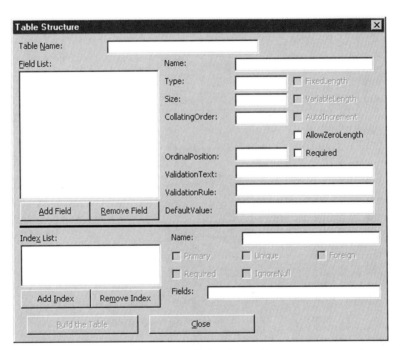

Figure 10.4. The Table Structure dialog box allows you to modify table fields and indices.

2   In the Table Name edit box, type **tblScore**.

3   Click the   Add Field   button to display the Add Field dialog box, as shown in Figure 10.5.
    This dialog allows you to set field properties.

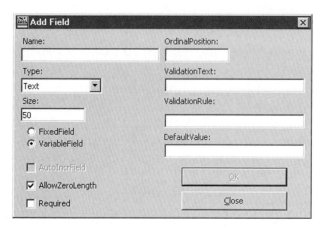

Figure 10.5. The Add Field dialog box allows you to add a new field to a table.

4 In the Name field, type **Name** and then click ⟨ OK ⟩ to add a second field.

5 Type **Score** in the Name field.

6 Change the Type to *Long.*

7 Click ⟨ OK ⟩ to add the field; then click ⟨ Close ⟩.
The dialog box will close.

8 Click the ⟨ Build the Table ⟩ button to create the tblScore table.

9 View the tblScore table by expanding it in the Database Window to show the Field names, as shown in Figure 10.6.

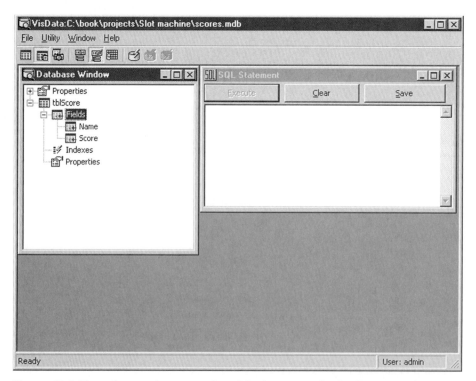

Figure 10.6 Now that you've created a table, it appears in the Database Window.

Adding Data to the Database

You can "seed" the database with sample data from VisData if you'd like. This will make it easier to test the database later from Visual Basic. To do so, simply double-click the table name in the Database Window. This will display the Dynaset:tblScore dialog box (Figure 10.7), which lets you add new records, modify existing records, or delete existing records. In following steps, you will add three new records to the database.

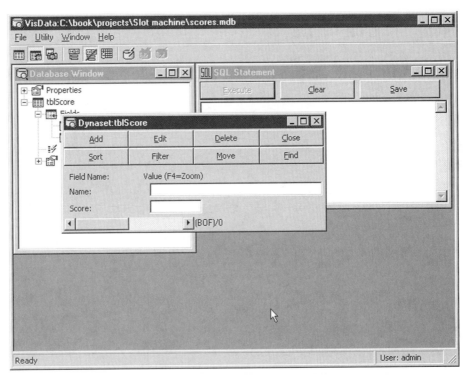

Figure 10.7 The table edit window allows you to add, modify, or delete records.

TASK 3: TO ADD DATA TO THE DATABASE WITH VISDATA

1   Double-click the tblScore entry in the Database Window.
    The table edit window will appear.

2   Click the [Add] button.

3   Type **Mark** in the Name field.

4   Type **2000** in the Score field.

5   Click [Update].
    A dialog box will appear and ask whether you'd like to save the new record (Figure 10.8). Click [Update].

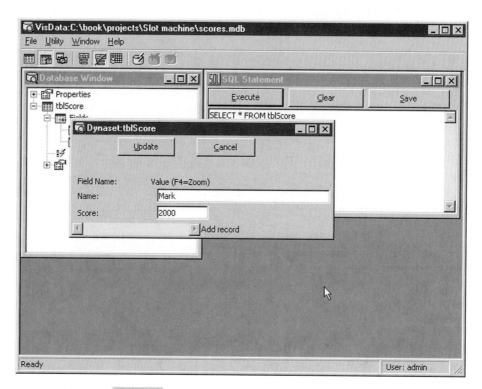

Figure 10.8 Click `Update` **to add the new record to the database.**

6   Click the `Add` button to add a second record.

7   Using the preceding steps, add the following two records:

Name	Score
Paul	**1500**
Steph	**1700**

8   When you are done, click the `Close` button to return to VisData.

9   Close the VisData window.

Accessing Databases from Visual Basic

Now that we have a database we can use for saving and displaying high scores, it's time to take a look at the ways you can access databases from Visual Basic. You may be surprised to know that there are numerous methods for doing so. In fact, over the years, Microsoft's prescribed method for accessing databases has changed with just about every version of Visual Basic.

In the past, Microsoft created data access ***object models***, a way to programmatically access databases using logical collections of objects and their properties, methods, and events. Such object models include ***Remote Data Objects (RDO)*** and ***Data Access Objects (DAO)***. For Visual Basic 6.0, however, Microsoft has created a new object model called ***ActiveX Data***

Objects (ADO) that incorporates the best features in RDO and DAO with additional benefits. This is the method we will use to access the high score database from the slot machine program.

Introduction to ActiveX Data Objects (ADO)

ActiveX Data Objects (ADO) is a simple object model that allows the Visual Basic programmer to access data in relational databases. It was designed to be easy to use, fast, and flexible. The ADO Object Model consists of the objects shown in Table 10.2.

Table 10.2   ADO Object Model

Object	Purpose
Connection	Maintains the connection to the database
Command	Handles database commands, such as data queries
Recordset	Stores a set of records returned from a table (or tables) in the database

Of these objects, the *Recordset* is the one we're most concerned with because it works most closely with the data we want. Consider the case of reading high scores from the database: A Recordset could be used to store the rows of data (literally, a set of records) that are contained in the tblScore table. Likewise, when we add a new high score to the database, what we're really doing is creating a new row in the Recordset with the name and high score information and then copying that information into the database as a new record.

Code versus Controls

There are two basic ways to add ADO functionality to your programs. You can add a visual control, such as the *Microsoft ADO Data Control*, which functions like the front panel on a VCR (Figure 10.9), or you can write code that accesses the ADO Object Model directly.

Figure 10.9 The Microsoft ADO Data Control offers a VCR-like menu for a Recordset.

The Microsoft ADO Data Control is nice because it offers a visual way for users to navigate through data. On the other hand, the times you would need such an interface are few; this control is pretty limited when you just need to quickly list some data from a table, like you will be doing.

That said, accessing the ADO Object Model through code introduces its own complexities. Although ADO code is fairly simple compared to older object models, it still involves writing some pretty dry, straight code. Much of the programming you do in Visual Basic is in response to events that happen to visual controls. Not so with the ADO Object Model: In this case, you will be writing code that accesses a database without using any of the typical niceties the Visual Basic IDE affords us.

To use the ADO Object Model, you will need to add a *reference* to your project. This is very similar to the way that you can add new components to your projects, but a reference is designed to provide access to code that has no visual element. The ADO Object Model is just such a reference.

Before you can do this, however, you will want to add the menu system that will enable the user interface for your high score system. Once that is in place, you can hook code into the ADO Object Model and access the data in your high score database. Let's get started.

Adding a Menu System

You've worked with menus in the past, so this section will simply describe the menu items you need to add.

TASK 4: TO ADD A MENU SYSTEM TO THE SLOT MACHINE

1. Open the Menu Editor and add a top-level menu item named **mnuGame** with a caption of **&Game**.

2. Add the following submenu items as sub-items below mnuGame (Figure 10.10):

Menu Name	Caption
mnuNewGame	**&New Game**
mnuHighScores	**&High Scores . . .**
mnuSep	**- (Dash, creates a separator)**
mnuQuit	**&Quit**

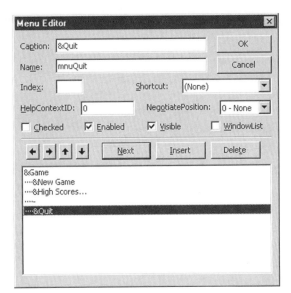

Figure 10.10 Use the Menu Editor to add a menu system to your slot machine.

3 When you're done, close the Menu Editor.

Starting and Quitting the Game

The first menu item we'll look at is the New Game functionality. This should hide the rectangular shapes around each reel, set the current and total score to 0, and set the display of the current score and total score labels to nothing. When our database functionality is ready, we will use this option to ask the user whether they'd like to save the total score (if it's greater than 0) to the high score database.

While we're at it, we'll also write code that will end the program if the user chooses Quit from the menu.

TASK 5: TO PROGRAM NEW GAME AND QUIT FUNCTIONALITY

1 In the Visual Basic IDE, click the [Spin!] button to open the code window.

2 Move the line of code that reads

```
Static CurrentScore, TotalScore As Integer
```

to the global declaration area (under Option Explicit) and change the word Static to **Dim**.
CurrentScore and TotalScore are now global to this module and can now be used in any procedure.

3 Click the New Game menu item to open the code window. In the *mnuNewGame_Click* event-handler, add the following code:

If MsgBox("Are you sure?", vbYesNo, "New Game") = vbYes Then

    lblCurrentScore.Caption = ""

    lblTotalScore.Caption = ""

```
        CurrentScore = 0
        TotalScore = 0


        shpReel1.Visible = False
        shpReel2.Visible = False
        shpReel3.Visible = False
End If
```

This will present a dialog box (MsgBox) to users and ask whether they're sure (Figure 10.11). If the user clicks [Yes], the scores will be set to 0, the labels will be erased, and the reel borders will be made invisible. It's functionally identical to what users see when they start the slot machine for the first time.

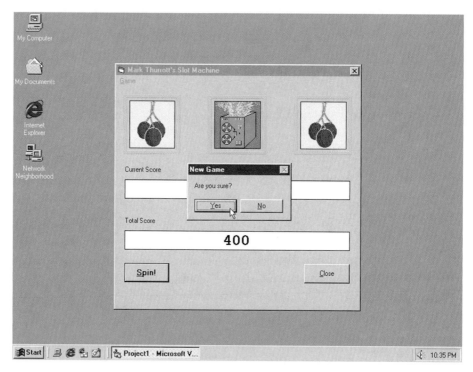

Figure 10.11 A MsgBox is used to make sure the user wants to start a new game.

4   Select mnuQuit from the menu system to open the event-handler for mnuQuit_Click. Add the following line of code:

Call cmdClose_Click

This calls the *Click* event-handler for cmdClose. Eventually, this code will also be modified to save the high score information to the database.

5   Save the project and test the New Game functionality.

Reading Information from a Database

Now we need to add a second form to the project. This form will be used to display the high score list that is stored in the database.

TASK 6: TO ADD A HIGH SCORE FORM TO THE PROJECT

1 Select *Add Form* from the Project window.
The Add Form window will appear.

2 Click the [Open] button to select the default choice, a simple blank form.

3 Save the new form as scores.frm.

4 Change the following properties to the following values:

Property	Value
Name	**frmScores**
Caption	**Slot Machine High Scores**
BorderStyle	**3 - Fixed Dialog**

5 Add a command button to the form and place it in the upper-right corner of the form, as shown in Figure 10.12. Change the following properties of the command button:

Property	Value
Name	**cmdOK**
Caption	**&OK**

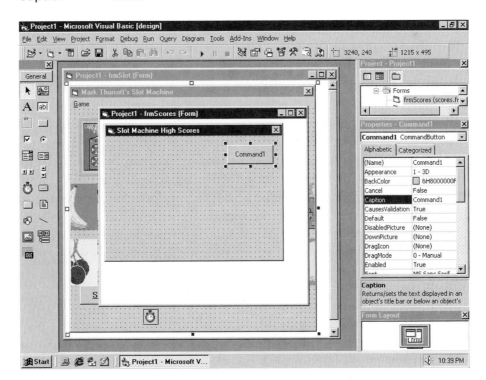

Figure 10.12 This command button will be used to close the dialog.

6 Add a list box control to the form and position it as shown in Figure 10.13. **List box controls** are used to provide a list of items to the user. It's perfect for the high score list.

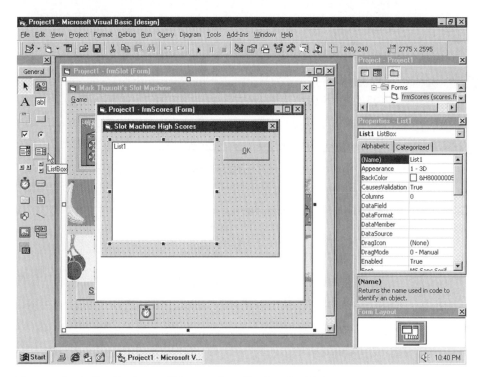

Figure 10.13 The list box will be used to display the high scores.

7 Change the (*Name*) property of the list box to **lstScore**.

Now it's time to write some code to access the database.

Using ActiveX Data Objects

Before we can access the ActiveX Data Objects Object Model, we will need to create a reference to it from within our project. Then, we can write code that runs when the high score form loads to display the information from the database into the list box.

TASK 7: TO ADD A REFERENCE TO THE ADO OBJECT MODEL

1 Choose *References* from the *Project* menu.
The References dialog box, shown in Figure 10.14, will appear.

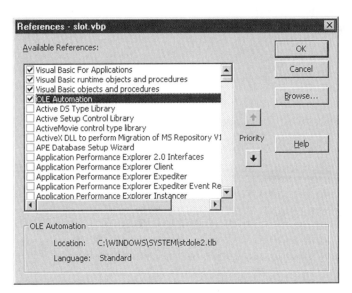

Figure 10.14 The References dialog box allows you to access other code libraries from your Visual Basic programs.

2 Scroll down the list of references until you find *Microsoft ActiveX Data Objects 2.0 Library.*

3 Check this option and click [OK] to close the dialog box.

You'll recall from our earlier discussion of the ADO Object Model that a Recordset object can be used to grab information from a database. In the following steps, we will use ADO to create a Recordset, connect to the database, and retrieve the contents of the tblScore table.

TASK 8: TO READ INFORMATION FROM THE DATABASE USING ADO

1 Double-click a blank area of frmScores to open the code window. An empty *Form_Load* event-handler appears.

2 Add the following code to the event-handler:

```
Dim MyRS As ADODB.Recordset
Set MyRS = New ADODB.Recordset

MyRS.Open "tblScore", _
    "Extended Properties=DBQ=<Full Path>\scores.mdb;" & _
    "Driver={Microsoft Access Driver (*.mdb)};DriverId=25;" & _
    "FIL=MS Access", adOpenForwardOnly, adLockReadOnly

Do Until MyRS.EOF
    lstScore.AddItem (MyRS("Name") & " - " & MyRS("Score"))
    MyRS.MoveNext
Loop
```

> **Note** The phrase <Full Path> in the above code must be changed to the actual full path on your system (including the drive letter) to the location your database is stored. This code will be explained in the next section.

3 Close the code window and double-click *cmdOK* [OK].

4 Add the following code to cmdOK_Click:

Unload frmScores

5 Close the code window and display frmSlot.

6 Click the High Scores menu item on frmSlot to display its *Click* event-handler.

7 Add the following line of code to this event-handler:

frmScores.Show vbModal

8 Save the project and test it.
When you choose High Scores from the Game menu, the High Scores dialog box should display with the high scores you entered into the database previously. This is shown in Figure 10.15.

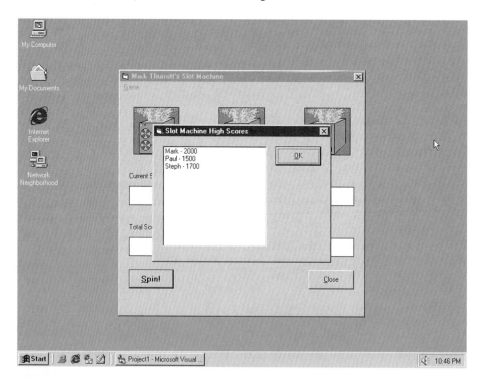

Figure 10.15 Here are the high scores, courtesy of our database.

9 Close the dialog box and the main window when you're done.

Understanding the ADO Code

Well, our ADO code seems to work fine, but *how* does it work? Looking over the code that you added to the *Form_Load* event-handler for frm-Scores, you should see a couple of new, and perhaps confusing, things going on. Let's take a look at it line by line.

```
Dim MyRS As ADODB.Recordset
```

This should be familiar: We are creating a new variable named MyRS (as in "my Recordset") that is of type Recordset. The Recordset object can be found in the ADODB library (the Microsoft ActiveX Data Objects 2.0 Library) to which you added a reference earlier. If you hadn't added a reference to this library, this code would cause an error message; Visual Basic doesn't know anything about the objects in the ADO Object Model unless you tell it where to find them.

```
Set MyRS = New ADODB.Recordset
```

This second line might be confusing. When you declare a variable with Dim, the next step is generally to assign the variable to some value. And indeed, this is what is done here. The different syntax is due to the fact that MyRS is an *object variable*. When you declare an object variable with Dim, the object (or, more exactly, the object reference) is not actually *created* in memory until you use the **Set statement** to assign the variable. This second line actually performs the function most people (incorrectly) associate with Dim: It *creates* the object we're working with ("MyRS" in this case).

```
MyRS.Open "tblScore", _
    "Extended Properties=DBQ=<Full Path>\scores.mdb;" & _
    "Driver={Microsoft Access Driver (*.mdb)};DriverId=25;" & _
    "FIL=MS Access", adOpenForwardOnly, adLockReadOnly
```

The **Open method** for the ADO Recordset object can be used in a variety of admittedly confusing ways. In this case, however, we are simply opening the tblScore table from the High Score database. The Recordset needs to know a few things about the database it is accessing, including the type of database (Microsoft Access), its physical location in the file system, the table to access, and some other information. The two parameters at the end indicate that the Recordset's *cursor*, which is an invisible marker used to enumerate through the various records in the Recordset, can only move forward and that the Recordset is to be open in read-only mode. Both of these options can speed up things considerably when you are only trying to read (and not modify) the data.

```
Do Until MyRS.EOF
    lstScore.AddItem (MyRS("Name") & " - " & MyRS("Score"))
    MyRS.MoveNext
Loop
```

This block of code loops through the list of records contained by the Recordset. The **EOF property** of the ADO Recordset indicates whether the cursor is positioned at the end of the Recordset (EOF stands for "end of file," which is an unfortunate term from the antiquities of BASIC. The Recordset is most certainly *not* a file). If it isn't, the Name and Score fields from the current Recordset are added to the list box and the cursor position is incremented with the **MoveNext method**. The loop will execute until the EOF condition is *False*.

> **Tip** Use the MSDN Library to find out more about the ADO Recordset and its properties and methods. The *Open* method, in particular, has an amazing assortment of options to explore.

Writing Information to a Database

Now that we can display information from the database, we'll need to write code that will add the current score to the database should the user wish to do so. This is also accomplished with the ADO Recordset and its properties and methods. Using code similar to that used in the previous section, we will connect to the database. But this time we will use a write-enabled, not read-only, Recordset. The Recordset's **AddNew method** allows us to add a new record to the Recordset. We will pass in the name (entered by the user), along with the high score, and then we will use the **Update method** to save the changes we've made back to the database.

Recording the High Score

The obvious time to write the high score to the database is when the user attempts to quit the game (or explicitly starts a new game using the menu). For this reason, we will handle the code for the [Close] button's *Click* event.

TASK 9: TO WRITE INFORMATION TO THE DATABASE

1 Double-click the *cmdClose* [Close] button to open the code window. The code simply reads End at this point.

2 Replace this code with the following:

```
Dim Name As String
Dim MyRS As ADODB.Recordset

If TotalScore > 0 Then
    If MsgBox("Save your score?", vbYesNo, "Save") = vbYes Then
        Name = InputBox("Please enter your name", "Name")

        Set MyRS = New ADODB.Recordset
        MyRS.Open "tblScore", _
            "Extended Properties=DBQ=D:\Program Files\Microsoft
                Visual Studio\My Projects\Slot Machine\scores.mdb;
                " & _
            "Driver={Microsoft Access Driver (*.mdb)}; Driver=25; "&_
            "FIL=MS Access", 1, 3
        MyRS.AddNew
        MyRS("Name") = Name
        MyRS("Score") = TotalScore
        MyRS.Update
        MyRS.Close
    End If
End If
End
```

3 Save the project and test the program by playing a round, quitting the
   game, and then restarting.
   When you view the High Scores dialog box, you should see that your scores
   have been added to the database.

4 When you are done, return to the Visual Basic IDE.

Finalizing the Solution

There's only one more thing that needs to be added now: When the users
choose to start a new game via the menu, they should be asked to save
their score to the High Score database before the new game begins. In the
following steps, you will add code to do this.

TASK 10: TO SAVE THE SCORE WHEN A NEW GAME BEGINS

1 In the Visual Basic IDE, open the code window and navigate to the event-
   handler for mnuNewGame_Click.

2   Make the following code changes. Note that new code is shown in bold type:

```
If MsgBox("Are you sure?", vbYesNo, "New Game") = vbYes Then

    Dim Name As String
    Dim MyRS As ADODB.Recordset

    If TotalScore > 0 Then
        If MsgBox("Save your score?", vbYesNo, "Save") _
        = vbYes Then
            Name = InputBox("Please enter your name", _
            "Name")
            Set MyRS = New ADODB.Recordset
            MyRS.Open "tblScore", _
                "Extended Properties=DBQ=<full path>\
                scores.mdb;" & _
                "Driver={Microsoft Access Driver(*.mdb)};
                DriverId=25;" & _
                "FIL=MS Access", 1, 3
            MyRS.AddNew
            MyRS("Name") = Name
            MyRS("Score") = TotalScore
            MyRS.Update
            MyRS.Close
        End If
    End If

    lblCurrentScore = " "
    lblTotalScore = " "

    CurrentScore = 0
    TotalScore = 0

    shpReel1.Visible = False
    shpReel2.Visible = False
    shpReel3.Visible = False

End If
```

Troubleshooting Tip Remember to substitute the actual path to the database for *<full path>* in the code listing.

3   Close the code window, save the project, and test the program.

The Conclusion

This was certainly a whirlwind tour through the features available in the ADO Object Model, most specifically the Recordset object, which you can use to retrieve data from or write data to a database. Visual Basic's prowess is easily observed as it offers a host of ways to access the sometimes complicated and enigmatic relational database.

Good work! You have completed Part Three and created a fully functional slot machine. In Part Four, you will build your own Web browser and include navigational features such as Go Back, Go Forward, and a fully functional Address bar.

Summary and Exercises

Summary

- A database is a file-based storage and retrieval system for data.
- Relational databases consist of tables and other objects.
- Tables are made up of rows of data called records. Each record is defined by columns called fields.
- The Visual Data Manager (VisData) allows you to create and modify Access databases from Visual Basic.
- ActiveX Data Objects (ADO) is an object model that provides objects to read and write to databases from Visual Basic code.
- The ADO Recordset is the primary object in the ADO Object Model.
- A reference can create a link between your Visual Basic code and a code library found elsewhere on your system.

Key Terms and Operations

Key Terms

ActiveX Data Objects (ADO)	*Open* method
AddNew method	record
ADO Recordset object	Recordset
cursor	reference
Data Access Objects (DAO)	relational database
database	Remote Data Objects (RDO)
EOF property	Set statement
field	Structured Query Language (SQL)
list box control	table
Microsoft ADO Data Control	Universal Data Access
MoveNext method	*Update* method
object model	Visual Data Manager (VisData)
object variable	

Operations

add data to a database
add tables and fields to a new database
create a new database
read records from a database with ADO code
use ADO code to access a database
use the Visual Data Manager
work with databases
write information to a database with ADO code

Study Questions

Multiple Choice

1. Microsoft Access is an example of a
   a. spreadsheet.
   b. database.
   c. word processor.
   d. personal information manager.

2. The columns in a database table are called
   a. fields.
   b. records.
   c. Recordsets.
   d. ADO.

3. The rows in a database table are called
   a. fields.
   b. records.
   c. Recordsets.
   d. ADO.

4. The Visual Data Manager (VisData) allows you to
   a. create new databases.
   b. update existing databases.
   c. create new databases and update existing databases.
   d. create its own proprietary type of database.

5. SQL stands for
   a. Sequential Query Language.
   b. Sorted Query Language.
   c. Structured Query Language.
   d. Standard Query Language.

6. ADO stands for
   a. ActiveX Data Objects.
   b. Active Data Objects.
   c. ActiveX Database Objects.
   d. Active Database Objects.

7. The ADO Recordset is used to
   a. create a new database.
   b. connect to a database and retrieve a set of records.
   c. connect to a database and retrieve table property information.
   d. work with the EOF marker to find out how big a table is.

8. The Set statement is used to
   a. dimension an integer variable.
   b. create an instance of an object variable in memory.
   c. replace the Dim statement.
   d. replace the *Static* keyword.

9. The ADO Recordset's *Open* method can be used to
   a. retrieve the data in a table.
   b. display information in a database.
   c. create the Recordset in memory.
   d. open a text file.

10. You can write information to a database with the ADO Recordset
    _____ methods.
    a. AddNew and Close
    b. Update and Close
    c. AddNew and Update
    d. Open and Update

True/False
1. Database is another word for spreadsheet.

2. Microsoft's strategy for data access is called Microsoft Data Access.

3. Microsoft Access is a relational database.

4. You can create Access databases in Visual Basic using the Visual Data Manager.

5. SQL stands for Server Query Language.

6. ADO allows you to access databases with Visual Basic code.

7. The ADO Recordset object allows you to gather data into rows for later use.

8. EOF stands for end of file.

9. You can use an ADO Recordset's *MoveNext* method to move to a new Recordset.

10. Instances of object variables are created in memory with Set.

Short Answer

1. How is information stored in a relational database?

2. What are the main objects in the ADO Object Model?

3. Which object in the ADO Object Model is the most important?

4. What is the name of the control that interacts visually with ADO?

5. What is the difference between a reference and a component?

6. How do you loop through the records in an ADO Recordset?

7. What does EOF stand for?

8. What is the ADO Recordset's *MoveNext* method used for?

9. Which ADO Recordset method is used to retrieve a table from a database?

10. What is an object model?

Group Discussion

1. Microsoft's Universal Data Access initiative is designed to give easy access to all kinds of different data sources—including information in databases, spreadsheets, email messages, and text documents—using the same set of objects, properties, and methods. Why is such an initiative important? Is this a good idea?

2. When there is a need to create code libraries that have no visual elements, developers often will create an object model that defines the objects in the library along with their properties, methods, and events. Database access is a great example of the need for an object model and, indeed, Microsoft has created numerous object models to deal with this task. What other object models do you think would be useful to the Visual Basic programmer?

3. In addition to reading and writing to databases, you can also use ADO to delete information in a database. Deleting data from a database can be dangerous, however. What steps should you take to ensure that nothing important gets deleted inadvertently (and permanently)?

Hands-On

Displaying employees from Northwind Traders

Visual Basic 6.0 ships with a sample Access database called Northwind Traders (nwind.exe; ask your instructor for its location). Use VisData to examine this database, specifically the Employees table. Create a Visual Basic program that connects to the Employees table in the Northwind Traders database and displays the first and last name of each employee in a list box.

On Your Own

1. Using SQL statements with Northwind Traders

In the Recordset *Open* method from the Hands-On exercise, you probably have a line of code that resembles the following:

```
MyRS.Open "Employees", _
    "Extended Properties=DBQ=<Full Path>\nwind.mdb;" & _
    "Driver={Microsoft Access Driver (*.mdb)};DriverId=25;" & _
    "FIL=MS Access", adOpenForwardOnly, adLockReadOnly
```

The portion of this code that reads tblScore can also be changed to gather more detailed information using SQL code. In fact, the term tblScore is really shorthand for the following SQL code:

```
SELECT * FROM Employees
```

What this says in English is "select all records from the tblScore table." The * is shorthand for "All."

You can also use code to limit or sort the data you receive. For example, the following code would sort the Recordset you retrieve by the employees' last names:

```
SELECT * FROM Employees ORDER BY LastName
```

Or you could sort by last name then first name:

```
SELECT * FROM Employees ORDER BY LastName, FirstName
```

Working with the program you created in the Hands-On exercise, add three new command buttons that will reconnect to the database. Create Recordsets with the following criteria (one for each command button):

1. Sorted by name (last then first)

SELECT * FROM Employees ORDER BY LastName, FirstName

2. Sorted by city, then state, then address

SELECT * FROM Employees ORDER BY City, State, Address

3. Sorted by title then hire date

SELECT * FROM Employees ORDER BY Title, 'Hire Date'

2. Northwind browser

Create a program similar to the Hands-On exercise that uses a text box rather than a list box. The program should also include two command buttons labeled *Go back* and *Go forward*. When the *Go Back* button is pressed, the text box should display the first and last names from the previous record. (*Hint*: Use MyRS.MovePrevious.) When the *Go Forward* button is pressed, the text box should display the names from the next record. To ensure that there isn't a problem if the *Go Back* button is pressed when the first record is being displayed (or, likewise, if *Go Forward* is pressed when the last record is displayed), use the code **On Error Resume Next** at the beginning of each *Click* event.

PART FOUR
Web Browser

11

PROJECT

Creating a Web Browser

Objectives

After completing this project, you will be able to:

➤ **Add the WebBrowser control to a Visual Basic program**

➤ **Work with WebBrowser control methods**

➤ **Navigate the WebBrowser control to the home page**

➤ **Automatically position a control to respond to the form resizing**

➤ **Use compound properties**

➤ **Retrieve the title of the document contained by the WebBrowser control**

The Challenge

As a Visual Basic programmer in a large company, you are often asked to deliver custom software solutions for various groups of employees. With the rise of Windows terminals and diskless workstations at your corporation, your boss has asked you to develop a lightweight, simple Web browser that encompasses a subset of the functionality in Internet Explorer or Netscape Navigator without the complexities of all the options in a high-end browser.

The Solution

When Microsoft programmers began working on Internet Explorer 3.0, they decided to implement the browser's functionality as an *ActiveX control* that could be embedded into any application, including those created in Visual Basic. An ActiveX control—like standard built-in VB controls such as the command button—is really just a unit of code that can be accessed in a consistent manner. ActiveX controls provide properties, methods, and events (just like the built-in controls). In addition, they can offer a user interface like visual controls or work behind the scenes like nonvisual controls (e.g., the timer control). In many ways they provide "black box" functionality where the "way" they work is unimportant. Internet Explorer 3.0 (and all future versions, including IE 4.0 and 5.0) is really just an application shell that hosts the Internet Explorer ActiveX control, which is responsible for providing all of the basic functionality for browsing the Web.

You will create a Web browser that includes basic functionality following these specifications:

- The Web browser will appear centered in the screen and occupy 80% of its width and height by default.

- The user will be able to resize the window if desired, and the controls on the form will then resize themselves accordingly.

- The Web browser will include navigational features, such as the ability to go back, go forward, refresh the page, stop the current transfer, and go to the home page.

- The Web browser will appear visually similar to current-generation Web browsers, with a toolbar utilizing buttons for the functions listed above.

- The toolbar will also feature a drop-down address bar that will record the sites visited in the current session. The user can type a Web address (URL) into the address bar, press (ENTER), and the Web browser will navigate to that address.

The Setup

Over the course of the projects in Part Four, you will add all of the features listed in the specifications. For this project, you will add only the most basic functionality as you learn about the WebBrowser control.

Using the WebBrowser Control

The Internet Explorer ActiveX control that provides the Web browsing functionality is aptly called the *WebBrowser control*. Before Microsoft created this control, creating a Web-enabled application was tedious at best. Microsoft has provided low-level Internet functionality for some time, but programmers had to handle all the details. Now, adding basic Web browsing capability to your applications is as simple as dropping a control on your form and handling a few events. Let's take a look.

Adding a Component to the Toolbox Window

Unlike the standard controls, which are available to the Visual Basic programmer from the toolbox window, the WebBrowser control must be explicitly added to a project before it can be used. In fact, there are many components you can use with your Visual Basic programs that do not appear in the toolbox. Because each new component added to a project increases the size of the program, Microsoft provides only the commonly used controls in the default and then allows you to add others as you need them.

In the following steps, you will add the WebBrowser control to a new Visual Basic project.

TASK 1: TO ADD THE WEBBROWSER CONTROL TO YOUR PROJECT

1 Start a new Visual Basic project, choosing *Standard EXE* as the project type.

2 Choose *Components* from the *Project* menu.
The Components dialog box, shown in Figure 11.1, will appear.

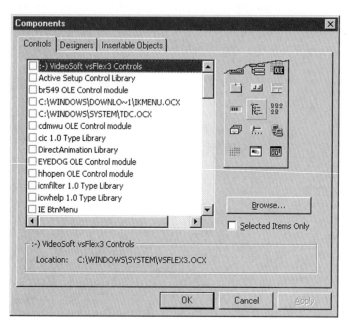

Figure 11.1 The Components dialog box allows you to add other components to your Visual Basic project.

3 Scroll down the list of components until you find *Microsoft Internet Controls*. This component contains the WebBrowser control.

> **Tip** If you are using Windows 98, the ***Microsoft Internet Controls component*** will contain two controls, including the WebBrowser control. In some systems, including some versions of Windows NT, you will see only the WebBrowser control when you add this component to a project.

4 Check *Microsoft Internet Controls* and click [OK] to close the dialog box. A new icon will appear on the Visual Basic Toolbox window, as shown in Figure 11.2.

Figure 11.2 Now that you've added the component, the controls in that component appear in the Toolbox window.

Using the WebBrowser Control

Now that the WebBrowser control is available to your project, you can add it to your form as you would any other control.

TASK 2: TO ADD THE WEBBROWSER CONTROL TO YOUR FORM

1 Double-click the WebBrowser control icon 🌐 in the Toolbox window. A new WebBrowser control will appear on the form, as shown in Figure 11.3.

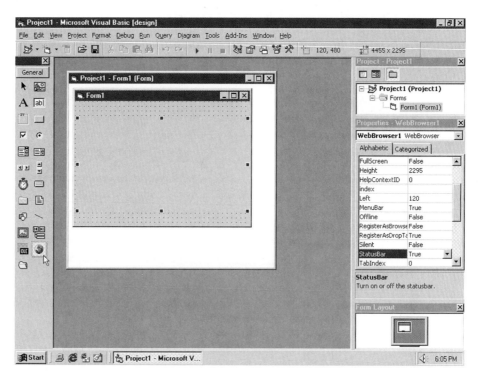

Figure 11.3 Double-click the icon to open your blank WebBrowser control.

2　Run the program.
As shown in Figure 11.4, nothing much happens; you must program the WebBrowser to do something first.

Figure 11.4 Your Web browser isn't much to look at yet.

3　Close the program.

4　Select the form (not the WebBrowser) and change its (*Name*) property to **frmWB**.

5　Change the (*Name*) property for the project to **WB**.

6　Select the WebBrowser control and change its (*Name*) property to **WB**.

7 Save the project, naming the form and project as **wb.frm** and **wb.vbp**, respectively. M,ake sure that you create a new folder for this new project.

Using WebBrowser Methods

The WebBrowser control supports a long list of properties, methods, and events. At this point, we are only interested in a few methods that will cause the WebBrowser to navigate to certain locations. These methods are shown in Table 11.1.

Table 11.1 WebBrowser Methods

Method	Purpose
GoBack	Navigates the browser to the previous Web page in the list of pages visited
GoForward	Navigates the browser forward one Web page in the list of pages visited
GoHome	Navigates to the current "home," or start page, as determined by Internet Explorer's options settings in the system Control Panel
Navigate	Navigates to a specific location on the Web
Refresh	Reloads the current Web page displaying in the Web browser
Stop	Stops downloading the Web page that is currently in the process of downloading

One of the most obvious things we want to add is the ability to navigate to the home page when the window appears. We do this by calling the Web-Browser's *GoHome method* when the form loads.

TASK 3: TO NAVIGATE THE BROWSER TO THE HOME PAGE

1 Double-click the form window (not the WebBrowser control) to bring up the Code window.
You should see the form's *Load* event-handler (if not, choose it from the drop-down lists at the top of the Code window.

2 Add the following line of code to Form_Load:

WB.GoHome

3 Save the project and run the program.
Your home page should load into the admittedly small browser window, as shown in Figure 11.5 (note that your home page will be different from the one shown in this figure).

> **Troubleshooting Tip** This may not be obvious, but you'll need to be connected to the Internet for this to work unless your browser's home page points to a file on your computer.

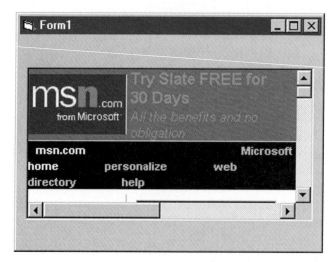

Figure 11.5 Isn't it cute? Your new, tiny Web browser in action.

4   Stop the program and return to the Visual Basic IDE.

Setting up the WebBrowser Control

Now that we know the Web browser is working, so to speak, this is a good time to think about some of the basic functionality that needs to occur. The size of the form window, for example, is obviously too small, so we will want to resize it in some way when the program starts.

According to the specifications for this project, the Web browser should appear centered in the screen and occupy 80% of the screen's width and height. In the following steps, you will add these features.

TASK 4: TO SET UP THE DEFAULT SIZE AND POSITION OF THE BROWSER

1   Find the Form Layout window in the Visual Basic IDE. If it isn't present, choose *Form Layout Window* from the *View* menu.

2   Right-click the representation of the form window in the monitor in this window and choose *Startup Position* then *Center Screen*. This is shown in Figure 11.6.

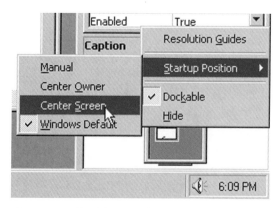

Figure 11.6 Position the form in the center of the screen.

3   Now resize the form window in the Visual Basic IDE so you have a little more room to work with (Figure 11.7).

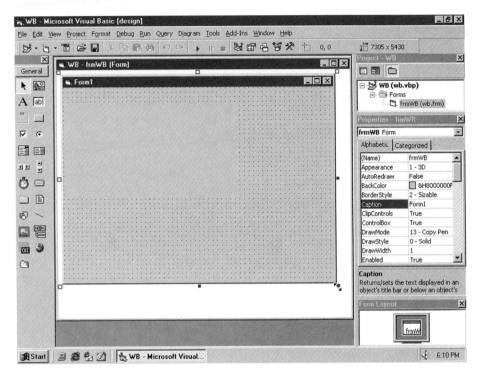

Figure 11.7 Now you have a little more breathing room.

4   Double-click an empty area of the form to open the Code window. In the form's Load event-handler, add the following code before the line that reads WB.GoHome:

frmWB.Width = Screen.Width * 0.8

frmWB.Height = Screen.Height * 0.8

5   Save the project and run the program.
As shown in Figure 11.8, the window will now size and position itself correctly (though that little WebBrowser control looks odd up in the corner).

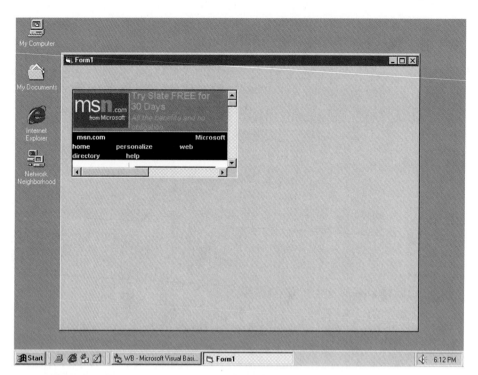

Figure 11.8 An obvious problem: The WebBrowser control doesn't know to resize itself with the form.

6 Close the program and return to the Visual Basic IDE.

Clearly, the WebBrowser control should occupy the entire surface of the form while the program is running. We could manually resize it in the Visual Basic IDE, but this presents a problem. If a user resizes the window while the program is running and WebBrowser control doesn't automatically resize itself with the resized form, the display will be messed up. Furthermore, since we've coded to automatically change the size of the form when the window loads, the display will be messed up from the start. So manually resizing the control won't work.

Obviously, we'll need to write some code to resize the WebBrowser control along with the form window. The easiest way to do this is to position the WebBrowser control at the top left corner of the form, handle the event that occurs when the form is resized, and size the control to match the form.

TASK 5: TO AUTOMATICALLY RESIZE THE WEBBROWSER CONTROL

1 Change the *Top* property of WB to **0**.

2 Change the *Left* property of WB to **0**.

3 Double-click a blank area of the form window in the Visual Basic IDE to bring up the Code window.
The Form_Load procedure will appear, but we want to write code to handle the *Resize* event.

4 Open the *Procedure* drop-down list at the top right of the Code window and choose *Resize,* as shown in Figure 11.9.
Visual Basic will add an empty Form_Resize procedure to the Code window.

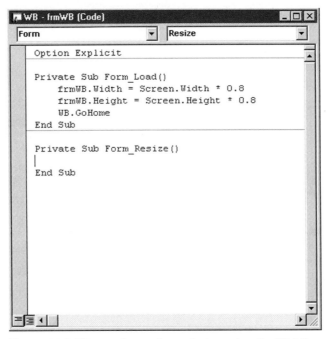

```
WB - frmWB (Code)                                   _ □ ×
Form                    ▼    Resize                 ▼
   Option Explicit                                   ▲

   Private Sub Form_Load()
        frmWB.Width = Screen.Width * 0.8
        frmWB.Height = Screen.Height * 0.8
        WB.GoHome
   End Sub

   Private Sub Form_Resize()
   |
   End Sub
                                                     ▼
═▐▌◄                                              ►
```

Figure 11.9 We need to write code to resize the WebBrowser control in the form's *Resize* event-handler.

5 Add the following code to the event-handler:

WB.Width = frmWB.ScaleWidth

WB.Height = frmWB.ScaleHeight

6 Save the project and run the program.
As shown in Figure 11.10, the WebBrowser control should now occupy the entire surface of the form. Resize the window in various dimensions to test this.

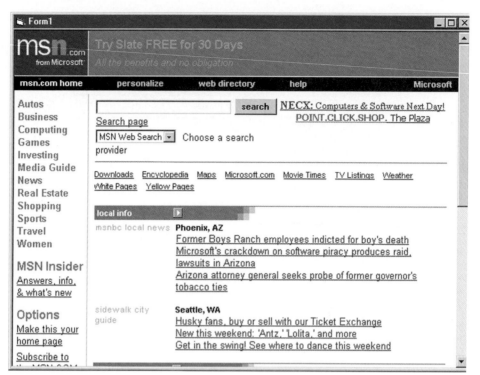

Figure 11.10 That's more like it.

7   When you're done testing, close the program and return to the Visual Basic IDE.

> **Tip** You can navigate in the browser by using (ALT)+(←) to go back and (ALT)+(→) to go forward. You can also right-click the surface of the WebBrowser control while the program is running to access a list of options.

Providing Feedback to the User

Before moving on to some of the more obvious improvements we need to make (such as adding a toolbar to the top of the form), we should take a minute to provide a more subtle visual improvement. Web browsers such as Netscape Navigator and Internet Explorer typically display the title of the current Web page in the caption of their title bars. We can add this basic functionality to our browser using the WebBrowser control's **Document property**.

Using Compound Properties

The WebBrowser's *Document* property is actually a reference to an object appropriately called the **Document object**, which exists in the **Dynamic HTML Object Model**. Microsoft provides this set of objects with their properties, methods, and events to Web developers so that developers can take advantage of the various features in both the Web pages and the Web browser that contains them. The *Document* property, then, can be considered a **compound property** because the object it represents—the Document object—has its own set of properties, methods, and events. In other words, a compound property represents another object. The **Title property** of the Document object contains the title of the currently loaded document; we will use this property to display the title in the form's caption.

One interesting side effect of using a compound property is the way it extends the familiar dot notation we use in Visual Basic code. Generally, to access the property of an object, we use code like this:

Object.Property

Using a compound property simply extends this notation like so:

Object.CompoundProperty.Property

So, for example, to set the caption of the form's title bar to the title of the current document, we could use the following line of code:

frmWB.Caption = WB.Document.Title

And in fact, this is very similar to the code we will use. The question, however, is where to put this code. The WebBrowser control offers various events that occur when the title of the document contained by the Web browser changes, including one called **TitleChange**. This is the obvious time to grab the title of the document and display it in the program's title bar.

TASK 6: TO SET THE FORM CAPTION

1 Select the form window and change its *Caption* property to **Web Browser**.

2 Double-click the WebBrowser control to display the Code window. The event-handler for the *StatusTextChange* event will appear, but this is not the event we want to handle.

3 Choose *TitleChange* from the *Procedure* drop-down list in the Code window. A blank event-handler will appear.

4 Add the following line of code to this event-handler:

frmWB.Caption = "WebBrowser - " & WB.Document.Title

5 Save the project and run the program. Your Web browser should now display an appropriate title (Figure 11.11) every time a page loads. Test this by clicking on various hyperlinks from your home page and observing how the form title changes.

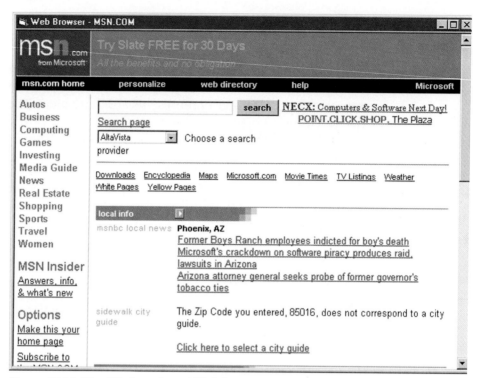

Figure 11.11 The title bar of your Web browser now displays the title of the current document.

6   Close the program when you are done and return to the Visual Basic IDE.

The Conclusion

While your Web browser is obviously not quite finished, you've made a good start. In the next project, you will add numerous new features to the Web browser, including a toolbar with several buttons, an address bar, and a status bar.

Summary and Exercises

Summary

- ActiveX controls are used to provide "black box" functionality to programs.
- The WebBrowser control allows you to provide Web browser functionality to your programs.
- You can add components to your Visual Basic project to add new features.
- The WebBrowser control must be manually positioned and sized in its container.
- Compound properties allow you to access other objects through an object's properties.
- The WebBrowser's *TitleChange* event occurs when the title of the document it contains has changed.

Key Terms and Operations

Key Terms
ActiveX control
compound property
Document object
Document property
Dynamic HTML Object Model
GoHome method
Microsoft Internet Controls
   component
Title property
TitleChange event
WebBrowser control

Operations
Add components to a project
Handle the *TitleChange* event
Navigate to the home page with the
   GoHome method
Resize a control when the form
   resizes
Use compound properties and
   extended dot notation
Use the WebBrowser control

Study Questions

Multiple Choice

1. The WebBrowser control is an example of a(n)
   a. ActiveX control.
   b. component.
   c. static function.
   d. form window.

2. The WebBrowser control is part of which component?
   a. WebBrowser component
   b. Microsoft Internet Controls component
   c. Microsoft Windows Common Controls 6.0 component
   d. Internet Explorer component

3. To add a component to your project, you must access
   a. Project then Components.
   b. Project then References.
   c. File then New Component.
   d. File then New.

4. The *Refresh* method of the WebBrowser control is used to
   a. navigate the browser to the home page.
   b. stop the current download.
   c. reload the current document.
   d. navigate to the previous document.

5. What event would you handle if you wanted to write code that executes when the form resizes?
   a. *OnResize*
   b. *Resize*
   c. *Reload*
   d. *ReDraw*

6. The Document property references the Document object in what object model?
   a. Dynamic HTML Object Model
   b. ActiveX Data Objects Object Model
   c.. Data Access Objects Object Model
   d. Remote Data Objects Object Model

7. A property that references an object is known as a(n)
   a. pointer.
   b. object.
   c. compound property.
   d. function.

8. The *TitleChange* event occurs when
   a. the caption of the Web browser application changes.
   b. the user clicks a hyperlink.
   c. the title of an Edit box changes.
   d. the title of the document contained by the browser changes.

True/False

1. An ActiveX control is an object that provides a consistent way to access its code.

2. Microsoft provides a WebBrowser control that provides Web browsing functionality.

3. You can add new controls to the Visual Basic Toolbox by choosing *Project* then *References* from the menu.

4. The WebBrowser control provides methods such as *GoBack* and *GoForward*.

5. The Document object contains information about the document contained by the WebBrowser control.

6. The *TitleChange* event occurs when the title of the document in the Web browser changes.

7. The WebBrowser control automatically resizes itself when the user resizes the form it resides on.

Short Answer

1. What navigational features does the WebBrowser control provide?

2. How can you use a control that isn't present in the Visual Basic Toolbox window?

3. What other control (besides WebBrowser) is available in the Microsoft Internet Controls component (in Windows 98)?

4. What does the *Navigate* method do?

5. How can you cause the browser to navigate to the home page?

6. What is the Dynamic HTML Object Model?

7. How do you access the properties of the object that is referenced by a compound property?

Group Discussion

1. Microsoft's decision to create its browser as an ActiveX control was a tremendous gift to developers. Netscape's browser, meanwhile, is hard-coded in C and C++. However, Netscape released the source to their browser to the public in 1998 in an attempt to get developers to help work on improvements. Is this approach superior, or inferior, to Microsoft's approach for developers that want to add browser functionality to their own programs? Explain your answer.

2. With the WebBrowser control, you could literally add Web browsing capabilities to any program. You could even add this feature to an About Box dialog if you were so inclined! Aside from creating an actual Web browser as we are doing, what other uses could this control have?

Hands-On

FTP browser

Create an FTP browser that navigates to a specific FTP site ("ftp://ftp.microsoft.com") when the form that contains the WebBrowser component first loads. (*Hint*: Look up the Navigate method in the MSDN Library). The form window should occupy 90% of the height and width of the screen and the browser control should resize to fit the form window if the user resizes it. The form's caption should be set to the location name of the document in the browser.

On Your Own

1. Improving the FTP browser

Enhance the FTP browser so that a second form loads when you run the program. This form should present a text box and a command button to the user. The text box will allow the user to type in the name of an FTP site they'd like to connect to. The command button, with a caption of "Go," will load the FTP site into the WebBrowser control on the main form.

A couple of notes: You can assume that the user will add the prefix **ftp://** to the address (and, indeed, when you test this program, you should always use that prefix). A more advanced version of this program would test for the existence of that prefix and add it if necessary. When the user clicks the *Go* button, the second form will unload itself and pass the text from the text box to the *Navigate* method of the WebBrowser control.

2. Completing the FTP browser

Enhance the FTP browser so that it checks for the existence of the prefixes **ftp://** and **http://** in the address entered by the user. If the ftp:// address is present, the browser should simply navigate to the address normally. If the http:// prefix is used, the browser should display a message to the user explaining that the address is invalid (see below). If neither prefix is present, the browser should add the prefix ftp:// to the address and attempt to load it for the user.

To notify the user of an invalid address, you could use the Visual Basic **MsgBox** (message box) function, which displays a dialog box to the user. This function is pretty versatile, allowing you to specify not only the message in the dialog but the command buttons that it uses as well. For example, if you wanted to provide a choice to the user, you could create a message box with "Yes" and "No" choices, or even "Yes," "No," and "Cancel." In this case, all you need to do is provide an error message and an *OK* button. The code to do so might look something like this:

```
Dim MyResponse As String
    If Left(strAddress, 7) = "http://" Then
        MyResponse = MsgBox("Sorry, Web addresses are invalid.", & _
        vbOKOnly, "Invalid Address")
End If
```

Troubleshooting Tip Look up the MsgBox function in the MSDN Library for more information about this useful way to provide information to the user.

12

Improving the Web Browser

Objectives

After completing this project, you will be able to:

➤ **Use the toolbar control to provide a toolbar**

➤ **Work with *Button* objects**

➤ **Use collections**

➤ **Use the image list control**

➤ **Handle the toolbar *ButtonClick* event and determine which button was clicked**

➤ **Execute code when a toolbar button is clicked**

➤ **Handle errors with the On Error statement**

The Challenge

In the previous project, you began work on a simplified Web browser, but more work needs to be done: A toolbar with *Back*, *Forward*, *Stop*, *Refresh*, and *Home* buttons must be added to the browser, and the Web browser should navigate accordingly when these buttons are clicked.

The Solution

We will use the specifications from Project 11 to determine what needs to be done. The following tasks will be completed in this project:

- A toolbar will be added to the Web browser.

- The toolbar will have five buttons: *Back*, *Forward*, *Stop*, *Refresh*, and *Home*.

- Code will be written to allow these buttons to navigate the browser accordingly.

- Images for the toolbar button will be stored in image list controls. There will be separate "enabled" and "disabled" images so that the buttons change appearance when the mouse cursor passes over them.

The Setup

In the next project, the remaining specifications for the Web browser will be completed and we will have a fairly full-feature Web browser to distribute. For now, however, we need to get cracking on the toolbar.

Using a Toolbar

Most professional Windows applications, such as Microsoft Word and Excel, contain extensive toolbars. **Toolbars**, which are generally composed of buttons and other elements such as drop-down lists, are designed to provide quick access to the commands that are used most often. In a program like Word, for example, the toolbar provides buttons to save the current document, open a new document, and print. Our Web browser toolbar will have buttons for go back, go forward, stop the current download, refresh the page, and go home. It will also contain an address bar like the one found in Internet Explorer.

Each button in a toolbar can contain a graphic and/or a text caption. Because the toolbar and its collection of buttons are treated as a single control, it's a little more difficult to access each of the individual buttons with Visual Basic code. In fact, you can think of the toolbar as a compound control, since you will have to access the properties of the individual buttons—which are themselves references to **Button objects**—through the extended version of dot notation we examined in Project 11.

Like the WebBrowser component, the **toolbar control** isn't provided in the Visual Basic Toolbox window by default, so you will need to add a component to the toolbox before you can use it. In this case, the toolbar control is included as part of the Microsoft Windows Common Controls 6.0 component, which also includes the controls shown in Table 12.1.

Table 12.1 Microsoft Windows Common Controls 6.0 Controls

Control	Purpose
TabStrip	Provides the ability to use a "tabbed" dialog such as the Display Properties dialog in Windows
StatusBar	Provides an area, generally at the bottom of a form, for status information (The Word and IE application windows use a status bar.)
ProgressBar	Provides a visual indication of progress during a lengthy operation (You'll see this when you copy files in Windows.)
TreeView	Provides a "tree" view for hierarchical data, such as the view of your system's file system in the left pane of Windows Explorer
ListView	Provides large icon, small icon, list, and detail views of data, such as the right pane of Windows Explorer
ImageList	Provides a way to group a list of graphical images into a single control (Recall that in the slot machine project we used separate image controls for each image: This control makes managing multiple images far easier.)
Slider	Provides a visual "slider," resembling a horizontal guage, that the user can drag and click to set a value (The Screen area portion of the *Settings* tab allows you to set your screen's resolution using a slider control.)
ImageCombo	Provides a special version of the standard combo box that supports the ability to display a graphical image next to each item in the combo box

Many components you add to Visual Basic will support multiple controls like this. We will be using a few of these other controls in this and future versions of the Web browser project. For now, let's add a toolbar to the Web browser.

TASK 1: TO ADD A TOOLBAR TO YOUR PROJECT

1   Open the Web browser project in Visual Basic and display the form window.

2   Select *Components* from the *Project* menu.
The Components dialog box will appear.

3   Scroll down the list of components and check *Microsoft Windows Common Controls 6.0*.

4   Click ⌐ OK ⌐ to close the Components dialog box.
Nine new controls (Figure 12.1) will be added to the Toolbox window.

Figure 12.1 You now have a host of common controls from which to choose.

5　Double-click the toolbar control ⟦⬚⬚⟧, as shown in Figure 12.2, to add a new toolbar to the form.

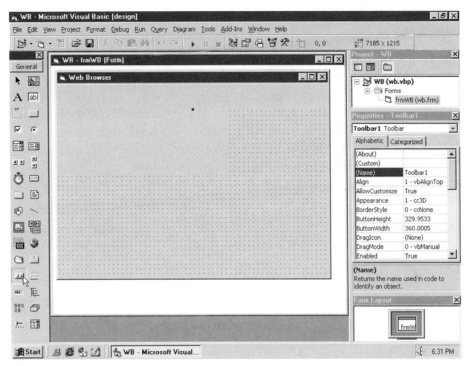

Figure 12.2 A blank toolbar is added to the top of the form by default.

6   Run the program.
Notice that the top of the WebBrowser control runs "under" the toolbar
(Figure 12.3). The WebBrowser control isn't smart enough to fit itself below
the toolbar, so we will need to add this functionality manually.

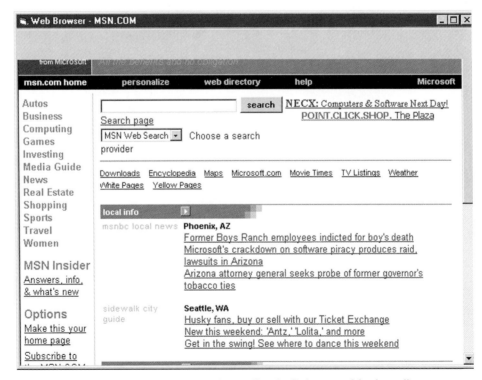

Figure 12.3 The WebBrowser control runs "under" the new, blank toolbar.

7 Close the program and return to the Visual Basic IDE.

Making Room for the Toolbar

We're going to need to reposition and resize the WebBrowser control to take into account the size and position of the toolbar. Because the Web-Browser *Top* property is currently se to 0, the toolbar is aligned, by default, with the very top of the form window. We need to set the *Top* property differently when the form loads. Likewise, when the form is resized, we will need to take into account the height of the toolbar when we set the height of the WebBrowser control. In both cases, we are concerned with the **Height property** of the toolbar control.

TASK 2: TO SIZE THE WEBBROWSER CONTROL TO FIT BELOW THE TOOLBAR

1 Change the *Name* property of the toolbar control to **Toolbar**.

2 Examine the *Height* property of Toolbar (420 on the system used to develop this project).

3 Change the *Top* property of the WebBrowser control to be the height of the toolbar + 1 (**421** in this case).
The screen should resemble Figure 12.4 when you are done.

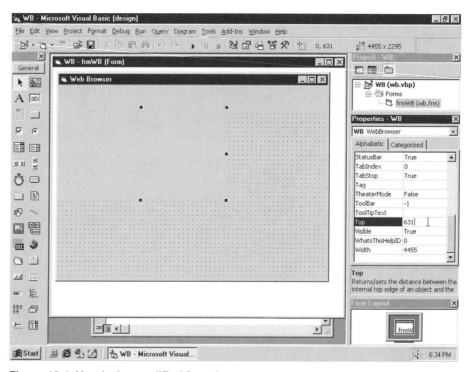

Figure 12.4 Here's the modified form layout.

4 Double-click a blank area of the form to display the Code window.

5 In the Form_Resize procedure, change the line of code that currently reads
WB.Height = frmWB.ScaleHeight
to

WB.Height = frmWB.ScaleHeight - Toolbar.Height

6 Save the project and run the program to test it. Resize the window to see how the WebBrowser control behaves. It should resize correctly with the form, taking into account the height of the toolbar (Figure 12.5).

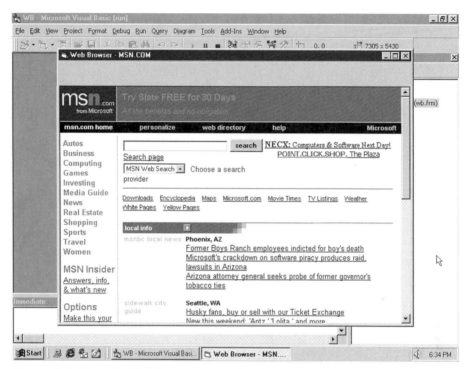

Figure 12.5 Now the WebBrowser control resizes correctly.

Working with Buttons

A toolbar without buttons isn't much of a toolbar, so let's add the required buttons. As mentioned previously, toolbar buttons are references to Button objects that have their own set of properties and methods. What Button objects don't have, however, are events of their own. Rather, you access the events of the toolbar itself—such as the *Click* event—and then determine which button was affected. It's a little complex since it isn't easy to access individual button events, but Visual Basic has a construct known as a *collection* that makes it a little easier.

Understanding Collections

A *collection* is a named list of other objects, which is similar to the programming construct called an *array*. The main difference between a collection and an array is that the objects in a collection can be different data types whereas the objects in an array must all be of the same data type. For that reason, a collection is far more powerful and useful than an array.

> **Troubleshooting Tip** For more information on arrays and collections, please examine the MSDN Library online help. Specifically, check out the Index entries for *arrays, described* and *collections, described, The Visual Basic Collection Object.*

A collection also offers different ways to get at the objects it contains. For example, you are probably familiar with array notation where MyArray(1) refers to the first object, or *member*, in an array called MyArray. You can also access collection members this way: MyCollection(1) refers to the first member in a collection called MyCollection. Toolbars have a *Buttons collection* that represents the list of button objects that toolbar contains. So, to access the first button in a toolbar named TB, you could use **TB.Buttons(1)**.

But you can also access Buttons collection members by the *Key* property. The *Key property* for each button in a Buttons collection is set to a unique string value so that you can, in effect, *name* each button. This makes it much easier to access buttons in a toolbar, especially in the *Click* event-handler for the toolbar. We will use the Key property to uniquely name each button in our toolbar.

Adding Buttons to the Toolbar

You can add buttons to the toolbar by accessing the toolbar's **Property Pages**, a dialog box made available by choosing *Properties* when you right-click the toolbar or by clicking *Custom* in the Properties window while the toolbar is selected. Either way, the Property Pages dialog box (Figure 12.6) offers a host of options for both the toolbar and the buttons it contains. In fact, Property Pages are used for any controls that have complicated options that are not easily exhibited in the Properties window.

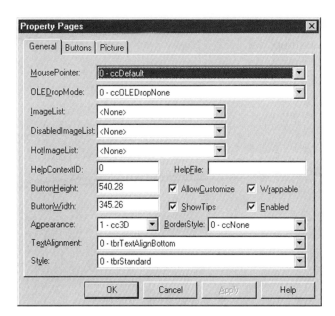

Figure 12.6 The Property Pages dialog box lets you set toolbar and button properties.

In the following steps, you will add five blank toolbar buttons.

TASK 3: TO ADD BUTTONS TO THE TOOLBAR

1   Right-click the toolbar on the form window and choose *Properties*. The Property Pages dialog box for the toolbar will appear.

2   Navigate to the *Buttons* page (Figure 12.7).

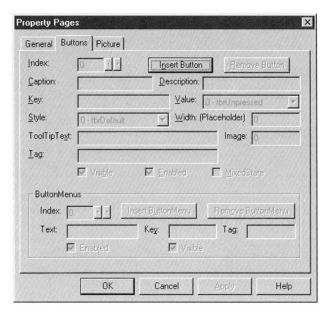

Figure 12.7 The *Buttons* page lets you add buttons and set properties.

3   Click ▐ Insert Button ▌ five times to add five blank command buttons. The buttons will appear on the toolbar, as shown in Figure 12.8.

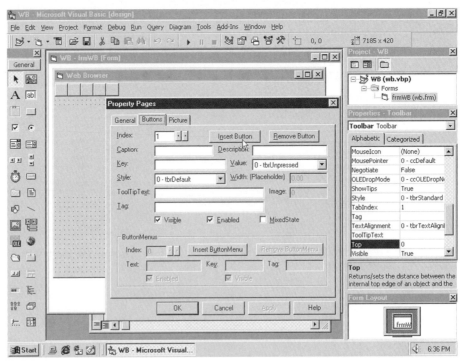

Figure 12.8 Adding buttons to the toolbar is as easy as clicking.

4   Navigate to the first button with the small arrow buttons next to the *Index* section and change the *Key* values of each button as shown in Table 12.2.

Table 12.2 Button Key Values

Button	Key value
1	**back**
2	**forward**
3	**stop**
4	**refresh**
5	**home**

5   Click ▐ OK ▌ to close the Property Pages dialog box, save the project, and run the program.

The toolbar buttons don't function yet because we haven't written any code to do so. Before we do that, we need to want to add an image to each button. For that, we'll first need to look at image lists.

Using the Image List control

You may recall from Part Three that we used a set of four image controls to hold images for the reels in the slot machine. While this simplifies matters somewhat, it isn't the most elegant way to store a group of images, especially when you have numerous images. In fact, Visual Basic supplies an *image list control* that is designed for just that purpose: It contains a collection of images that can be referred from other controls that need access to many images, such as our toolbar.

The image list control is part of the Microsoft Windows Common Controls 6.0 component that you added previously so it's already in the toolbox, ready for use. Like the timer control, it is a nonvisual control that the user will never "see." Instead, the images are displayed by other controls.

In the following steps, you will add an image list control to your project and add images to the toolbar control. (Your instructor will supply these images to you; you should copy them into the folder that you use to store your project.)

TASK 4: TO ADD AN IMAGE LIST TO THE PROJECT

1   Double-click the image list control icon ▭ in the toolbox to add an image list control to the center of the form. It doesn't matter where you place the control because the user will not see it when the program runs (Figure 12.9).

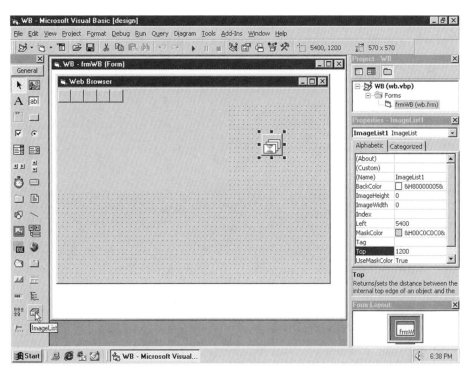

Figure 12.9 The image list is a nonvisual control.

2 Change the (*Name*) property of the image list to **ilDisabled**.
The images in this image list will be used to display the disabled images for the toolbar buttons.

3 Right-click on the image list control to bring up its Property Pages, as shown in Figure 12.10. (Alternatively, you could choose *Custom* from the Properties window.)

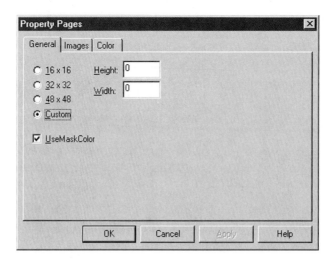

Figure 12.10 As with the toolbar, you can set image list options from its Property Pages.

4 Navigate to the *Images* page (Figure 12.11).

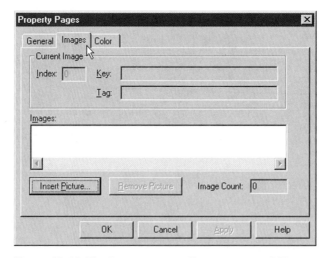

Figure 12.11 The Images page allows you to add images to the control.

5 Click Insert Picture... to add an image to the image list control.
The Select Picture dialog box will appear, as shown in Figure 12.12.

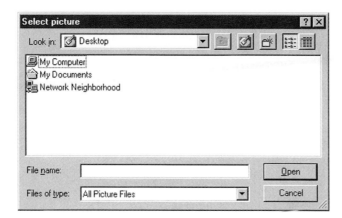

Figure 12.12 The Select Picture dialog box works like other Open and Save dialog boxes.

6   Navigate to the folder where you store your Web browser project and choose *backoff.bmp*.
    The image will appear in the list of images (Figure 12.13).

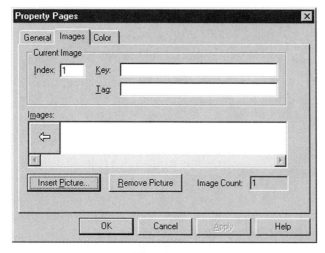

Figure 12.13 This image will be used whenever the *Back* button is disabled or not selected.

7   Using the preceding steps as a guide, add the remaining four images as shown in Table 12.3.
    When you're done, the screen should resemble Figure 12.14.

Table 12.3

Image Number	Image Name
2	**Forwardoff.bmp**
3	**Stopoff.bmp**
4	**Refreshoff.bmp**
5	**Homeoff.bmp**

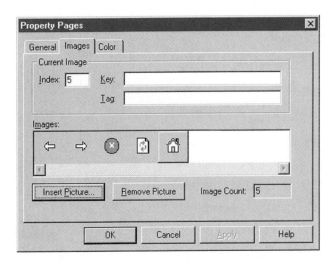

Figure 12.14 When you're done, you should have five images in the image list control.

8 Click ____OK____ to close the Property Pages dialog box when you are done.

Now you must create a second image list to hold the enabled button images.

TASK 5: TO ADD A SECOND IMAGE LIST CONTROL

1 Double-click the image list icon 🗗 in the Toolbox window to add a second image list to the project. If it covers your first image list, move it off to the side.

2 Name the second image list **ilEnabled**.

3 Using the steps in Task 4, add the images in Table 12.4 (in this order shown) to the list.

Table 12.4

Image Number	Image Name
1	**back.bmp**
2	**forward.bmp**
3	**stop.bmp**
4	**refresh.bmp**
5	**home.bmp**

4 Click ____OK____ to close the Property Pages dialog box when you're done, and save the project.

Adding Images to the Toolbar Buttons

To use the images in the image list controls with your toolbar, you will need to associate the image list controls with the toolbar. This is done with the toolbar's **ImageList property**. You set this property from the toolbar's Property Pages dialog box.

TASK 6: TO ADD IMAGES TO THE TOOLBAR BUTTONS

1 Right-click the toolbar and choose *Properties*. On the *General* page of the Property Pages dialog box, choose *ilDisabled* from the drop-down list next to *ImageList* (Figure 12.15).

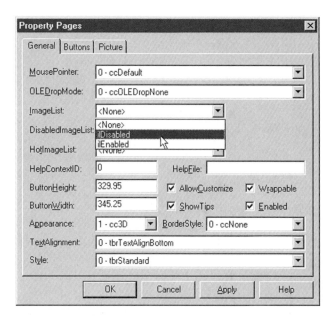

Figure 12.15 Once you have an image list control, you can tell the toolbar to use it for its images.

2 Choose *ilDisabled* from the drop-down list next to *DisabledImageList*.

3 Choose *ilEnabled* from the drop-down list next to *HotImageList*.

4 Choose *1 - tbrFlat* from the drop-down list next to *Style*.
This will give your toolbar a nice Microsoft Office-style flat toolbar.

5 Navigate to the *Buttons* page and change the *Image* value for Button 1 to **1** and click ⌊ Apply ⌋.
As shown in Figure 12.16, the disabled back arrow image will appear on the first toolbar button. This is because you've associated the first toolbar button (Button 1) to the first image in the image list (Image 1).

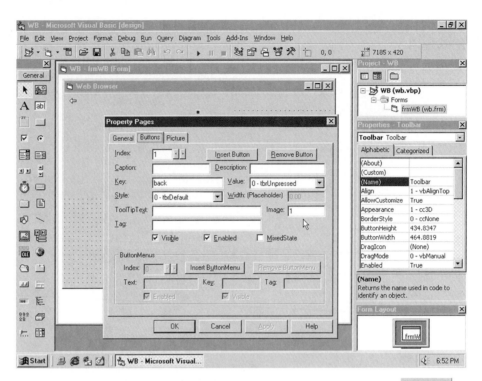

Figure 12.16 As you add images to the toolbar buttons, you can click `Apply` **to make sure you're using the right images.**

6 Using the preceding steps and Table 12.5 as a guide, change the *Image* value for each button to the appropriate value (note that you can use the right arrow button next to the *Index* value to navigate to each button). When you're done, the screen should resemble Figure 12.17.

Table 12.5

Button	Image Value
2	2
3	3
4	4
5	5

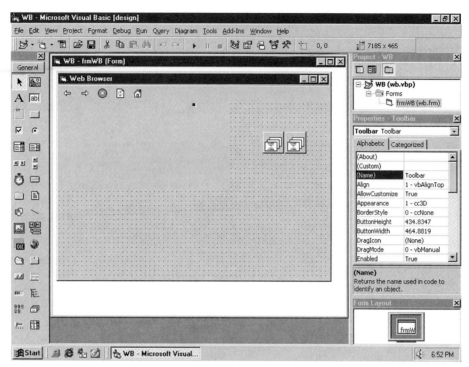

Figure 12.17 The completed toolbar should include all five disabled button images.

7 Click OK to close the Property Pages dialog box, and save the project.

8 Run the program, moving the mouse cursor over the toolbar buttons. Notice how they become "enabled" as you move the cursor over them, as shown in Figure 12.18. But notice that there's a small problem: Because the height of the toolbar changed when you added the images, the top of the WebBrowser control now sticks under the toolbar a bit.

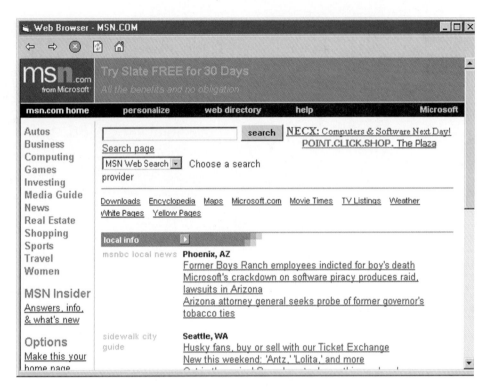

Figure 12.18 Behold the professional Office-like toolbar!

9 Stop the program and examine the *Height* property of the toolbar. (In the case of the system used to create the project, this value is 465.)

10 Change the *Top* property of WebBrowser so that it is equal to the height of the toolbar + 1 (466, in this case), and save the project.

Programming the Toolbar Buttons

Now that you have a wonderful-looking toolbar, it's time to add some browser functionality to it. To do this, you simply have to handle the ***ButtonClick event*** for the toolbar (which occurs when any toolbar button is clicked), figure out which button was clicked, and call the appropriate WebBrowser control method. For example, when you press the *Back* button, your browser should navigate to the previous document.

Let's add this functionality now, using those *Key* values we added to the buttons earlier. The *ButtonClick* event-handler looks like this:

```
Private Sub Toolbar_ButtonClick(ByVal Button As MSComctlLib.Button)

End Sub
```

The Button parameter passes the button that was pressed to the procedure, so we can use a Select Case statement to determine which button we're dealing with. Since it might be hard to maintain a list of buttons by number, we'll use the *Key* property to make our Select Case block easier to read.

TASK 7: TO PROGRAM THE TOOLBAR BUTTONS

1 In the Visual Basic IDE, double-click the toolbar to bring up the Code window. It should display an empty ButtonClick procedure by default. Add the following code to this procedure after the existing first line:

Select Case Button.Key

   Case "back"

      WB.GoBack

   Case "forward"

      WB.GoForward

   Case "stop"

      WB.Stop

   Case "refresh"

      WB.Refresh

   Case "home"

      WB.GoHome

End Select

2 Save the project and run the program. Test the functionality of the buttons and... oops!
As shown in Figure 12.19, there's a problem if you try to go back (or forward) when there is no previous (or next) document.

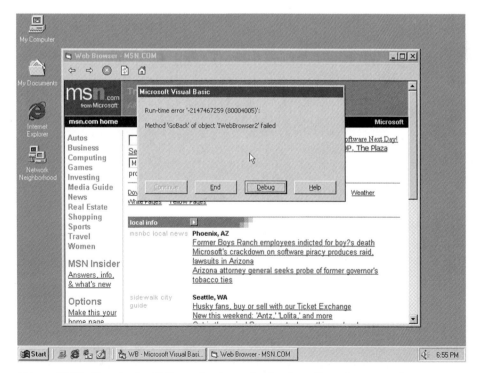

Figure 12.19 Abort, abort! If you try to go back when there is no previous document, you'll get an error.

3 Close the program and return to the Visual Basic IDE.

Handling Errors

There is an elegant way to determine whether the back or forward button can be clicked, and we will implement that in the next project. For now, you can simply handle the error and prevent the error message dialog box from appearing. To do this, you must use Visual Basic's **On Error statement**. On Error is used to specify what to do when an error occurs in a procedure. You can redirect the code to an error-handling routine elsewhere in the procedure or simply tell Visual Basic to ignore the error. We will use the latter approach. Then if the user clicks the *Back* button and there is no previous document to navigate back to, the browser should simply do nothing.

To implement this functionality, you will need to add the following as the first line of code in the ButtonClick procedure:

On Error Resume Next

This tells Visual Basic to simply resume code execution at the next line of code should it encounter an error, thus keeping the program running. In Project 13, we will look more closely at On Error, examine some of its other options, and develop a more elegant solution to this problem. For now, let's handle the error in the ButtonClick procedure.

TASK 8: TO HANDLE ERRORS IN THE BUTTONCLICK PROCEDURE

1 Double-click the toolbar to open the Code window.

2 Add the following line of code as the first line in the procedure, directly above the Select Case statement:

On Error Resume Next

3 Close the Code window, save the project, and run the program. You shouldn't see any more error messages.

The Conclusion

Your little Web browser has come a long way, with a nice working toolbar that supports mouse-overs and the expected browser functionality. In the next project, you will further refine the browser with the addition of a full-featured address bar. Additionally, you will code the browser to more elegantly handle the Go Back and Go Forward functionality. You will also work with new controls, including the coolbar, the drop-down combo box, and the status bar.

Summary and Exercises

Summary

- Most professional Windows applications supply a toolbar with buttons that act as shortcuts to commonly used functions.
- Buttons on a toolbar are contained in a Buttons collection.
- An image list control can hold numerous images that are accessed by their position in a collection or by their *Key* name.
- Image lists can be associated with toolbars to provide graphics for the toolbar buttons.
- A single *ButtonClick* event-handler handles all of the buttons on a toolbar.
- The On Error statement is used to trap errors so that the user doesn't see an error dialog.

Key Terms and Operations

Key Terms	Operations
Button object	add buttons to a toolbar
ButtonClick event	add images to an image list
Buttons collection	associate an image list with a toolbar
collection	handle errors with the On Error
Height property	statement
image list control	program browser functionality
ImageList property	program toolbar buttons
Key property	use a toolbar
member	use an image list control
On Error statement	use collections
Property Pages	
toolbar	
toolbar control	
Top property	

Study Questions

Multiple Choice

1. The toolbar control is found in which component?
   a. The standard toolbox control list
   b. Microsoft Windows Common Controls 6.0
   c. Microsoft Windows Common Controls-3 6.0
   d. Microsoft Internet Controls

2. Each button on a toolbar is a
   a. Button object.
   b. command button.
   c. TabStrip control.
   d. member of the CommandButton collection.

3. A collection is
  a. the same as an array.
  b. a list of identical objects.
  c. a named list of objects.
  d. a series of related events.

4. Objects in a collection are referred to as collection
  a. indices.
  b. items.
  c. properties.
  d. members.

5. The Buttons collection is a collection of the
  a. command buttons in a frame or form container.
  b. *Key* values of a toolbar.
  c. buttons in a toolbar.
  d. images that can be used with toolbar buttons.

6. An image list control is used when you
  a. need to work with many images.
  b. need to work with a single image.
  c. want to add audio capabilities to your program.
  d. want to place images in a list box.

7. To determine which button on a toolbar was clicked, use the _____ event-handler.
  a. *Click*
  b. *OnClick*
  c. *ButtonClick*
  d. *WhichButton*

8. The On Error statement is used to
  a. simply skip over errors.
  b. simply redirect the code to an error-handler when an error occurs.
  c. specify what to do should an error occur.
  d. do none of the above.

True/False

1. The buttons in a toolbar are considered controls.

2. Toolbar buttons are references to Button objects.

3. Toolbars align with the left edge of the form by default.

4. A collection is the same thing as an array.

5. The *Key* property of a Button object allows you to assign the button a unique value that effectively "names" the button.

6. The image list control displays a group of images in a list box.

7. *On Error Resume Next* allows you to skip to the next error.

Short Answer

1. What can each button on a toolbar contain?

2. How do you access the properties of the individual buttons on a toolbar from the Visual Basic IDE?

3. Where does a toolbar align itself by default?

4. How is a collection different from an array?

5. Why would you want to utilize the *Key* properties in a collection?

6. When would you use an image list control instead of an image control?

7. Do Button objects have their own *Click* events?

8. What does *On Error Resume Next* do?

Group Discussion

1. It may seem odd that you can't directly access individual *Click* events for each button in a toolbar. Microsoft did this for a simple reason: The toolbar is the control; the buttons are a *feature* of that kind of control; and only a control can handle events. Should Microsoft have implemented the toolbar as a simple container instead and allowed programmers to add command buttons to create toolbars? Why or why not? (*Note*: Before the toolbar control existed, programmers had to emulate a toolbar using many command buttons sitting on a panel control.)

2. The ability to basically skip over errors with On Error introduces an interesting problem for the programmer. When one is testing a program and error dialogs are being generated, it is sometimes tempting to just add this line of code to the beginning of every procedure to prevent error dialogs from ever appearing. Is this a good idea? Why or why not?

Hands-On

Toolbar design
Break out your copy of Microsoft Word and examine one of its many toolbars. Think about the different elements that are there and try to determine how you might create a duplicate of that toolbar in Visual Basic. Look through the Property Pages of a toolbar in VB to determine some of the more difficult controls that are added, such as drop-down lists. How does Microsoft add this functionality?

On Your Own

1. Working with toolbars
Create a new project and add a toolbar with five buttons. Assign unique *Key* values to each button. The buttons should have the captions shown in Table 12.6.

Table 12.6

Button	Caption
1	**Height**
2	**Width**
3	**Top**
4	**Left**
5	**Caption**

Handle the *ButtonClick* event of the toolbar so that clicking each button displays a message box indicating the text value of the form property indicated by the button caption. The caption in the title bar of the message box should display the caption of the button as well. For example, if the user clicks the first button, the message box titled "Height" should display the height of the form window as the message text along with an [OK] button.

> **Tip** The MsgBox function was discussed in the On Your Own section of Project 11. If you're not familiar with this powerful and useful function, refer to the MSDN Library for details.

2. Advanced FTP browser

Using the FTP browser from the Hands-On and On Your Own exercises in Project 11 as a starting point, add a quick-link toolbar to the program. The toolbar should contain buttons with text aligned to the right so that the button captions appear next to, not below, the images. Use the same image for each button and assign the buttons the functionality shown below in Table 12.7.

Table 12.7

Button number	Navigate to	Caption	Key
1	ftp://ftp.microsoft.com	**Microsoft**	**microsoft**
2	ftp://ftp.netscape.com	**Netscape**	**netscape**
3	ftp://ftp.cdrom.com	**Walnut Creek**	**cdrom**

For example, if the user clicks the first button, the WebBrowser control will navigate to the Microsoft FTP site.

3. A more radical Web browser

Create a version of the Web browser that uses a wildly different color scheme and look, perhaps red and gray on black. Create your own toolbar button graphics that emphasize the look of your new browser. The idea is to move as far away as possible from the standard dull gray look and feel of Windows so that your browser is truly a unique—but still usable—experience. Make sure that each image you create for your image lists and toolbars are the exact same size. You can also experiment with different toolbar button styles so that the graphics you create—which could resemble nonrectangular shapes—form the visual boundaries of your buttons.

13

Fine-Tuning the Web Browser

Objectives

After completing this project, you will be able to:

> ➤ Handle the WebBrowser control's *CommandStateChange* event to properly handle GoBack and GoForward

> ➤ Add button captions and tooltips to a toolbar

> ➤ Use controls within a coolbar control

> ➤ Use the combo box control

> ➤ Add address bar functionality to the Web browser project

> ➤ Use the status bar control

> ➤ Change the project icon

The Challenge

In the two previous projects you created a fine foundation for a simple Web browser. In this project, you will finish implementing the specifications for this program. You will create an address bar and a status bar, which will provide download progress feedback. And you will fine-tune the GoBack and GoForward functionality of the browser's toolbar so that those buttons become properly enabled and disabled.

The Solution

This project will complete the specifications as outlined in Project 11. Specifically, the following features will be added:

4   Add the following code to this event-handler:

Select Case Command
    Case 1
        ' The forward button's state has changed
        Toolbar.Buttons(2).Enabled = Enable
    Case 2
        ' The back button's state has changed
        Toolbar.Buttons(1).Enabled = Enable
End Select

This sets the *Back* and *Forward* buttons' *Enabled* properties to the same value as the Enable parameter that is passed when the event fires.

5   Save the project and run the program.
Once the home page has loaded, you should notice that the *Forward* and *Back* buttons are disabled, so that they cannot be clicked. However, they will become enabled—and disabled—as needed as you use the browser.

6   When you are done testing the browser, close the program and return to the Visual Basic IDE.

Adding Other Toolbar Button Features

Before moving on to the address bar, let's make some small changes to the toolbar buttons that will make them more closely resemble the buttons used by Internet Explorer and Navigator: button captions and tooltips. For example, the *Back* button should have a caption of **Back** and a tooltip, perhaps saying "**Navigate to the previous document.**" In the following steps, you will add these features to each of the toolbar buttons.

TASK 2: TO ADD ADDITIONAL TOOLBAR BUTTON FEATURES

1   Right-click the toolbar button and choose *Properties*.
The Property Pages dialog box for the toolbar will appear.

2   On the *General* page, ensure that the *TextAlignment* option is set to **0 - tbrTextAlignBottom**.

3   Navigate to the *Buttons* page and use the following table to add button captions and tooltips using the *Caption* and *ToolTipText* options, respectively, for each button:

Table 13.1

Button	Caption	ToolTipText
1	**Back**	**Navigate to the previous document**
2	**Forward**	**Navigate to the next document**
3	**Stop**	**Stop downloading**
4	**Refresh**	**Reload the current document**
5	**Home**	**Return to the home page**

When you're done, close the Property Pages dialog box. The screen should resemble Figure 13.2. Notice that because the height of the toolbar has changed, you will need to adjust the *Top* property of WebBrowser yet again (touchy, isn't it?).

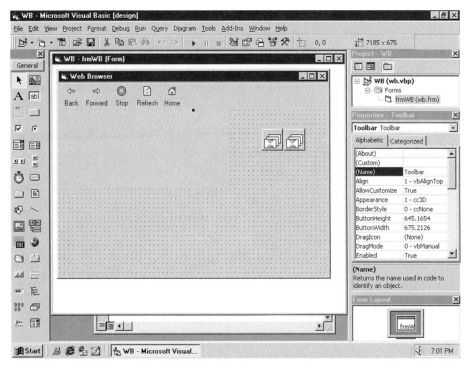

Figure 13.2 That's what we want: a nice, browser-like toolbar.

4 Note the value of the *Height* property for the toolbar (on this system, 675).

5 Change the value of the WebBrowser's *Top* to **WebBrowser.Height + 1** (676 in this case.

6 Save the project and run the program, testing the toolbar buttons and the reaction of the WebBrowser control to the resizing of the form window. All should be working properly at this point.

7 When you're done testing, close the program and return to the Visual Basic IDE.

Adding the Address Bar

Web browsers typically include an *address bar* (called a *location bar* by Netscape browsers) that displays the Web address of the current Web site. The Web address, also known as a **URL** or **Uniform Resource Locator,** is similar to your street address in that each address is unique, ensuring that no two sites use the same address. Most Web addresses begin with the odd prefix http:// (other prefixes include ftp:// for FTP sites and file:// for files on your local system), but modern browsers (including the IE Web-Browser control we're using) will fill in that part if the user leaves it out.

> **Web Tip** In fact, modern browsers will fill in most of a URL if you just know the important part. Consider the URL http://www.microsoft.com: If you just type **microsoft** into the address bar of Internet Explorer or Netscape Navigator, it will load the Microsoft Web site found at http://www.microsoft.com.

In addition to providing a place to view the sometimes cryptic Web address of the current site, most address bars provide a drop-down list so that users can easily return to a site already visited. Also, when the user types in a Web address and presses (ENTER), the browser should be able to load that page. To encompass all of this functionality in our own Web browser, we will need to use the *combo box control*. The combo box is a combination of a text box, which allows user-entered text, and a drop-down list box, which presents a list of items to the user. Technically, the control we're creating here is a drop-down combo box, which is essentially a combo box that only displays one line of text at a time, offering the rest of the list items (Web addresses in our case) when the user clicks a down-arrow on the control.

Using a Coolbar Control

Before we can add our address bar, however, we need to create a container for it. Typically, the address bar occupies its own area—below a browser's toolbar and above the document that is displayed by the browser. There are three ways we could add the address bar to our Web browser program: We could add it directly to the form; we could add a second toolbar that would sit below the first toolbar; or we could add it to a *coolbar*, which is a special kind of toolbar introduced with Internet Explorer 3.0. Coolbars typically consist of one or more segments, called *bands*, that can be resized and reshuffled as the user likes. If you've used newer versions of Internet Explorer, you've used coolbars.

There is one simple reason not to use the combo box directly on the form or as part of a standard toolbar: the size of the address bar would have to be manually adjusted every time the user changed the width of the browser window. In the case of the coolbar, however, we can set up the combo box to automatically resize itself with the coolbar, which would itself automatically resize itself with the form. The less work, the better: Let's use a coolbar.

By default, any coolbar you add to a Visual Basic project has three bands. Since we will only need one band, after adding the coolbar we will remove two of the bands.

TASK 3: TO ADD A COOLBAR TO THE WEB BROWSER

1 Select *Components* from the *Project* menu.
The Components dialog box will appear.

2 Navigate to *Microsoft Windows Common Controls-3 6.0*. Check this option and click the ___OK___ button.
This adds the coolbar control to the project.

3 Double-click the coolbar icon in the Toolbox window to add a new coolbar to the center of the form.
Notice that it has three bands, as shown in Figure 13.3.

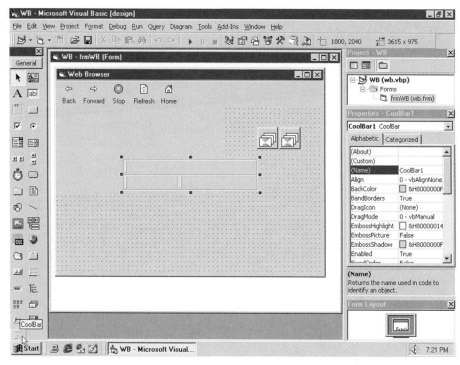

Figure 13.3 The default coolbar is not aligned to an edge of the form and consists of three bands.

4 Change the (*Name*) property of the coolbar to **coolAddress**.

5 Right-click the coolbar and choose *Properties*.
The Property Pages dialog box will appear.

6 On the *Bands* page, delete two of the bands. You can do this by clicking the *Remove Band* button twice.

7 In the Caption option box, type **Address** and then close the Property Pages dialog box by clicking the ___OK___ button.

8 Change the coolbar's *Align* property to **1 - vbAlignTop** to align the coolbar with the top of the form.
The screen should resemble Figure 13.4.

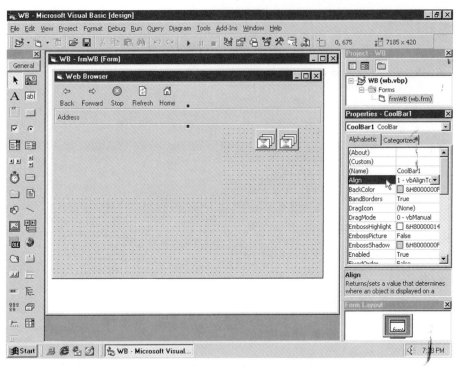

Figure 13.4 Now all we have to do is add the address bar to the coolbar.

Now we want to add the combo box and paste it into the coolbar so that the coolbar, rather than the form, becomes the container of the combo box. This allows us to use a special functionality of the coolbar to automatically size the combo box to fit within the coolbar.

TASK 4: TO ADD A COMBO BOX TO THE COOLBAR

1 Locate the combo box icon 🔲 in the Toolbox window.

2 Double-click the combo box icon 🔲 to add a new combo box to the center of the form window.

3 Change its (*Name*) property to **cmboAddress** and its *Text* property to an empty string.

4 Right-click the combo box and choose *Cut* from the pop-up menu.

5 Right-click the coolbar and choose *Paste* from the pop-up menu.
The combo box will appear within the coolbar, as shown in Figure 13.5.

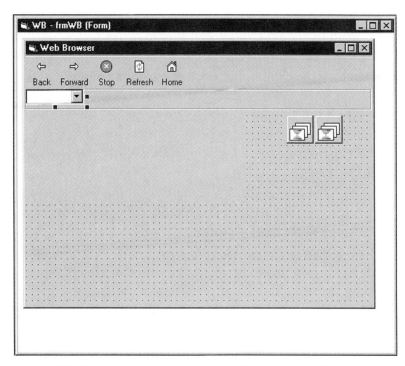

Figure 13.5 It isn't pretty yet, but the coolbar now contains the combo box.

6 Right-click the coolbar and choose *Properties*.

7 Navigate to the *Bands* page, choose **cmboAddress** from the *Child* drop-down list box, and click OK.
The screen should resemble Figure 13.6. Notice that the combo box now fits the exact size of the coolbar.

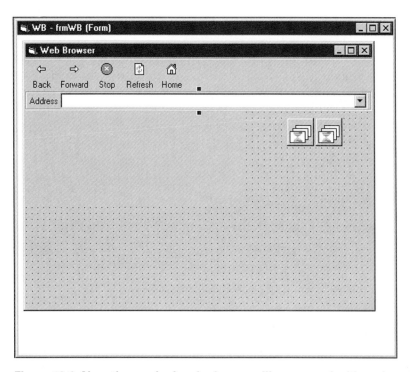

Figure 13.6 Now the combo box looks more like a normal address bar.

8 Save the project and run the program, testing to see how the address bar reacts to resizing the window. It should resize automatically to match the width of the browser window.

9 When you're done testing, close the program and return to the Visual Basic IDE.

Once again, the position of the WebBrowser control has been usurped by the addition of another control, in this case, the new coolbar control. In the following steps, you will fix this.

TASK 5: TO RESIZE THE WEBBROWSER CONTROL PROPERLY

1 Double-click a blank area of the form and examine the Form_Resize procedure in the Code window.

2 Change the line of code that currently reads
WB.Height = frmWB.ScaleHeight - Toolbar.Height
to

WB.Height = frmWB.ScaleHeight - Toolbar.Height - _

    coolAddress.Height

This accounts for the height of the coolbar.

3 Add the height of the toolbar (675 on this system) and the height of the coolbar (375) to arrive at a total (**1050**). Change the *Top* property of the WebBrowser control to this value.

4 Save the project, and run and test the program.

5 Quit the program and return to the Visual Basic IDE when you are done.

Programming the Address Bar

Now that we've got a decent-looking address bar, the next obvious step is to enable it to record the URL of the currently loaded document. This is easy enough: All we need to do is use the WebBrowser control's *LocationURL property*, which records this value, and copy it into the combo box's *Text property*. The obvious time to do this is in the event-handler for the Web Browser's *TitleChange* event, since we are already handling this event.

TASK 6: TO DISPLAY THE CURRENT URL IN THE ADDRESS BAR

1 Double-click the WebBrowser control to open the Code window.

2 Navigate to the *WB_TitleChange* event-handler and add the following line of code below the code that is already present there:

cmboAddress.Text = WB.LocationURL

3 Close the Code window and save the project.

4 Run the program, noting that the address bar displays the address of the current document (Figure 13.7).

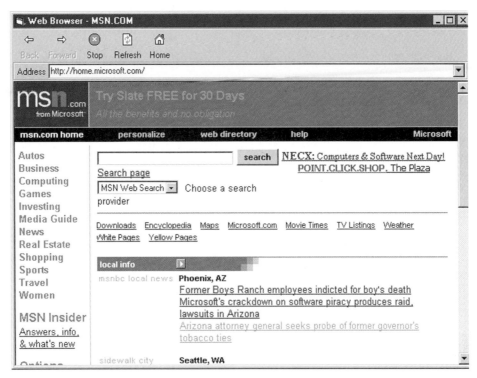

Figure 13.7 The current URL is displayed in the address bar.

5   Quit the program when you are done and return to the Visual Basic IDE.

Recording Previously Visited Addresses

The next step is to program the address bar to store the URLs of every Web site the user has browsed to in the current session (that is, while the program has been running). We could simply add the URL of the current Web site to the address bar every time a page download completed, but that would result in repeated entries every time the user returned to a site. Instead, we should check to see if the current address is in the list of items in the address bar. If it is, we won't add it to the list again; otherwise, we will add it.

The WebBrowser control has an obvious event we can handle for this purpose—the ***DownloadComplete event***. This event fires whenever a Web page is completely downloaded, either when the page does indeed fully download or when the user halts the site download by clicking the *Stop* button.

In the following steps, you will write code that handles this event and adds addresses to the list of URLs held by the address bar.

TASK 7: TO ADD THE CURRENT ADDRESS TO THE ADDRESS BAR'S ADDRESS LIST

1   Double-click the WebBrowser control on the form to open the Code window.

2   Using the *Procedure* drop-down list, choose the *DownloadComplete* event-handler.

3   Add the following code to this event-handler:

```
Dim x As Integer
Dim AddressExists As Boolean
AddressExists = False
For x = 0 To cmboAddress.ListCount
    If cmboAddress.Text = cmboAddress.List(x) Then
        AddressExists = True
        Exit For
    End If
Next
If AddressExists = False Then
    cmboAddress.AddItem WB.LocationURL
End If
```

4   Save the project and run the program, navigating to as many sites as possible. Notice that the address of each site is added to the combo box's drop-down list (Figure 13.8). In fact, you can select an address from the list and make it appear as the text in the combo box. Of course, we haven't added any "go to" functionality yet to make it possible to navigate to that address; that's coming in the next section.

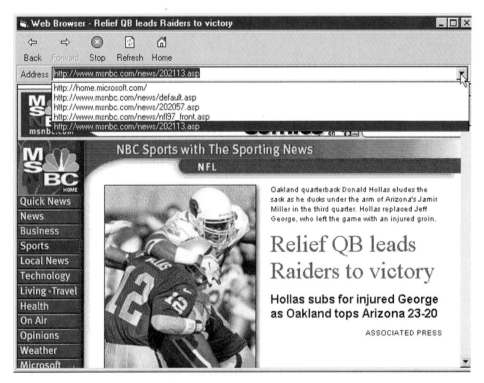

Figure 13.8 After navigating to a few sites, you will see how the combo box list fills up.

5   Close the program when you are done and return to the Visual Basic IDE.

Adding "Go To" Functionality

For the final bit of address bar functionality, we will add the ability for the user to type in an address, press (ENTER), and have the browser attempt to load that address. In addition, the user should be able to select a previously visited address from the address bar drop-down list, press (ENTER), and have the browser reload that page. This is similar to the code we wrote in the *Hello, world!* project in Part One, where a test was made for a particular key press, in this case the (ENTER) key. We can add the same functionality here by using the ***Navigate method*** of the WebBrowser control, which navigates to the URL it is given. We'll use the *Navigate* method to navigate to the URL specified in the address bar.

TASK 8: TO ADD "GO TO" FUNCTIONALITY TO THE ADDRESS BAR

1   Double-click the address bar combo box to display the Code window.

2   Choose *KeyPress* from the *Procedure* drop-down list box to add an event-handler for the *KeyPress* event.

3   Add the following code to this procedure:

If KeyAscii = 13 Then

  If cmboAddress.Text <> "" Then

    WB.Navigate (cmboAddress.Text)

  End If

End If

4   Save the project and run the program. Test the functionality of your Web browser by typing several known URLs into the address bar and pressing (ENTER) after each (Figure 13.9). Also, when you've navigated to enough sites, choose a site from the address bar's drop-down list and press (ENTER) to reload that page.

Figure 13.9 Now the address bar is complete.

5 When you're done testing, close the program and return to the Visual Basic IDE.

Adding a Status Bar

Most Windows programs, including office applications such as Microsoft Word and system tools such as My Computer, offer a ***status bar*** that sits at the bottom of the window displaying data. The ***status data*** displayed in a status bar is application-dependent. For example, the status bar in Microsoft Word displays the current page and cursor location, as well as a host of other information for creating documents. On the other hand, a My Computer status bar may display the size of the currently selected hard drive or a count of the number of currently selected objects.

In our Web browser application, we will use the status bar to provide a visual progress indication to show the state of the current download. That way, while a page is still downloading it will be obvious that the browser is doing something. When a page is completely downloaded, however, the status bar will display a "Ready" message.

Status bars consist of one or more ***panel objects***, which can contain text and/or graphics. For our purposes, a simple one-panel status bar will be sufficient. The Visual Basic status bar supports a special one-panel mode that is enabled by its ***Style property***. Setting *Style* to sbrNormal gives you a typical multipanel status bar; setting *Style* to sbrSimple gives you a simpler, one-panel status bar. You can then set the text display of the status bar with the **SimpleText property**.

In the following steps, you will add a simple status bar to the Web browser.

TASK 9: TO ADD A STATUS BAR TO THE WEB BROWSER

1 Locate the StatusBar icon ⬚ in the Visual Basic Toolbox window. (This control is added with *Microsoft Windows Common Controls 6.0.*)

2 Double-click the StatusBar icon ⬚ to add a new status bar to the form window.
By default, the status bar will appear aligned with the bottom of the windows, as shown in Figure 13.10.

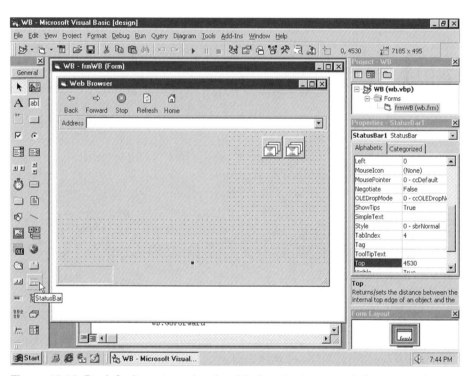

Figure 13.10 By default, a status bar is added to the bottom of the current form window.

3 Resize the status bar a bit so that it is not so tall. (The default status bar in Visual Basic is about one grid line too tall for some reason.)

4 Change the (*Name*) property to **Status**.

5 Change the *Style* property to **1 - sbrSimple**.

6 Save the project and run the program.
Once again, the WebBrowser control needs to be resized because we've added another control to the form's surface.

7 Close the program and change the last line of code in Form_Resize to the following:

WB.Height = frmWB.ScaleHeight - Toolbar.Height _

- coolAddress.Height - Status.Height

8 Save and test the project. When you're done, close the program and return to the Visual Basic IDE.

Programming the Status Bar

Now that we've got a decent-looking status bar that seems to work well with the rest of the controls on the form, we'll need to add code that will update the text in the status bar to provide status information about the current download. This will require three code additions. First of all, when the browser begins downloading, we will set the *SimpleText* property of the status bar to a blank string (""). When the download is complete, we will display the text "Ready." The interesting part, however, occurs *while* the browser is downloading a page.

The WebBrowser control supports a ***ProgressChange event*** that fires as a Web page is downloaded. More specifically, this event occurs when the progress of a download is updated, so it can fire multiple times during a page download. The longer the download, the more times it fires. The code we'll be adding will simply check to see what the text in the status bar is. If it's the "Ready" text, then it will do nothing. Otherwise, it will append a plus ("+") character to the end of the text that is already displayed there. Since only the plus character can be written to the status bar while a page is downloading, the user will see a group of plus signs ("+++++") as a page downloads. When the download is complete, the user will see the "Ready" message.

In the following steps, you will add this progress functionality.

TASK 10: TO ADD PROGRESS FUNCTIONALITY TO THE STATUS BAR

1 Double-click the WebBrowser control to open the Code window.

2 Choose *DownloadBegin* from the *Procedure* drop-down list and add the following line of code to that procedure:

Status.SimpleText = ""

3 Locate the *WB_DownloadComplete* event-handler and add the following line of code as the last line in the procedure:

Status.SimpleText = "Ready"

4 Choose *ProgressChange* from the *Procedure* drop-down list and add the following code to this procedure:

If Status.SimpleText <> "Ready" Then

    Status.SimpleText = Status.SimpleText & "+"

End If

5 Run the program and observe the status bar as documents load into the browser. Notice that a line of plus signs appears during long downloads (Figure 13.11) and that the "Ready" text appears when downloads are complete.

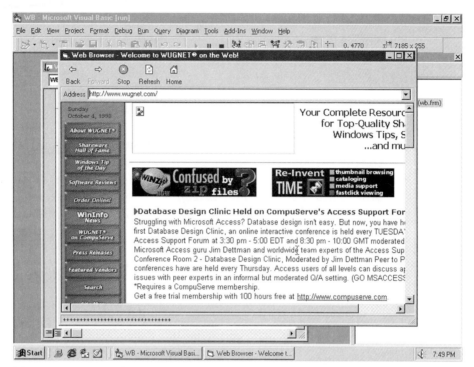

Figure 13.11 Now the user has a visual cue that the browser is doing something.

Changing the Project Icon

You've probably noticed by now that the same default icon has been used for all of the projects we've created so far. (If you haven't, look for the icon in the far left of the form window's title bar and in the taskbar button for the program while it's running.) In the following steps, you will change the icon used for the form window and for the project itself using the *Icon property*.

TASK 11: TO CHANGE THE PROJECT ICON

1 Select the form window and then locate the *Icon* property in the Properties window.

2 Double-click the *Icon* property to display the Load Icon dialog box. Navigate to the **Entirnet.ico** file, which by default is located in C:\Program Files\Microsoft Visual Studio\Common\Graphics\Icons\Win95 (if not, ask your instructor or lab assistant for the location of this file).

3 Select *Entirnet.ico* and click Open to choose this icon. The icon for the form will change.

4   Select *WB Properties* from the *Project* menu to display the Project Properties dialog box.

5   In the *Make* page, choose *frmWB* for the *Icon* option. Click `OK` to apply the choice.

6   Save the project.

The Conclusion

Well done! Microsoft and Netscape Communications may have nothing to fear from your entry into the browser wars, but you must admit that the possibilities presented by the WebBrowser control are almost limitless. Microsoft's decision to make its Web browser available as an ActiveX control was a major coup for developers, and it's only a matter of time before a host of third parties and private developers release their own personal versions of Internet Explorer. In fact, you can find a really cool example of this at the NeoPlanet Web site (http://www.neoplanet.com/). Now that's something to work toward, but there's no reason *you* couldn't create it in Visual Basic. You have the skills. Go for it!

Summary and Exercises

Summary

- The WebBrowser control's *CommandStateChange* event-handler handles the event that occurs when the state of the GoBack and GoForward functions change.
- The combo box is a combination of a text box and a drop-down list box.
- The coolbar is a new kind of toolbar that was introduced with Internet Explorer 3.0.
- Coolbar segments are called bands.
- You can add a control to each coolbar band and it will automatically size to match the size of the band.
- The WebBrowser's *Navigate* method navigates to a URL that is passed to the method.
- A status bar control is used to display status data. It generally aligns with the bottom of a window.

Key Terms and Operations

Key Terms

band
combo box control
Command argument
CommandStateChange event
coolbar
DownloadComplete event
Enable argument
Icon property
LocationURL property
Navigate method
panel object
ProgressChange event
SimpleText property
status bar
status data
Style property
Text property
Uniform Resource Locator (URL)

Operations

add captions and tooltips to toolbar buttons
change the icon for a form
change the icon for the project
copy text into a combo box's list
disable and enable the *Back* and *Forward* buttons
handle the *CommandStateChange* event
use the coolbar control
use the drop-down combo box control
use the *Navigate* method to browse Web addresses
use the status bar to display progress data

Study Questions

Multiple Choice

1. The *CommandStateChange* event concerns itself with which two browser functions?
   a. GoBack and Stop
   b. Stop and Refresh
   c. GoBack and GoForward
   d. GoHome and Refresh

2. Which WebBrowser control method would you call to return to the previous document?
   a. *Navigate*
   b. *GoHome*
   c. *PreviousURL*
   d. *GoBack*

3. URL stands for
   a. Uniform Resource Locator
   b. Uniform Resource Location
   c. Uninformed Resource Locator
   d. Untitled Resource Location

4. A coolbar is a new type of
   a. window dressing.
   b. title bar.
   c. combo box.
   d. toolbar.

5. Coolbar segments are called
   a. bands.
   b. rebars.
   c. sections.
   d. panels.

6. Text is displayed on a simple status bar
   a. with the *Text* property of the Panel object.
   b. with the status bar's *SimpleText* property.
   c. with the status bar's *Text* property.
   d. with the status bar's *Caption* property.

7. The sections in a status bar are known as
   a. segments.
   b. bands
   c. panels.
   d. sections.

8. The captions of toolbar buttons are set from
   a. the Properties window.
   b. the Property Pages for the Button objects.
   c. the Property Pages for the toolbar.
   d. the Property Pages for the form window.

True/False

1. The *CommandStateChange* event tells the WebBrowser control that it is now possible for the user to refresh the current page.

2. Button captions are added from the Property Pages of the Toolbar control.

3. A combo box provides the features of both a text box and a drop-down list box.

4. The coolbar control replaces the toolbar control.

5. Coolbar segments are called sections.

6. The location of the current document in a WebBrowser control is contained by its *LocationURL* property.

7. The *DownloadDone* event fires whenever a Web page is completely downloaded.

8. A status bar is used to alert the user, like a dialog box.

Short Answer

1. If it becomes possible for the browser to "go back," what values will be passed to the *CommandStateChange* event-handler through its Command and Enable parameters?

2. Which WebBrowser method allows you to download a particular Web page?

3. Which control combines the features of a drop-down list box and a text box?

4. How do you remove bands from a coolbar in the Visual Basic IDE?

5. Which WebBrowser method stores the address of the current document?

6. Which WebBrowser method stores the title text of the current document?

7. Which event fires when a Web page has finished downloading?

8. Which property do you change to make a status bar a simple, single-panel status bar?

Group Discussion

1. The Windows user interface marches on: Windows has had a toolbar for some time and Internet Explorer 3.0 introduced the coolbar. But there is now an even newer kind of toolbar available—the *command bar*. Menus and toolbars can be added to command bars, which debuted with Office 97. In fact, the menus and toolbars in Visual Basic are actually implemented with command bars, not coolbars. Sadly, Visual Basic offers no easy way to add command bars to your programs, though you can add them through some pretty complicated code if you'd like. Using the MSDN Library as a reference, explain how command bars work and why they're different from other types of toolbars.

2. Bill Gates once described the Web browser as a "trivial piece of software," but you might agree that this isn't the case. While the IE-based WebBrowser control is amazingly useful, some obvious features—such as a way to access Favorites—are glaringly missing. What other functionality is missing from the WebBrowser control? (*Hint*: Use the MSDN Library for research, while examining Internet Explorer.)

Hands-On

Working with personalization

As discussed in the next project, personalization is an important but often overlooked feature in software design. Users typically take for granted the fact that their application programs remember to open at the same position and size that the user chooses. Browsers such as Internet Explorer also remember to save toolbar settings, such as whether the user chooses to display the Links toolbar. With a complex control such as the coolbar, however, browsers also have to remember how the controls contained by the coolbar are arranged: The user can move, resize, and restack the contents of a coolbar at will. This creates an interesting problem: How do you "know" the positions of the various bands in the coolbar and how would you restore the coolbar to these settings when your program restarts? (*Hint*: Check the MSDN Library for help.)

On Your Own

1. Advanced coolbar use

The toolbar in Internet Explorer 4.0 is housed along with the address bar and menu in a coolbar control with various bands. In this exercise, you will move the toolbar into the coolbar so that you can position and size the toolbar and address bar as you can with Internet Explorer. This will require some careful cutting and pasting, so be sure to back up the files in your Web browser project before attempting this.

Here are the steps in simple terms:

- Change the *Align* property of the toolbar to **none** and move the toolbar to the center of the form.

- Cut the address bar combo box and paste it onto the form. Resize it so that it is less wide.

- Delete coolAddress and create a new coolbar. Name it coolAddress and remove the third band. Align the coolbar with the top of the form.

- Cut the address bar again and paste it onto the coolbar as you did earlier in this project. On the *Bands* page of the coolbar's Property Pages, set the *Child* property to the combo box.

- Cut the toolbar and paste it onto the coolbar. On the *Bands* page of the coolbar's Property Pages, set the *Child* property to the toolbar. Change the toolbar's *Appearance* property to **flat**.

If all goes well, you should have a functioning coolbar toolbar (so to speak). There is one problem, however: when you resize the coolbar, the WebBrowser component isn't sized correctly and its *Top* property is wrong! Now, how would you go about fixing *that*?

2. Preventing an address bar overflow

If you use the Web browser you've created for a long time and browse to numerous Web sites, the address bar is going to fill up pretty quickly. In this exercise, you will limit the address bar to 20 entries. To do this, your program will need to check the number of entries in the combo box before adding a new entry. If there are fewer than 20 entries, the new entry can simply be added as usual. If there are already 20 entries, then the oldest entry will need to be deleted and then the new entry added. (*Hint*: You can get the number of combo box entries by examining the *ListCount* property; the *RemoveItem* method removes an entry. Check the MSDN Library for details.)

3. Creating an advanced status bar

The status bar used in this program provides only a single panel that uses the *SimpleText* property to display status information to the user. But most status bars are more complicated than that and provide multiple panels for status information.

Create a new program and add a status bar control. Use the status bar's Property Pages to add two new panels (for a total of three panels). Set the *AutoSize* property of the third panel to *sbrSpring* so that it automatically fills all of the remaining space on the status bar as the form resizes. The first panel should display the time (check the panel's *Style* property for appropriate values) and the second panel should display the status of the (NUM LOCK) key on the keyboard. Display a text message in the third panel, using the MSDN Library to figure out how that will work.

Personalizing the Web Browser

Objectives

After completing this project, you will be able to:

➤ **Save personalized settings using the Windows Registry**

➤ **Retrieve personalized settings from the Registry**

➤ **Handle the maximized window state**

➤ **Work with a multiband coolbar**

➤ **Create a pop-up menu**

The Challenge

Thus far you have created a simple Web browser that offers some pretty exciting functionality thanks to Microsoft's WebBrowser control. But to be like professional Windows applications your browser should also remember user settings such as the size, shape, and position of the main window. Additionally, the toolbar of your browser should be customizable, and any customizations made should be retained along with the other personalized settings.

The Solution

To personalize your Web browser, the following list of features will be needed:

- The position, height, and width of the Web browser window will be saved when the program quits.

- When the program is started, this information will be retrieved and the Web browser will display in the correct size and in the correct location onscreen.

- A new View menu item will be added to the main menu. This menu will have options to determine whether the toolbar, toolbar button captions, and/or the address bar will be displayed.

- The View menu will also be available as a pop-up menu that appears when the user right-clicks the toolbar or coolbar.

- User-set toolbar configuration options will be saved when the program closes and restored when the program starts.

The Setup

One of the nicest features of a good Windows program is its ability to remember such *personalized settings* as window position and size, toolbar configuration, and the like. There are numerous ways to programmatically save and retrieve this information. In the olden days (when Windows 3.1 still roamed the earth), this type of information was stored in various *INI files*, which are specially formatted text files. In fact, Windows still uses INI files for some things in a nod toward backward compatibility. But Windows 95, 98, and NT, as well as most modern application programs, use a far more elegant way to store and retrieve user settings and other configuration information—the Windows Registry. Let's take a look.

Introducing the Windows Registry

Rather than store important configuration information in simple—and easily erased or ruined—text files, Microsoft created a special kind of database called the *Windows Registry* (or simply the Registry), which is accessible to any program. The Windows Registry is a central repository for various system and application program configuration settings. Windows builds the Registry when your system starts, using other configuration files and auto-detection routines to establish the current state of the Registry.

The structure of the Registry resembles a hierarchical database. Tools such as the Windows Registry Editor (regedit.exe) allow users to view and modify the Registry if desired, as shown in Figure 14.1. This is not recommended however: While it is unlikely, it is nonetheless possible for you to render your system unbootable by messing around in the Registry.

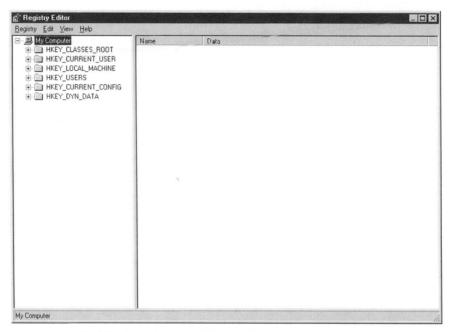

Figure 14.1 The Windows Registry Editor allows you to examine and modify the Registry. But be careful!

Registry keys, such as HKEY_CLASSES_ROOT, establish the top, or *root*, of the hierarchical structure of the Registry. Within these keys are various subkeys that can themselves contain other subkeys. In this way, the structure of the Registry resembles the file system of your system, where the root keys are similar to hard drives and the subkeys are analogous to folders within the hard drives. Folders can contain other folders, just like subkeys in the Registry can contain subkeys (Figure 14.2).

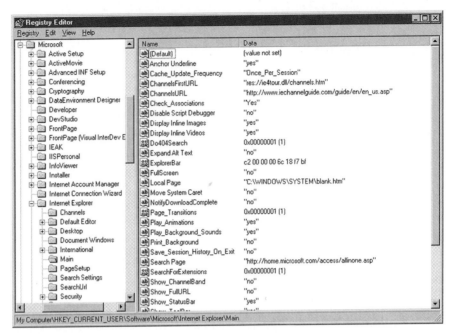

Figure 14.2 The structure of the Registry is similar to the file system of your computer system.

Application programs such as Microsoft Word and Windows store configuration information in the Registry. As a Visual Basic programmer, you can store this kind of information in the Registry as well. In the following sections, we will write code that saves the size and position of the Web browser window to the Registry and then reads it back when the program starts. That way, when users take the time to configure the size and shape of the Web browser, they won't need to do it each time they run the program; the registry will "remember" these settings.

Writing to the Registry

The first step, then, is to write code that will save information to the Registry when the user exits the Web browser program. As you might expect, Visual Basic supplies a form event for this action—the **Form_Unload event**. The Form_Unload event, which occurs when the form window closes, or *unloads*, is, of course, the opposite of Form_Load, which occurs when the form first appears. The form unloads when the user clicks the close window button in the titlebar, or you can cause it to happen programmatically, either with the End statement (if the form is the main form) or with the Unload statement (which we used to close an About Box dialog box).

Accessing the Registry from Visual Basic is disarmingly simple. There are only a handful of functions in the entire Visual Basic language that might be needed, and we'll only be needing two of them: *SaveSetting* and *GetSetting*.

The *SaveSetting function* is used to save a single setting to the Windows Registry and takes the following form:

SaveSetting appname, section, key, setting

The `appname` argument should contain the name of the application, which is wb in our case. The section argument identifies the Registry sub-key where the setting should be stored. The key and setting arguments contain the *name* of the setting (the `key`) and the *value* of the setting (the `setting`).

We will need to store four values initially: the position of the top of the Web browser window, the position of the leftmost edge of the window, the window's width value, and the window's height value. In the following steps, you will add this functionality to the program.

TASK 1: TO WRITE CONFIGURATION DATA TO THE REGISTRY

1   Start Visual Basic and load the Web browser project.

2   Open the Code window and create a new, blank Form_Unload procedure for frmWB.

3   Inside this procedure, add the following code:

SaveSetting "wb", "StartupTop", "StartupTop", frmWB.Top

SaveSetting "wb", "StartupLeft", "StartupLeft", frmWB.Left

SaveSetting "wb", "StartupWidth", "StartupWidth", frmWB.Width

SaveSetting "wb", "StartupHeight", "StartupHeight", frmWB.Height

This will create a key in the Registry for our Web browser application (if it doesn't already exist) with four subkeys and values. We assign the appropriate form properties to the keys with the SaveSetting functions.

4   Right-click on the representation of the form in the Form Layout window and choose *Startup Position* and then *Manual*. This will prevent the Web browser from automatically starting in the center of the screen.

5   Save the project and run the program.
Nothing happens per se, although the values for the form *Top*, *Left*, *Width*, and *Height* properties are written to new keys in the Windows Registry. To test this, we'll need to read these values back from the Registry when the program first starts. We'll tackle that next.

Reading the Registry

The *GetSetting function* reads information from the Registry and takes the following form:

GetSetting(appname, section, key)

The arguments correspond to the same values used with the SaveSetting function. To read back the value of the Web browser window's height, we will use:

```
frmWB.Height = GetSetting("wb", "StartupHeight", "StartupHeight")
```

Notice that we are applying the return value of the GetSetting function to the height of the form. The only question is *when* to do this. We could use the familiar *Form_Load* event-handler, but to ensure that the various properties are set before the form is visible, we will use the handler for the **Form_Initialize event** instead. This event occurs right before the *Load* event, and it's designed for the very reason we're using it—to set initialization data such as form properties. Since we'll be setting the *Top*, *Left*, *Width*, and *Height* values of the form window programmatically, this is the obvious place to do it.

TASK 2: TO READ DATA FROM THE WINDOWS REGISTRY

1 Open the code window and create a new, blank Form_Initialize procedure for frmWB.

2 Inside this procedure, add the following code:

frmWB.Top = GetSetting("wb", "StartupTop", "StartupTop")

frmWB.Left = GetSetting("wb", "StartupLeft", "StartupLeft")

frmWB.Width = GetSetting("wb", "StartupWidth", "StartupWidth")

frmWB.Height = GetSetting("wb", "StartupHeight", "StartupHeight")

3 To test this, size the Web browser to an odd shape, tall and skinny, for example. Then stop the program and restart it. The tall and skinny Web browser should load, as shown in Figure 14.3.

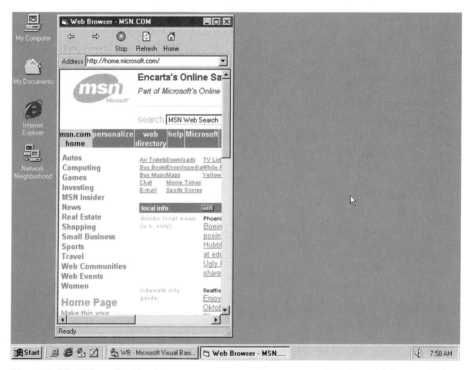

Figure 14.3 Using the Registry, your program can remember its position and size.

4   Maximize the Web browser and then close it. Rerun the program and examine the window (Figure 14.4).
Although the browser does indeed occupy the entire screen, it's not really maximized because we aren't handling the maximize window feature correctly. We'll correct that next.

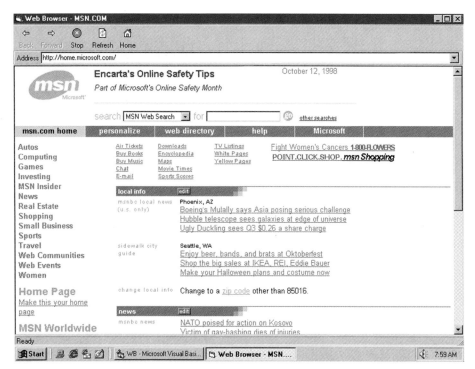

Figure 14.4 Is it or isn't it? Although the window is full screen, it isn't truly maximized.

5   Close the window.

Working with the Maximize Window Feature

Visual Basic provides a *WindowState property* for each form window that helps you determine the *state* of the window. A form window can be in a normal, minimized, or maximized state. Since it's unlikely that a user would want to save the state of a minimized window, we won't worry about that state. We do need to worry about the maximized window, however.

When a window is correctly maximized, the system changes a few window attributes. For example, if the window is normally resizable (like the Web browser we're creating), the resize handle on the lower right of the window will disappear when the window is maximized. Note, however, that the handle is present in Figure 14.4. Note also that the *Restore Window* button in the title bar should be activated but is not.

To correct this and truly maximize our window, we can use a simple If-Then-Else block. If the window is maximized when it is closed, we will write a "*True*" value to a Registry key. If it isn't maximized, we will write a

"*False*" value to that key and then write the *Top, Left, Width,* and *Height* values as we did before. When the program starts, a similar test will ensue. First, the maximized key will be checked. If it is "*True*," then we will simply maximize the form. If it is "*False*," however, we will read the *Top, Left, Width,* and *Height* values and apply them to the appropriate form properties. In the following steps, you will perform these actions.

> **Tip** Please note that the "*True*" and "*False*" values we are reading and writing to the Registry are strings, not true Boolean values. We are using "*True*" and "*False*" rather than something nonsensical, such as "0" and "1," for readability only.

TASK 3: TO HANDLE A MAXIMIZED FORM WINDOW

1 Open the code window and navigate to the *Form_Unload* event-handler.

2 Change the code to the following. Note that the new code appears in bold.

If frmWB.WindowState = vbMaximized Then

    SaveSetting "wb", "StartUpMaximized", "StartUpMaximized", "True"

Else

    SaveSetting "wb", "StartUpMaximized", "StartUpMaximized", "False"

    SaveSetting "wb", "StartupTop", "StartupTop", frmWB.Top

    SaveSetting "wb", "StartupLeft", "StartupLeft", frmWB.Left

    SaveSetting "wb", "StartupWidth", "StartupWidth", frmWB.Width

    SaveSetting "wb", "StartupHeight", "StartupHeight", frmWB.Height

End If

3 Run the program so that the Registry values are written and then close it and return to the Visual Basic IDE.

4 Navigate to the *Form_Initialize* event-handler and change the code as follows (again, new code is in bold):

If GetSetting("wb", "StartUpMaximized", "StartUpMaximized") = "True" Then

    frmWB.WindowState = vbMaximized

Else

    frmWB.Top = GetSetting("wb", "StartupTop", "StartupTop")

    frmWB.Left = GetSetting("wb", "StartupLeft", "StartupLeft")

    frmWB.Width = GetSetting("wb", "StartupWidth", "StartupWidth")

```
frmWB.Height = GetSetting("wb", "StartupHeight",
    "StartupHeight")
```

End If

WB.GoHome

5 Save the project and test the program by quitting it when the window is both maximized (Figure 14.5) and normal (nonmaximized). It should restart using the correct shape either way.

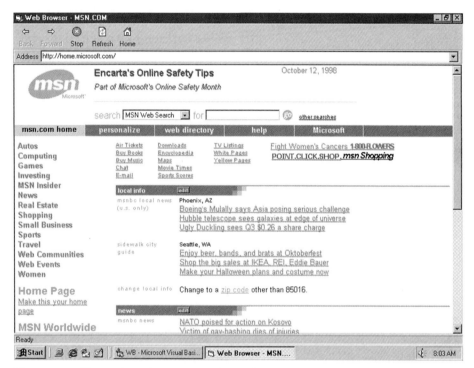

Figure 14.5 Now when the program is maximized, it saves the setting correctly.

6 Close the program when you are done testing and return to the Visual Basic IDE.

Personalizing the Toolbar

Now let's work on the toolbar. If you consider the Internet Explorer toolbar, you'll see that a user can choose whether to display the toolbar, the address bar, and the toolbar button captions. This would be a nice customizable feature to add to our Web browser, and we'll do so using the SaveSetting and GetSetting functions. But first, we need to make a change to the toolbar/coolbar combo we're now using: Before we can make the toolbar customizable, we'll have to place it inside of the coolbar along with the address bar.

> **Tip** If you completed the Hands-On exercises at the end of Project 12, you will already have placed the toolbar inside of the coolbar. If you have, skip to the section entitled Working with Pop-up Menus. If you have not, please note that you must be very careful when completing these steps as you will be cutting and pasting controls. To be safe, back up your project before you begin.

TASK 4: TO PLACE THE TOOLBAR INSIDE OF THE COOLBAR

1 Close the Code window if it is open and make sure the form window is visible.

2 Select *coolAddress* and change its *Align* property to **0 - vbAlignNone**.

3 Select *Toolbar* and change its *Align* property to **0 - vbAlignNone**.

4 Drag *Toolbar* to the middle of the form, as shown in Figure 14.6.

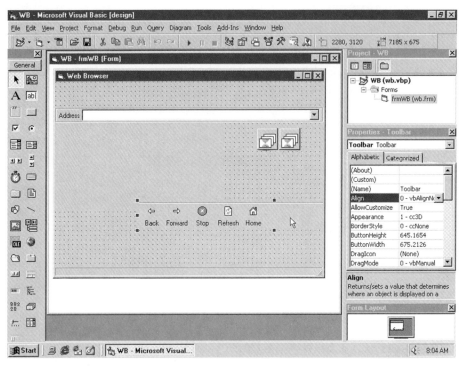

Figure 14.6 Once the toolbar is no longer aligned to the top of the form, you can move it elsewhere temporarily.

5 Right-click *cmboAddress* and select *Cut*.
The address bar will disappear from the coolbar.

6 Select a blank area of the form window, right-click, and choose *Paste*.
When the area appears on the form, drag it near the center of the form, as shown in Figure 14.7.

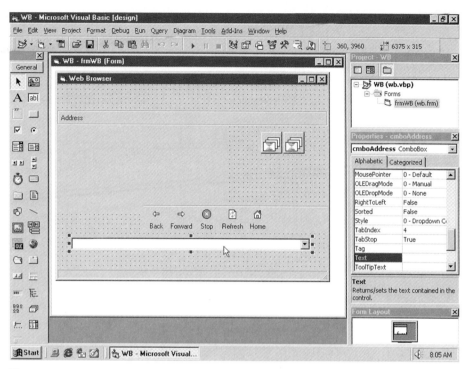

Figure 14.7 Now that the address bar has been removed from the coolbar, you can add a second band.

7   Change the *Align* property of *coolAddress* to **1 - vbAlignTop**.
The coolbar will align with the top of the form again.

8   Display the Property Pages for the coolbar and navigate to the *Bands* page.

9   Click *Insert* to add a second band and check the *New Row* checkbox so that the new band appears on its own row (Figure 14.8). Click ⬚ OK ⬚ to close the Property Pages.

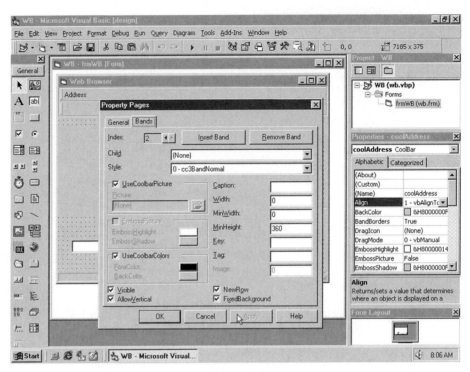

Figure 14.8 Ensure that the second band occupies its own row in the coolbar.

10 *Cut* the *Caption* (Address) on Band 1 and *Paste* it to Band 2.

11 *Cut* the toolbar again and *Paste* it onto the coolbar.

12 *Cut* the cmboAddress drop-down combo box and *Paste* it onto the coolbar as well.

13 Open the Property Pages for the coolbar again and navigate to the *Bands* page.

14 Assign *Toolbar* to the *Child* property of the first band, as shown in Figure 14.9.

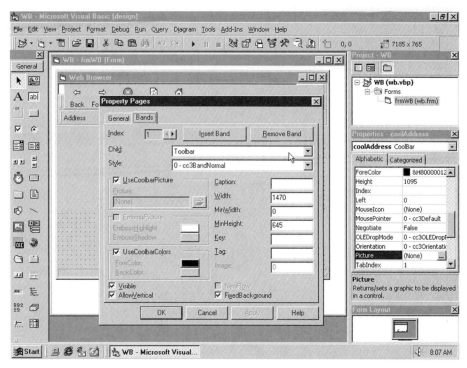

Figure 14.9 Now the toolbar is assigned to the first band on the coolbar.

15 Assign *cmboAddress* to the *Child* property of the second band and click
`OK` to close the Property Pages.
The toolbar will be aligned within the first band of the coolbar and the
combo box will be aligned within the second band.

16 Change the toolbar's *Appearance* property to **0 - ccFlat**.

17 Find the *Form_Resize* event-handler and change the line of code that
currently reads

```
WB.Height = frmWB.ScaleHeight - Toolbar.Height - coolAddress.Height -
    Status.Height
```

to

WB.Height = frmWB.ScaleHeight - coolAddress.Height - Status.Height

We don't need to worry about the height of the toolbar anymore because it
is contained inside the coolbar.

18 Run the Web browser to test it (Figure 14.10).

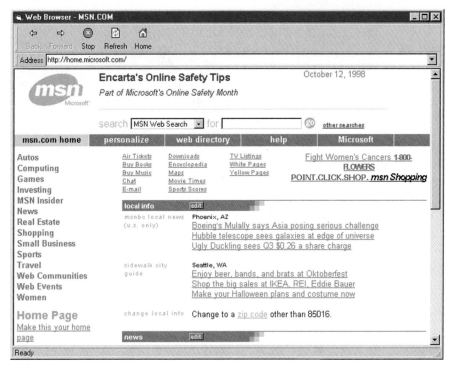

Figure 14.10 Now the toolbar and address bar are contained within the coolbar control.

Working with Pop-up Menus

When you're using Internet Explorer, you can modify toolbar configuration settings by right-clicking the toolbar and displaying a *pop-up menu* like the one shown in Figure 14.11. A ***pop-up menu***, or ***context menu*** as it's sometimes called, is a special kind of menu that appears when you right-click an object. It seems to float over the object you right-clicked, and its top-right corner typically displays at the mouse pointer position. Pop-up menus are pervasive in Windows; a typical example is the one you see when you right-click the desktop.

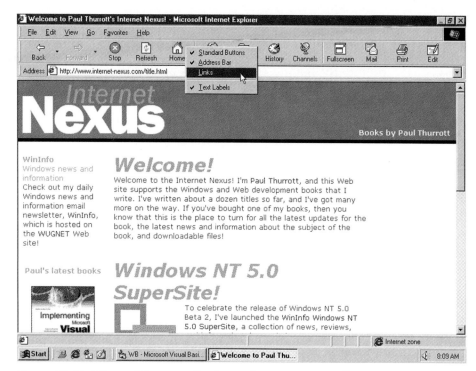

Figure 14.11 Microsoft Internet Explorer allows you to configure the toolbar from a pop-up menu.

You can add pop-up menus to your own programs as well, although Visual Basic only offers a fairly convoluted way to do so. Since you can create only one menu per form window through the Visual Basic Menu Editor, you have to add your pop-up menu to the existing menu system. If you don't want it to appear in the main menu, you have to mark your pop-up menu as not visible by unchecking the *Visible* option in the Menu Editor. However, there are times where you may indeed want the pop-up menu to be available from the main menu, as is the case with the pop-up menu we'll be creating.

We will add a View menu item to the Web browser's main menu with the following submenu items:

- *Standard Toolbar* Determines whether the toolbar (actually, the first coolbar band, which contains the toolbar) is displayed.

- *Address Bar* Determines whether the address bar (actually, the second coolbar band, which contains the address bar) is displayed.

- *Button Text* Determines whether the toolbar buttons have text captions.

Each of these menu items will be checked if the option is enabled. In other words, if the toolbar is visible, then the Standard Toolbar menu item will be checked. Otherwise, it will be unchecked.

The reason we want this menu to appear on the main menu as well as on a pop-up menu is simple: If the user removes the toolbar and the address bar, there will be nothing on which to right-click to display the pop-up menu! By having these options available from the main menu as well, they will always be available since the main menu can't be hidden.

The first step then is to create a basic menu. In the following steps, you will do this, using the familiar Menu Editor.

TASK 5: TO ADD A VIEW MENU TO THE WEB BROWSER

1   Open the Visual Basic Menu Editor.

2   Add a new menu item called **mnuFile** with a caption of **&File**.

3   Add a submenu under *File* with a name of **mnuClose** and a caption of **&Close**.

4   Add a new main menu item named **mnuView** after *File*. It should have the caption **&View**.

5   Add the submenu items shown in Table 14.1 below mnuView.

Table 14.1

Menu Caption	Menu Name	Checked
&Standard Toolbar	**mnuStandardToolbar**	Yes
&Address Bar	**mnuAddressBar**	Yes
(Separator—no caption)	**-mnuSep**	No
&Button Text	**mnuButtonText**	Yes

6   Close the Visual Basic Menu Editor.
The screen should resemble Figure 14.12 when you run the program and display the View menu.

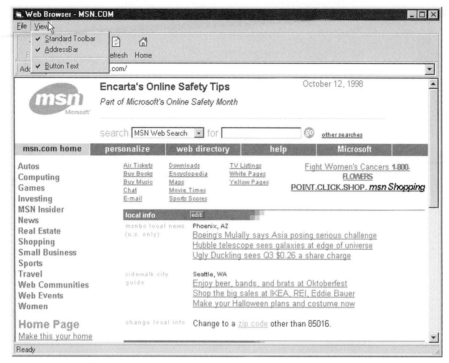

Figure 14.12 The View menu doesn't do much yet, but we'll fix that.

Displaying a Pop-Up Menu

Now that you've got a working menu, you need to write code that will display it as a pop-up menu. This is done with the Pop*UpMenu method*. You pass this method the name of a menu (such as mnuView) and it will display the menu as a pop-up menu. Because we want to tie this to a right-click, we will want to handle the ***MouseUp event*** for the toolbar and the coolbar. The *MouseUp* event occurs when the user releases one of the mouse buttons. The event-handler for this event is passed the number of the mouse button that was pressed and then released. In our case, the right mouse button (or more correctly, the *secondary mouse button*) is clicked, we will display the View menu as a pop-up menu. Let's write the code to do this.

TASK 6: TO DISPLAY A POP-UP MENU

1   Open the Code window and create a blank *MouseUp* event-handler for the toolbar.

2 Add the following code to this event-handler:

If Button = vbRightButton Then

   PopupMenu mnuView

End If

3 Add the same code to the *MouseUp* event-handler for *coolAddress*.

4 Save the project and run the program. Right-click the toolbar or coolbar to display the View menu as a pop-up menu, as shown in Figure 14.13.

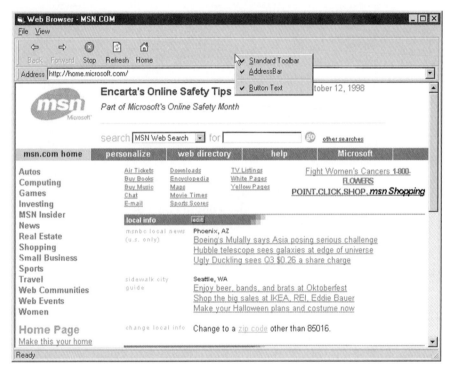

Figure 14.13 It's pretty, but still useless until we write code for those menu items.

5 Close the program when you are done and return to the Visual Basic IDE.

Coding the Pop-up Menu

Since the pop-up menu is also available as a menu item in the main menu, coding it is straightforward: Select the View submenu items for which you want to write code and add that code to their *Click* event-handlers. Let's consider the three options we're using here.

- *View Standard Toolbar* If this option is checked, the toolbar (or more correctly, the first band of the coolbar, which contains the toolbar), is displayed. When the user selects this item, the first band of the coolbar should disappear. Checking it again will redisplay the first coolbar band.

- *View Address Bar* If this option is checked, the second coolbar band, which contains the address bar, is visible. When the user selects this item, the second coolbar band should disappear. Checking it again will redisplay the second coolbar band.

- ***View Button Text*** This option will toggle the text caption under the toolbar buttons. When it is checked, the text captions will display. Otherwise, there will be no text captions.

This all makes sense, but there is a hidden problem here. Our coolbar has two bands. If we change the *Visible* property of one of these bands to *False*, then the band disappears and the coolbar appears to have only one band. Then, when there is only one band displaying in the coolbar, changing its *Visible* property to *False* will not make the coolbar disappear, which is the desired effect.

To solve this, the *Click* event-handlers for mnuStandardButtons and mnu-AddressBar will need to check to see whether the other band is visible. If it is, all we need to do is make the appropriate band invisible. However, if the band we are working with is the only visible band, then we will need to write code that disables the coolbar itself and makes it invisible.

This may seem a little confusing, but it will become more clear when we write the code. Let's take a look.

TASK 7: TO HANDLE THE POP-UP MENU *CLICK* EVENTS

1 Open the *mnuClose* event-handler and add the following code:

End

2 Open the *mnuStandardToolbar_Click* event-handler and add the following code:

```
If mnuStandardToolbar.Checked = True Then
    mnuStandardToolbar.Checked = False
    If coolAddress.Bands(2).Visible = True Then
        coolAddress.Bands(1).Visible = False
    Else
        coolAddress.Bands(1).Visible = False
        coolAddress.Enabled = False
        coolAddress.Visible = False
        coolAddress.Height = 0
        Call Form_Resize
    End If
Else
    If coolAddress.Bands(2).Visible = True Then
        coolAddress.Bands(1).Visible = True
    Else
        coolAddress.Bands(1).Visible = True
```

```
            coolAddress.Enabled = True
            coolAddress.Visible = True
        End If
        mnuStandardToolbar.Checked = True
    End If
    Call Form_Resize
```

3 Open the *mnuAddressBar_Click* event-handler and add the following code:

```
If mnuAddressBar.Checked = True Then
    mnuAddressBar.Checked = False
    If coolAddress.Bands(1).Visible = True Then
        coolAddress.Bands(2).Visible = False
    Else
        coolAddress.Bands(2).Visible = False
        coolAddress.Enabled = False
        coolAddress.Visible = False
        coolAddress.Height = 0
    End If
Else
    If coolAddress.Bands(1).Visible = True Then
        coolAddress.Bands(2).Visible = True
    Else
        coolAddress.Bands(2).Visible = True
        coolAddress.Enabled = True
        coolAddress.Visible = True
    End If
    mnuAddressBar.Checked = True
End If
Call Form_Resize
```

4 Open the *mnuButtonText_Click* event-handler and add the following code:

```
Dim x As Integer
If mnuButtonText.Checked = True Then
    mnuButtonText.Checked = False
    For x = 1 To Toolbar.Buttons.Count
        Toolbar.Buttons(x).Caption = ""
    Next
Else
    mnuButtonText.Checked = True
    Toolbar.Buttons(1).Caption = "Back"
    Toolbar.Buttons(2).Caption = "Forward"
    Toolbar.Buttons(3).Caption = "Stop"
```

```
        Toolbar.Buttons(4).Caption = "Refresh"
        Toolbar.Buttons(5).Caption = "Home"
End If
coolAddress.Bands(1).MinHeight = Toolbar.ButtonHeight
Call Form_Resize
```

We change the **MinHeight property** of the coolbar so that the coolbar re-sizes properly when the captions are added or removed. *MinHeight* determines the minimum height to which the coolbar can be sized.

5   Because the coolbar height can vary, we will want to write code in the *Form_Resize* event-handler that places the top of the WebBrowser control one pixel below the coolbar while allowing the coolbar to properly resize. To do this, add the following lines of code to the bottom of the Form_Resize event-handler:

```
WB.Top = coolAddress.Height + 1
coolAddress.Bands(2).MinHeight = Toolbar.Buttons(1).Height
coolAddress.Bands(1).MinHeight = Toolbar.Buttons(1).Height
```

6   Save the project and run the program, testing each of the pop-up menu's options. If you make the coolbar disappear entirely (Figure 14.14), remember that you can always access these options from the *View* menu as well.

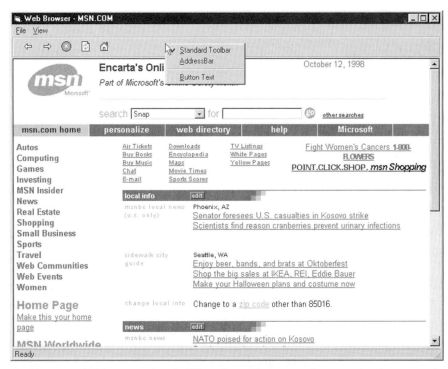

Figure 14.14 With some simple VB code, we've created a completely customizable toolbar.

7   Close the program and return to the Visual Basic IDE when you're done.

Personalizing the Web Browser toolbar

Now that you've got a functioning pop-up menu that lets the user configure the toolbar, you'll need to save user-entered changes to the Registry and retrieve them when the program starts. This way, the user's personalized toolbar will be retained each time the program runs in the same manner as the window size and position.

The process of saving and retrieving these values is very similar to the work you completed earlier in this project.

TASK 8: TO SAVE AND RETRIEVE TOOLBAR CONFIGURATION SETTINGS

1 Open the Code window and navigate to the *Form_Unload* event-handler.

2 Add the following code below the existing code:

```
' Write Coolbar settings
SaveSetting "wb", "CoolBar", "CoolBar", CStr(coolAddress.Visible)
SaveSetting "wb", "Toolbar", "ToolBar", _
    CStr(coolAddress.Bands(1).Visible)
SaveSetting "wb", "AddressBar", "AddressBar", _
    CStr(coolAddress.Bands(2).Visible)


' Write Toolbar Button Text settings
If Toolbar.Buttons(1).Caption = "" Then
    SaveSetting "wb", "ToolBarText", "ToolBarText", "False"
Else
    SaveSetting "wb", "ToolBarText", "ToolBarText", "True"
End If
```

3 Run the program and close it to save the customization settings to the Registry.

4 Navigate to the *Form_Initialize* event-handler and add the following code below the existing code in the procedure:

```
Dim x As Integer


' Grab Coolbar settings
coolAddress.Visible = CBool(GetSetting("wb", "CoolBar", "CoolBar"))
If coolAddress.Visible = False Then coolAddress.Height = 0
    coolAddress.Bands(1).Visible = CBool(GetSetting("wb",
        "Toolbar", _ "ToolBar"))
    mnuStandardToolbar.Checked = coolAddress.Bands(1).Visible
    coolAddress.Bands(2).Visible = CBool(GetSetting("wb", _
        "AddressBar", "AddressBar"))
```

```
mnuAddressBar.Checked = coolAddress.Bands(2).Visible
' Grab Toolbar Button Text settings
If GetSetting("wb", "ToolBarText", "ToolBarText") = "True" Then
    mnuButtonText.Checked = True
    Toolbar.Buttons(1).Caption = "Back"
    Toolbar.Buttons(2).Caption = "Forward"
    Toolbar.Buttons(3).Caption = "Stop"
    Toolbar.Buttons(4).Caption = "Refresh"
    Toolbar.Buttons(5).Caption = "Home"
Else
    mnuButtonText.Checked = False
    For x = 1 To Toolbar.Buttons.Count
        Toolbar.Buttons(x).Caption = ""
    Next
End If
```

5 Save the project and test the new configurable toolbars by closing the program with various toolbar settings enabled.

The Conclusion

With the configuration options added in this project, your Web browser now presents a powerful and feature-filled alternative to the leading browsers of the day. Watch out, Microsoft!

Summary and Exercises

Summary

- Personalized settings and configuration information are stored in the Windows Registry.
- Information is written to the Registry with the SaveSetting function.
- Information is read from the Registry with the GetSetting function.
- The *Form_Initialize* event occurs before the *Form_Load* event and is designed to set initialization data such as form properties before the form becomes visible.
- The form's *WindowState* property determines whether the form is maximized, minimized, or normal.
- A pop-up menu is a floating menu that appears when an object is right-clicked.
- The *PopUpMenu* method displays a pop-up menu.
- The *MouseUp* event occurs when the user releases one of the buttons on the mouse.

Key Terms and Operations

Key Terms
Form_Initialize event
Form_Unload event
GetSetting function
INI files
MinHeight property
MouseUp event
personalized settings
pop-up menu (context menu)
PopUpMenu method
Registry key
SaveSetting function
Windows Registry
WindowState property

Operations
handle the *Form_Initialize* event
handle the *Form_UnLoad* event
handle the various window states
read information from the Registry
save information to the Registry
store and retrieve personalization
   information
use a coolbar with two bands
use a pop-up menu

Study Questions

Multiple Choice

1. Before the Windows Registry achieved prominence in Windows 95, developers stored configuration information in
   a. INI files.
   b. TXT files.
   c. CNF files.
   d. NFO files.

2. The Windows Registry is a special kind of
   a. file structure.
   b. INI file.
   c. database or central repository.
   d. file system.

3. The structure of the Registry is divided into _____ that act like the folders and files in your file system.
   a. units
   b. keys
   c. delimiters
   d. nodes

4. The *Form_Initialize* event occurs _____ the *Form_Load* event.
   a. alongside
   b. after
   c. before
   d. instead of

5. What are other registry methods besides SaveSetting and GetSetting that you can use with Visual Basic? (*Hint*: Check the MSDN Library.)
   a. DeleteSetting and GetAllSettings
   b. ParseSetting and FindSetting
   c. ExistsSetting and FindSetting
   d. QuerySetting and GetNode

6. The three possible window states are
   a. normal, reference, and toplevel.
   b. normal, maximized, and minimized.
   c. display, icon, and fullscreen.
   d. display, hidden, and visible.

7. The CBool function
   a. converts an expression to a Boolean value.
   b. converts a Boolean value to a 1 or a 0.
   c. converts an expression to a 1 or a 0.
   d. converts a Boolean value to a string.

8. What method is used to display a pop-up menu?
   a. *DisplayPopup*
   b. *PopupMenu*
   c. *Popup_Display*
   d. *ShowMenu*

True/False

1. Personalized settings should be stored in INI files.

2. The Windows Registry is like a hierarchical database.

3. The *Form_Unload* event fires when a form window closes.

4. GetSetting retrieves information from an INI file.

5. The form *WindowState* property determines whether a form window is capable of being minimized.

6. A pop-up menu generally appears when an object is clicked with the left, or primary, mouse button.

7. A pop-up menu is sometimes called a context menu.

8. A pop-up menu appears when its *Show* method is called.

Short Answer

1. Why is the Registry better for storage than multiple INI files?

2. What are the uppermost keys in the Registry referred to as?

3. What method do you use to read information from the Registry?

4. Which form property determines the state of the window?

5. Which coolbar property is used to associate a control with a particular band on the coolbar?

6. What method do you use to write information to the Registry?

7. What does the *Checked* property do for a menu item?

Group Discussion

1. The *MouseUp* event might seem like an odd choice when you want to handle a right mouse button click. Why can't you just use the *Click* event instead?

2. Personalizing the Web browser as we have introduces some interesting options. What other personalization settings do you think would be valuable to users?

3. In some ways, coolbars seem overly complex. You can only associate one control with each band, for example, and you cannot place a menu inside one even though programs like Office 97 and Visual Basic appear to do so. (As described earlier, these are actually command bars, not coolbars, but they appear similar to the user.) What other features would be appropriate for coolbars?

Hands-On

Creating a pop-up menu

Create a program with a pop-up menu that appears when you right-click the form. The menu should not appear as a main menu but should be invisible until the form is right-clicked. Use the options shown in Table 14.2 for your pop-up menu:

Table 14.2

Menu caption	Purpose
Red	Changes the form to red.
Blue	Changes the form to blue.
Green	Changes the form to green.
(Separator—no caption)	
Ex**i**t	Exits the program.

If you're not sure how to make the pop-up menu not appear as a main menu, consult the MSDN Library.

On Your Own

1. Creating hi-res toolbar buttons

Using images supplied by your instructor, create three more image list controls (**imlEnabled_Hi**, **imlDisabled_Hi**, and **imlNormal_Hi**) that contain high-resolution images for the Web browser toolbar. Allow the user to choose between normal and high-resolution button images as another personalization option on the View menu. The menu should be named **mnuHiResButtons** and it should have a caption of **&Hi-res buttons**.

Here's a hint: When programming the switch between the *Hi-res* and *Normal* buttons, you will first need to set each of the image list associations to **Nothing**, which is a special Visual Basic keyword that disassociates an object variable from an actual object. The following pseudocode is representative of the code you will need to place in the *mnuHighResButtons_Click* event-handler:

```
Dim x As Integer

Toolbar.ImageList = Nothing
Toolbar.DisabledImageList = Nothing
Toolbar.HotImageList = Nothing

If mnuHighResButtons is Checked Then
    Uncheck mnuHighResButtons
    Toolbar.ImageList = imlDisabled
    Toolbar.DisabledImageList = imlDisabled
    Toolbar.HotImageList = imlEnabled
Else
    Check mnuHighResButtons
    Toolbar.ImageList = imlNormal_Hi
    Toolbar.DisabledImageList = imlDisabled_Hi
    Toolbar.HotImageList = imlEnabled_Hi
End If

For x = 1 To the number of buttons in the toolbar
    Set the Image property of the current button to x
Next

coolAddress.Bands(1).MinHeight = Toolbar.ButtonHeight
```

2. Personalizing the hi-res buttons

Using the preceding exercise as a starting point, add code to the *Form_Unload* event-handler that will write the hi-res button settings to the Registry. To com-

docked   A style of sub-window (or "child window") in the Visual Basic IDE. Child windows can be docked, that is, attached to one side of the IDE, or float freely within the IDE.

Document object   An object in the Dynamic HTML Object Model that represents the document currently loaded into the Web browser.

dot notation   The type of coding style used in Visual Basic where an object's methods and properties can be referred to following the name of the object and a period or "dot."

Dynamic HTML Object Model   An object model that allows Web developers to take advantage of the features found in Web pages.

Enable argument   A parameter of the WebBrowser control's CommandStateChange method that determines whether the command that changed is now enabled.

Enabled property   Determines whether the object is enabled, or accessible.

EOF   End of File.

error-handler   A block of code that is executed in response to an error condition.

event   Something that happens to an object in an object-based language such as Visual Basic. You can write code in Visual Basic that responds to, or handles, events.

event-driven programming   A style of programming where the code you write is largely responsible for responding to specific events.

event-handler   A sub-routine containing code that will execute in response to an event.

EXE   Short for "executable" as in "executable file."

executable file   A program that can be executed by the user.

execute   To "run" a program on a computer.

field   A column in a database table. A field represents an attribute of a row, or record.

focus   A state that determines whether an object is selected or active. If it is selected, the object is said to have the focus.

Font property   Determines the font and font styles used to display text in an object.

ForeColor property   Determines the foreground color of an object.

form   A window in Visual Basic.

Format function   A function that formats a number using a variety of styles.

Fortran   An early English-like programming language that is similar to BASIC.

frame control   A Visual Basic control that creates a visual frame around other controls.

FRM file   A file with a .frm extension that representes a Visual Basic form window.

function   A named subroutine that returns a value.

GetSetting method   A Visual Basic function that retrieves data from the Windows Registry.

global variable   A variable that is accessible anywhere in a form or module.

GoHome method   A method of the WebBrowser control that causes the browser to navigate to its home page.

hard-code   The process of writing certain values directly into a program so that they cannot be easily changed later.

Hungarian Notation   A naming convention developed by Microsoft programmer Charles Simonyi that attaches three-letter prefixes to object names.

hypertext   A special text format, employed on the Web and the MSDN Library help system, where marked portions of text called hyperlinks can be clicked to navigate to another document.

IBM PC   The original Personal Computer. All personal computers sold today are said to be compatible with the IBM PC.

Icon property   The Form property that determines which icon is used to represent the form window.

If-Then-Else statement   A Visual Basic statement that allows you to make decisions with code.

Image control   A Visual Basic control that allows you to display a bitmapped graphic.

Image list control   A Visual Basic control that allows you to store a number of images that will be displayed by other controls.

INI files   A text file used by older versions of Windows to store personalized settings and configuration information.

Initialize event   A form event that occurs right before the Load event. This is the first event that fires when a form is created at runtime.

Int function   A function that retrieves the integer portion of a value.

Integer   A data type that represents a whole number.

Internet   A vast network of networks that can be connected to from almost anywhere in the world.

Interval property   A property of the Timer control that determines how often its timer event fires.

Java   A high-level object-oriented programming language that is similar to C++. Java is designed to run on any operating system, but it's harder to learn and use than Visual Basic.

Key property   A property for each button in a Buttons collection is set to a unique string value so that you can, in effect, name each button.

KeyPress event   The event that occurs when an object is selected and a key on the keyboard is pressed by the user.

Label control   A Visual Basic control that displays read-only text.

list box control   A Visual Basic control that provides a list of text.

Load event   The event that occurs when a form window first loads.

local variable A variable that is available only within the subroutine it is declared within.

LocationURL property A property of the WebBrowser control that determines the URL of the document currently loaded into the browser.

machine language The native, low-level language that is understood by a computer.

Menu Editor A tool in Visual Basic that allows you to add a main menu and/or pop-up menus to your application.

method A function, or sub-routine that typically returns a value, that is associated with a particular object.

Microsoft ADO Data Control A Visual Basic control that interfaces with ADO to provide a simple way of accessing data in a database or other data source.

Microsoft Internet Controls component A system component you can access from Visual Basic that provides Web browsing functionality.

MinHeight property A property of a band object that determines the minimum height of the band.

MITS The company from Albuquerque, New Mexico that created the Altair, the first personal computer.

Modal A style of window/dialog box that requires you to close the window before focus can return to the window that called it.

module A special type of Visual Basic file that can contain Visual Basic code but no form window.

MouseUp event The event that occurs when the user releases a mouse button.

MoveNext method A method of the ADO Recordset that allows you to move the cursor forward to the next record.

MSDN Library The help system for Visual Basic and the entire Visual Studio suite.

MS-DOS Microsoft's first operating system. It was later merged into Windows with the release of Windows 95 in 1995.

Name property Determines the name used to reference an object in Visual Basic code.

Navigate method A method of the WebBrowser control that causes the browser to navigate to a new location.

non-modal A style of window/dialog box that allows you to switch back to other windows at any time.

non-visual control A Visual Basic control that is not seen by the user, such as the Timer and ImageList controls.

object An entity in an object-oriented or object-based programming language that has properties, methods, and events that you can access programmatically.

Object drop-down list box A drop-down list in the code window that allows you to choose from a list of available objects.

object model A logical collection of objects and their properties, methods, and events.

object variable A variable that represents an object.

On Error statement A Visual Basic statement that allows you to specify what to do when an error occurs in a procedure.

Open method A method of the ADO Recordset that copies the results of a query into the recordset.

option button control A Visual Basic control that is typically used in a group with other option buttons to represent a range of possible values.

panel object An object that represents a segment of a status bar control.

parameter An argument.

Pascal A high-level programming language similar to C that provides a highly structured programming model for developers.

Personal Computer (PC) A computer that is said to be compatible with the IBM PC, that is, a computer that runs DOS and/or Windows.

personalized settings User-configurable settings such as window position and size, toolbar configuration, and the like.

Picture property Determines which image is displayed by the object.

pixel The smallest dot or image unit you can see on a computer screen.

pop-up menu A special kind of menu that appears when you right-click an object. Pop-up menus are sometimes called context menus.

PopUpMenu method A method that displays a pop-up menu for the current object.

Private A Visual Basic keyword that declares a variable or subroutine as being available only to the code in the form or module in which it is declared.

procedure A block of Visual Basic code that can be called by name.

Procedure drop-down list box A drop-down list in the code window that allows you to choose from a list of event handlers that are specific to the object displayed in the Object drop-down list box.

program A sequence of code that instructs the computer to perform certain tasks. Programs are typically executed, or run, by a user that wishes to accomplish something specific; Microsoft Word is a program that provides word processing functionality.

programmer A person that creates computer programs using programming languages.

programming language A special kind of written language, or code, used by a programmer to create programs.

project A collection of files that constitutes a Visual Basic program.

property An attribute of an object.

Property Page A dialog box that displays options for an object in the Visual Basic IDE. A Property

---

Page is used when the Properties window is inadequate for displaying all of the properties of an object.

Public A Visual Basic keyword that declares a variable or subroutine as being available to all forms and modules in the project in which it is declared.

RAD Acronym meaning "Rapid Application Development."

Randomize statement The Visual Basic statement that initializes the random number generator.

Rapid Application Development A visual style of programming where programs can be quickly created and debugged.

record A row in a database table. A record represents a collection of field data.

Recordset A set of database records.

reference A way to refer to code that exists in other files.

Registry Key A unit of storage in the Windows Registry.

relational database A database that stores data in tables that can interrelate to each other.

Remote Data Objects (RDO) An older object model for accessing databases.

reserved word A word that is part of the reserved list of Visual Basic keywords.

resolution The dimensions of your computer screen, usually measured in pixels.

Rnd function A function that returns a random number between 0 and 1.

run *See* execute.

SaveSetting method A Visual Basic function that saves information to the Windows Registry.

Scope The visibility and lifetime of a variable or subroutine. Scope is determined by the way these entities are declared.

Select Case A Visual Basic statement that is designed as a more readable alternative to multiple nested If-Then-Else statements. Select Case allows you to programmatically make decisions.

Set statement A Visual Basic statement that creates an instance of an object at runtime.

Shape control A Visual Basic control that provides simple geometric shapes.

Show method Used to display a form window.

SimpleText property The status bar control property that determines the text to display in a single-panel status bar.

solution A collection of one or more Visual Studio projects that represents a single entity.

SQL Structure Query Language.

Static keyword The Visual Basic keyword that is used to declare a static variable.

static variable A special kind of variable that retains its value even after the subroutine it was declared within is exited.

status bar control A Visual Basic control that typically sits at the bottom of a form window and provides status information to the user.

status data Information that is displayed by a status bar.

Step The process of executing a program one line at a time in the debugger so that you can watch variables change values.

String A data type representing a collection of alpha-numeric characters.

Structured Query Language The native language of relational databases.

Style property A property of the status bar control that determines whether the status bar is a simple, one-panel style.

system colors A collection of named colors that are guaranteed to work on any Windows system, even when the user changes the color scheme.

tab order A value that determines an object's position in the list of objects that can receive the focus.

TabIndex The property that determines an object's position in the tab order.

table A collection of related columns (fields) and rows (records).

text box A Visual Basic control that allows you to display text that can be edited by the user.

Text property Determines the text displayed by an object.

Timer control A Visual Basic control that responds to the passage of time.

timer event The event that occurs when a specific amount of time has passed.

Title property A property of the WebBrowser control that retrieves the title of the document currently loaded into the browser.

TitleChange event The event that occurs when the title of the document currently loaded by the WebBrowser control changes.

toolbar control A Visual Basic control that represents a Windows toolbar.

twip A unit of measurement that is 1/20th of a printer's point; 1440 twips is one inch wide.

Uniform Resource Locator (URL) A Web address. Each document on the Web has a unique URL.

Universal Data Access Microsoft's strategy for creating a programmatic way to access different kinds of data from a consistent interface.

Unload event The event that occurs when a form window is closed.

Update method A method of the ADO Recordset that saves any changes to the current record.

URL *See* Uniform Resource Locator.

variable A named value that can change at any time.

VBP file A file with a .vbp that represents a Visual Basic project.

Visible property   Determines whether the object is visible to the user. Don't confuse Visible with Enabled: An object (such as a control) can be enabled but not visible.

Visual C++   A Microsoft development tool that lets programmers work with the C and C++ programming languages.

Visual Data Manager   A tool included with Visual Basic that allows you to create and modify Microsoft Access databases.

Visual J++   A Microsoft development tool that lets programmers work with the Java programming language.

Visual Studio   A collection of Microsoft development tools that is sold as a single package.

watch window   A window used by the Visual Basic debugger to display the values of variables while your program executes.

WebBrowser control   A Visual Basic control that is included in the Microsoft Internet Controls component.

Windows   The most popular operating system ever created for personal computers. Windows provides a graphical user interface that is easier to use than command-line operating systems such as DOS. The most recent version of Windows is currently Windows 98.

Windows Registry   A central repository in Windows for various system and application program configuration settings.

WindowState property   Determines the "state" of a form window. A form window can be in a normal, minimized, or maximized state.

Index

Notes

Notes

Notes

Notes

Notes

Notes

Notes

END-USER LICENSE AGREEMENT FOR MICROSOFT SOFTWARE

IMPORTANT—READ CAREFULLY: This Microsoft End-User License Agreement ("EULA") is a legal agreement between you (either an individual or a single entity) and Microsoft Corporation for the Microsoft software product identified above, which includes computer software and may include associated media, printed materials, and "online" or electronic documentation ("SOFTWARE PRODUCT"). The SOFTWARE PRODUCT also includes any updates and supplements to the original SOFTWARE PRODUCT provided to you by Microsoft. Any software provided along with the SOFTWARE PRODUCT that is associated with a separate end-user license agreement is licensed to you under the terms of that license agreement. By installing, copying, downloading, accessing or otherwise using the SOFTWARE PRODUCT, you agree to be bound by the terms of this EULA. If you do not agree to the terms of this EULA, do not install , copy , or otherwise use the SOFTWARE PRODUCT.

SOFTWARE PRODUCT LICENSE

The SOFTWARE PRODUCT is protected by copyright laws and international copyright treaties, as well as other intellectual property laws and treaties. The SOFTWARE PRODUCT is licensed, not sold.

1. GRANT OF LICENSE. This EULA grants you the following rights:

1.1 **License Grant**. You may install and use one copy of the SOFTWARE PRODUCT on a single computer. You may also store or install a copy of the SOFTWARE PRODUCT on a storage device, such as a network server, used only to install or run the SOFTWARE PRODUCT over an internal network; however, you must acquire and dedicate a license for each separate computer on or from which the SOFTWARE PRODUCT is installed, used, accessed, displayed or run.

1.2 **Academic Use**. You must be a "Qualified Educational User" to use the SOFTWARE PRODUCT in the manner described in this section. To determine whether you are a Qualified Educational User, please contact the Microsoft Sales Information Center/One Microsoft Way/Redmond, WA 98052-6399 or the Microsoft subsidiary serving your country. If you are a Qualified Educational User, you may either:

   (i) exercise the rights granted in Section 1.1, OR

   (ii) if you intend to use the SOFTWARE PRODUCT solely for instructional purposes in connection with a class or other educational program, this EULA grants you the following alternative license models:

     (A) <u>Per Computer Model</u>. For every valid license you have acquired for the SOFTWARE PRODUCT, you may install a single copy of the SOFTWARE PRODUCT on a single computer for access and use by an unlimited number of student end users at your educational institution, provided that all such end users comply with all other terms of this EULA, OR

     (B) <u>Per License Model</u>. If you have multiple licenses for the SOFTWARE PRODUCT, then at any time you may have as many copies of the SOFTWARE PRODUCT in use as you have licenses, provided that such use is limited to student or faculty end users at your educational institution and provided that all such end users comply with all other terms of this EULA. For purposes of this subsection, the SOFTWARE PRODUCT is "in use" on a computer when it is loaded into the temporary memory (i.e., RAM) or installed into the permanent memory (e.g., hard disk, CD ROM, or other storage device) of that computer, except that a copy installed on a network server for the sole purpose of distribution to other computers is not "in use." If the anticipated number of users of the SOFTWARE PRODUCT will exceed the number of applicable licenses, then you must have a reasonable mechanism or process in place to ensure that the number of persons using the SOFTWARE PRODUCT concurrently does not exceed the number of licenses.

2. DESCRIPTION OF OTHER RIGHTS AND LIMITATIONS.

- **Limitations on Reverse Engineering, Decompilation, and Disassembly**. You may not reverse engineer, decompile, or disassemble the SOFTWARE PRODUCT, except and only to the extent that such activity is expressly permitted by applicable law notwithstanding this limitation.

- **Separation of Components**. The SOFTWARE PRODUCT is licensed as a single product. Its component parts may not be separated for use on more than one computer.

- **Rental**. You may not rent, lease or lend the SOFTWARE PRODUCT.

- **Trademarks**. This EULA does not grant you any rights in connection with any trademarks or service marks of Microsoft.

- **Software Transfer**. The initial user of the SOFTWARE PRODUCT may make a one-time permanent transfer of this EULA and SOFTWARE PRODUCT only directly to an end user. This transfer must include all of the SOFTWARE PRODUCT (including all component parts, the media and printed materials, any upgrades, this EULA, and, if applicable, the Certificate of Authenticity). Such transfer may not be by way of consignment or any other indirect transfer. The transferee of such one-time transfer must agree to comply with the terms of this EULA, including the obligation not to further transfer this EULA and SOFTWARE PRODUCT.

- **Termination**. Without prejudice to any other rights, Microsoft may terminate this EULA if you fail to comply with the terms and conditions of this EULA. In such event, you must destroy all copies of the SOFTWARE PRODUCT and all of its component parts.

4. COPYRIGHT. All title and intellectual property rights in and to the SOFTWARE PRODUCT (including but not limited to any images, photographs, animations, video, audio, music, text, and "applets" incorporated into the SOFTWARE PRODUCT), the accompanying printed materials, and any copies of the SOFTWARE PRODUCT are owned by Microsoft or its suppliers. All title and intellectual property rights in and to the content which may be accessed through use of the SOFTWARE PRODUCT is the property of the respective content owner and may be protected by applicable copyright or other intellectual property laws and treaties. This EULA grants you no rights to use such content. All rights not expressly granted are reserved by Microsoft.

5. BACKUP COPY. After installation of one copy of the SOFTWARE PRODUCT pursuant to this EULA, you may keep the original media on which the SOFTWARE PRODUCT was provided by Microsoft solely for backup or archival purposes. If the original media is required to use the SOFTWARE PRODUCT on the COMPUTER, you may make one copy of the SOFTWARE PRODUCT solely for backup or archival purposes. Except as expressly provided in this EULA, you may not otherwise make copies of the SOFTWARE PRODUCT or the printed materials accompanying the SOFTWARE PRODUCT.

6. U.S. GOVERNMENT RESTRICTED RIGHTS. The SOFTWARE PRODUCT and documentation are provided with RESTRICTED RIGHTS. Use, duplication, or disclosure by the Government is subject to restrictions as set forth in subparagraph (c)(1)(ii) of the Rights in Technical Data and Computer Software clause at DFARS 252.227-7013 or subparagraphs (c)(1) and (2) of the Commercial Computer Software—Restricted Rights at 48 CFR 52.227-19, as applicable. Manufacturer is Microsoft Corporation/One Microsoft Way/Redmond, WA 98052-6399.

7. EXPORT RESTRICTIONS. You agree that you will not export or re-export the SOFTWARE PRODUCT, any part thereof, or any process or service that is the direct product of the SOFTWARE PRODUCT (the foregoing collectively referred to as the "Restricted Components"), to any country, person, entity or end user subject to U.S. export restrictions. You specifically agree not to export or re-export any of the Restricted Components (i) to any country to which the U.S. has embargoed or restricted the export of goods or services, which currently include, but are not necessarily limited to Cuba, Iran, Iraq, Libya, North Korea, Sudan and Syria, or to any national of any such country, wherever located, who intends to transmit or transport the Restricted Components back to such country; (ii) to any end-user who you know or have reason to know will utilize the Restricted Components in the design, development or production of nuclear, chemical or biological weapons; or (iii) to any end-user who has been prohibited from participating in U.S. export transactions by any federal agency of the U.S. government. You warrant and represent that neither the BXA nor any other U.S. federal agency has suspended, revoked, or denied your export privileges.

8. NOTE ON JAVA SUPPORT. THE SOFTWARE PRODUCT MAY CONTAIN SUPPORT FOR PROGRAMS WRITTEN IN JAVA. JAVA TECHNOLOGY IS NOT FAULT TOLERANT AND IS NOT DESIGNED, MANUFACTURED, OR INTENDED FOR USE OR RESALE AS ON-LINE CONTROL EQUIPMENT IN HAZARDOUS ENVIRONMENTS REQUIRING FAIL-SAFE PERFORMANCE, SUCH AS IN THE OPERATION OF NUCLEAR FACILITIES, AIRCRAFT NAVIGATION OR COMMUNICATION SYSTEMS, AIR TRAFFIC CONTROL, DIRECT LIFE SUPPORT MACHINES, OR WEAPONS SYSTEMS, IN WHICH THE FAILURE OF JAVA TECHNOLOGY COULD LEAD DIRECTLY TO DEATH, PERSONAL INJURY, OR SEVERE PHYSICAL OR ENVIRONMENTAL DAMAGE.

MISCELLANEOUS

If you acquired this product in the United States, this EULA is governed by the laws of the State of Washington. If you acquired this product in Canada, this EULA is governed by the laws of the Province of Ontario, Canada. Each of the parties hereto irrevocably attorns to the jurisdiction of the courts of the Province of Ontario and further agrees to commence any litigation which may arise hereunder in the courts located in the Judicial District of York, Province of Ontario. If this product was acquired outside the United States, then local law may apply. Should you have any questions concerning this EULA, or if you desire to contact Microsoft for any reason, please contact Microsoft, or write: Microsoft Sales Information Center/One Microsoft Way/Redmond, WA 98052-6399.

LIMITED WARRANTY

LIMITED WARRANTY. Microsoft warrants that (a) the SOFTWARE PRODUCT will perform substantially in accordance with the accompanying written materials for a period of ninety (90) days from the date of receipt, and (b) any Support Services provided by Microsoft shall be substantially as described in applicable written materials provided to you by Microsoft, and Microsoft support engineers will make commercially reasonable efforts to solve any problem. To the extent allowed by applicable law, implied warranties on the SOFTWARE PRODUCT, if any, are limited to ninety (90) days. Some states/jurisdictions do not allow limitations on duration of an implied warranty, so the above limitation may not apply to you.

CUSTOMER REMEDIES. Microsoft's and its suppliers' entire liability and your exclusive remedy shall be, at Microsoft's option, either (a) return of the price paid, if any, or (b) repair or replacement of the SOFTWARE PRODUCT that does not meet Microsoft's Limited Warranty and that is returned to Microsoft with a copy of your receipt. This Limited Warranty is void if failure of the SOFTWARE PRODUCT has resulted from accident, abuse, or misapplication. Any replacement SOFTWARE PRODUCT will be warranted for the remainder of the original warranty period or thirty (30) days, whichever is longer. Outside the United States, neither these remedies nor any product support services offered by Microsoft are available without proof of purchase from an authorized international source.

NO OTHER WARRANTIES. TO THE MAXIMUM EXTENT PERMITTED BY APPLICABLE LAW, MICROSOFT AND ITS SUPPLIERS DISCLAIM ALL OTHER WARRANTIES AND CONDITIONS, EITHER EXPRESS OR IMPLIED, INCLUDING, BUT NOT LIMITED TO, IMPLIED WARRANTIES OR CONDITIONS OF MERCHANTABILITY, FITNESS FOR A PARTICULAR PURPOSE, TITLE AND NON-INFRINGEMENT, WITH REGARD TO THE SOFTWARE PRODUCT, AND THE PROVISION OF OR FAILURE TO PROVIDE SUPPORT SERVICES. THIS LIMITED WARRANTY GIVES YOU SPECIFIC LEGAL RIGHTS. YOU MAY HAVE OTHERS, WHICH VARY FROM STATE/JURISDICTION TO STATE/JURISDICTION.

LIMITATION OF LIABILITY. TO THE MAXIMUM EXTENT PERMITTED BY APPLICABLE LAW, IN NO EVENT SHALL MICROSOFT OR ITS SUPPLIERS BE LIABLE FOR ANY SPECIAL, INCIDENTAL, INDIRECT, OR CONSEQUENTIAL DAMAGES WHATSOEVER (INCLUDING, WITHOUT LIMITATION, DAMAGES FOR LOSS OF BUSINESS PROFITS, BUSINESS INTERRUPTION, LOSS OF BUSINESS INFORMATION, OR ANY OTHER PECUNIARY LOSS) ARISING OUT OF THE USE OF OR INABILITY TO USE THE SOFTWARE PRODUCT OR THE FAILURE TO PROVIDE SUPPORT SERVICES, EVEN IF MICROSOFT HAS BEEN ADVISED OF THE POSSIBILITY OF SUCH DAMAGES. IN ANY CASE, MICROSOFT'S ENTIRE LIABILITY UNDER ANY PROVISION OF THIS EULA SHALL BE LIMITED TO THE GREATER OF THE AMOUNT ACTUALLY PAID BY YOU FOR THE SOFTWARE PRODUCT OR U.S.\$5.00; PROVIDED, HOWEVER, IF YOU HAVE ENTERED INTO A MICROSOFT SUPPORT SERVICES AGREEMENT, MICROSOFT'S ENTIRE LIABILITY REGARDING SUPPORT SERVICES SHALL BE GOVERNED BY THE TERMS OF THAT AGREEMENT. BECAUSE SOME STATES/JURISDICTIONS DO NOT ALLOW THE EXCLUSION OR LIMITATION OF LIABILITY, THE ABOVE LIMITATION MAY NOT APPLY TO YOU.